VIETNAM

Vietnam

Rising Dragon

Bill Hayton

YALE UNIVERSITY PRESS
NEW HAVEN AND LONDON

For information about this and other Yale University Press publications, please contact:
U.S. Office: sales.press@yale.edu   www.yalebooks.com
Europe Office: sales@yaleup.co.uk   www.yalebooks.co.uk

Set in Arno by IDSUK (DataConnection) Ltd
Printed in Great Britain by TJ International Ltd, Padstow, Cornwall

Library of Congress Cataloging-in-Publication Data

Vietnam: Rising Dragon/Hayton, Bill
    p. cm.
  Includes bibliographical references and index.
  ISBN 978–0–300–15203–6 (ci: alk. paper)
1. Social change—Vietnam. 2. Vietnam—History—1975– 3. Vietnam—Politics and government—1975–4. Vietnam—Economic conditions—1975– 5. Vietnam—Social conditions—1975– 6. <ang cong san
Viêt Nam. I. Title.
  DS559.912.H39 2010
  959.704′4—dc22

                                                              2009026502

A catalogue record for this book is available from the British Library.

10 9 8 7 6 5 4 3 2 1

For Pam, Tess and Patrick
the lights of my life

Contents

Illustrations and Maps

Illustrations

Unless otherwise acknowledged all pictures belong to the author.

Maps

Acknowledgements

This book could not have been written without the participation, support and insight of a great many people inside and outside Vietnam. My thanks must go first to everyone who appears in the following pages: the assembly-line workers, tea-pickers, politicians, scientists and all the others who interrupted their efforts to feed their families or develop the country to answer my questions patiently.

When I first arrived in Vietnam I was amazed how easy it was to stop people on the streets and ask questions but the answers I received in such public encounters rarely breached the official meniscus. My understanding of what was told and seen came only from time spent in quiet conversation with the few people prepared to act as agents of scholarly osmosis, transferring molecules of knowledge through the membrane. I would like to thank them all here in print. It is sad indication of the constraints upon intellectual life in Vietnam that almost all the people who helped me there (whether Vietnamese or expatriate) have asked not to be identified.

Further illumination came from reading the work of the small number of western academics who have spent years diligently researching aspects of Vietnamese life. Many of them are mentioned or referenced in the text but I would like to thank them here specifically: Chapter One made much use of the published work or advice of Scott Cheshier, Ari Kokko, Jago Penrose, Jonathan Pincus, Martin Rama, Carrie Turk, Brian Van Arkadie and, in particular, Adam Fforde; Chapter Two of Pam McElwee and Mike di Gregorio; Chapter Three of Lisa Drummond, Erik Harms and Mandy Thomas; Chapter Four of Mark Sidel, David Koh and Jonathan London;

Chapter Five of Regina Abrami, Eddy Malesky, Martin Gainsborough, Martin Painter, Mark Sidel and Thaveeporn Vasavakul; Chapter Six of Zachary Abuza; Chapter Nine of Ramses Amer, Diane Fox, Alexander Vuving, Tuong H. Vu and, in particular, Carl Thayer; and Chapter Ten of Hue-Tam Ho Tai, Oscar Salemink and Philip Taylor. Many of these people are also members of the Vietnam Studies Group online list, whose discussions are a frequent source of enlightenment and encouragement.

The small band of foreign journalists in Hanoi was an early source of information and advice. My thanks go, in particular, to Didier Lauras, Catherine McKinley, Roger Mitton, Matt Steinglass and Frank Zeller. As any journalist knows, the people who do the real work are our fixers and translators and I was very lucky to be able to benefit from the great skills of Ngo Xuan Tung, Nguyen Anh Thu, Do Minh Thuy, Tran Thi Ngoc Lan and Vu Trong Khanh. Many local journalists became friends and advisors including Bui Cam Ha, Le Quoc Minh, Nguyen Hong Ngan and Pham Trung Bac. I thank the others anonymously. The BBC Vietnamese Service was a source of succour throughout my time in Vietnam and subsequently. My thanks, in particular, go to Nguyen Giang, Nguyen Hoang, Nguyen Thi Bich Ngoc and Hong Nga. Giang and Nga read and corrected parts of my manuscript. I'm also very grateful to Jacob Gamelgaard, Mike Coleman, Ross Hughes, Tim Knight, Nora Luttmer, David Payne, Scott Robertson and Michael Turner, plus others already mentioned and more who don't wish to be – for their advice and counsel. My editor at Yale University Press, Heather McCallum, deserves double thanks, firstly for saying yes to this book, and secondly for improving it through her ever-positive criticism.

My teachers Pham Quoc Dat and Tran Hanh An first opened the doors to the richness of Vietnamese language and culture, Le Thi Ly and the lovely staff of Rainbow School looked after our children, and Grainne and Julian, Charlie and Michelle rescued me in Hong Kong when I failed to get through Vietnamese immigration controls. Families always come last in these lists but if it hadn't been for mine there wouldn't have been an expedition to Vietnam or a book. My love and thanks to them.

Colchester, England
September 2009

Introduction: Another Vietnam

'The Hidden Charm' is Vietnam's seductive tourist slogan. Many Vietnamese don't like it, but it teases foreigners' yearning for adventure and discovery. The phrase conjures an image which sums up the country: the peasant girl looks up, tips back the brim of her conical hat and reveals her shy smiling face beneath. The straw-coloured hat, the bright green paddy fields and the black buffalo grazing all around – a world pure and beautiful, hidden and charming. Make the effort, implies the slogan, and your reward will be a vision of tranquillity, grace and beauty. This Vietnam promises everything your modern world has left behind: delicate women, simple living and unspoilt landscapes. The country once torn apart in prime time has been reborn, its essence untouched by the predations of foreigners. Now it is available to the discerning visitor with the patience to find it.

Those without the time or the patience can still capture it – on canvas in one of the big-city sidewalk ateliers. Paint, tapestry and photography reproduce images of a country we know instantly is Vietnam: bicycle-riding girls in white *ao dai*, sun-aged women porting bamboo shoulder poles, boys astride buffalo and sampans piled high with fruit. It's overwhelmingly an aesthetic of details – paddy fields, peasants and pagodas – not wide landscape shots. The image of Vietnam we foreigners seek is a close-cropped study in 'otherness'. Zoom out from the girl in the conical hat and the newly erected pylon intrudes on the view. Turn away from the buffalo boy and the scene is 'spoiled' by his parents' new concrete house. Vietnamese development planners don't share the western tourist aesthetic. Call it socialist, call it proletarian or just call it ugly; they'd rather see an electricity substation than a pre-industrial rural landscape. The people want progress and prosperity. The fantasy country we seek is the one they want to leave behind.

We care about Vietnam for one reason above all. Through all the horrors the modern world could throw at it, it prevailed. No other country name has the same resonance: 'the lesson of Vietnam', 'the ghost of Vietnam', 'another Vietnam' – we know instantly all that these phrases imply. This 'Vietnam' has become an abstract place, trapped in a blood-soaked decade between 1965 and 1975. It lives on in daily discourse. 'Vietnam' has become a shorthand reference for so many cleavages within American society that on most days searching the newswires for 'Vietnam' will return more stories about the United States than Southeast Asia. A civil rights law will be described as 'Vietnam-era legislation', a motorist in an accident might be routinely described as a 'Vietnam veteran' and politicians and commentators wield 'the lessons of Vietnam' as a blunt instrument to defend their position on a gamut of foreign policy issues. Americans understand that these phrases imply far more than simply a faraway country.

This book isn't about that 'Vietnam'; it's about a country in Southeast Asia with almost 90 million inhabitants, the 13th most populous country in the world, the country which moved and inspired me and where I lived for a while until I was told to leave. It doesn't claim to be a view of the country untainted by all the different visions others have projected upon it, nor a vision of some 'essential' Viet Nam which exists behind these projections. Vietnam keeps its secrets well. Foreigners can live there a long time and fail to understand why things happen the way they do until Vietnamese friends patiently explain what, to them, is blindingly obvious – and things slowly fall into place. Many times I would finish a news report and think that I had made a breakthrough, that this time I *really* understood what was going on – only to have a friend or colleague, often from the BBC's Vietnamese Service, point out some vital element of the story that I had no idea even existed. Many times I felt I was just describing ripples on the surface, while beneath great currents were at work. This book is an attempt to describe those currents.

Vietnam is in the middle of a revolution: capitalism is flooding into a nominally communist society, fields are disappearing under new industrial parks, villagers are flocking to booming cities and youth culture is blooming. Dense networks of family relationships are being strained by demands for greater personal freedom and traditions are being eroded by the lure of modern living.

It's one of the most breathtaking periods of social change anywhere, ever. Vietnam is a very different place, even from a decade ago. When Robert Templer wrote *Shadows and Wind* in the late 1990s, Vietnam was a sclerotic country mired in economic crisis and unwilling to make the changes necessary to unleash its innate dynamism. It still faces mighty challenges and it does so with a severely strained political system but it is also a country in the middle of – to use the official slogan – renovation. There is ambition everywhere: from the kids crammed into after-school English classes to the political leaders who want their country to catch up with the Tigers of East Asia. The question is whether the leaders' ambitions will match those of the masses. Can Communist Party-ruled Vietnam meet the aspirations of its people?

The signs, so far, are broadly positive. Vietnam has made great strides – delivering basic education, healthcare and a rising standard of living to almost everyone. Political leaders have passed on power without violence or crisis and are actively thinking about what they must do to remain in change of a young, vibrant and ambitious society. Vietnam is proof that development can work; that a poor society can become better-off, and in a dramatically short period of time. International development agencies flourish there, basking in the reflected glory of the country's achievements. They hold up Vietnam as a model of economic liberalisation and political reform. The truth is not so straightforward.

Many people have assumed that, with billions of dollars of foreign investment piling into Vietnam, political change will inevitably follow. But liberalisation only began because of the need to feed and employ a burgeoning population and even now its limits are rigorously policed. The trappings of freedom are apparent on every city street but, from the economy to the media, the Communist Party is determined to remain the sole source of authority. Beneath the great transformation lurks a paranoid and deeply authoritarian political system. Vietnam's prospects are not as clear as they might first appear to outsiders. The risks of economic mismanagement, of popular dissatisfaction and environmental damage – made more dangerous by an intolerance of public criticism – mean the country's prospects are far from assured. Everything depends upon the Communist Party maintaining coherence and discipline at a time when challenges to stability are growing by the day.

The problem for the Party leadership is how to stay in control. The Party has never been a monolithic organisation; its rule depends on balancing the competing interests of a range of factions – from the army, to the bosses of state-owned enterprises and its rank and file members. In the past this gave it the flexibility to adapt and survive but now seems to prevent it from confronting the new elite who are twisting the country's development in their own favour and laying the ground for future crisis. As well-connected businesspeople build top-heavy empires with cosy links to cheap money and influence, people at the bottom are being squeezed by increases in the cost of living. The system often looks like, in the words of Gore Vidal, 'free enterprise for the poor and socialism for the rich'.[1]

Vietnam has come a long way in the past 30 years but its evolution has often been through crisis. The contradictions inherent in simultaneously having communist control and eating capitalist cake have come to breaking point near the end of each decade: 1979, 1988, 1997 and 2008. Each time, the Party has found a peaceful way through but the resolution has only set the stage for the next battle. Future outcomes will depend on the balance of forces within the Communist Party and between the Party and outsiders. Anyone who has witnessed the motorised armadas of youth which circulate Vietnamese cities at weekends can appreciate the challenge the Party leaders face. Over the next few years a less hobbled society and vested interests will test and re-test the limits of what is possible while the Party centre tries to recapture power. Every day, petty conflicts are being fought in fields, cybercafés and offices. Whatever happens next is unlikely to be dull.

1 A General Map of Vietnam.

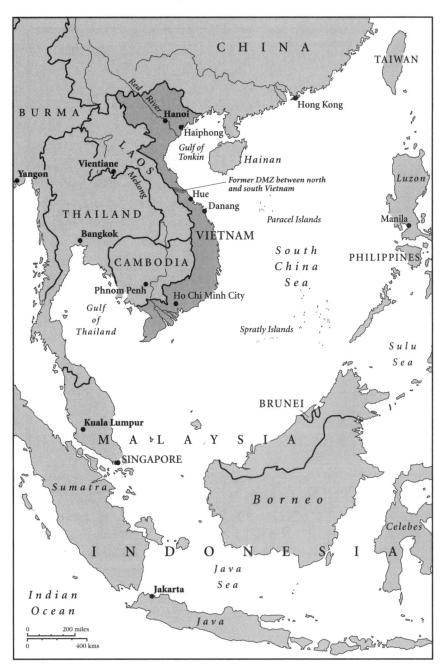

2 Vietnam, the frontier between East and Southeast Asia. The South China Sea (or as Vietnamese call it, the East Sea) is highly contested territory.

3 Map by the German geographer Herman Moll drawn in 1720 of the European perception of 'Indochina'. It shows Cambodia in control of the Mekong Delta and the now defunct kingdom of Champa in southeastern Vietnam.

1

The communist capitalist playground

Autumn is wedding season in Vietnam. The temperatures dip, the humidity slackens, everyone's ready for a party. It was a Sunday evening and the streets of central Saigon were filled with the weekend parade – the motorised celebration of youth, noise and exhaust fumes. Young men and women biked down the wide boulevards, exulting in the freedoms of their new urban culture. Starting on Le Duan Street, named after Vietnam's last Stalinist leader; they rode past the United States Consulate (the old embassy long demolished); up to the gates of the Reunification Palace, the old Saigon seat of power; down to the huge traffic circle by Ben Thanh Market and then a triumphal roar up Le Loi Street to the Opera House – completed by the French colonists in 1900, once home to the National Assembly of the old southern regime and now hosting music again. At the Opera House they divided. Some went north, past the Continental Hotel – where Graham Greene sat on the veranda to write *The Quiet American* – and up towards the Notre Dame Cathedral to rejoin the crowds at Le Duan. It was a tour of Vietnam's recent past: from partition and war, through poverty and out into new-found prosperity. Those who headed south down Dong Khoi Street – the old Rue Catinat – might just have caught sight of a wedding party arriving at the Caravelle, Saigon's first luxury hotel and once home to newsmen and women covering the 'American War'. But as they sped down to the Saigon River it's unlikely they gave too much thought to the significance of the couple getting married.

Although the Caravelle is no longer the only luxury hotel in town, it sits at the pinnacle of aspiration for Saigon's new elite. (Few people in Saigon call the place Ho Chi Minh City.) The elegance of its interior, the quality of its catering and its sheer exclusivity mean there is nowhere smarter to get married and the hotel can charge a small fortune. With every expense included, a wedding here can easily cost $40,000. But if you invite the right guests, the costs can be covered by the contents of the envelopes they leave behind. On 16 November 2008 the young couple who came to celebrate their match weren't short of cash. The groom was 36-year-old Nguyen Bao Hoang, Managing General Partner of an investment firm, IDG Ventures Vietnam, and his bride was 27-year-old Nguyen Thanh Phuong, Chairperson of another investment firm, VietCapital. Between them, their two companies controlled around $150 million of investments in Vietnam. That two such young people should be in charge of such huge amounts of money is evidence of the extraordinary change in Vietnam over the past two decades. More than half the population is under the age of 26, the country is yearning to catch up with its Asian neighbours, life is improving rapidly for most of its people and those who are best placed to make the most of the opportunities are the young.

But there was something more than a bit special about this wedding. Nguyen Thanh Phuong isn't just an investment banker; she's the daughter of the Prime Minister, Nguyen Tan Dung – and the man she was marrying isn't just an investment banker either; he's an American citizen, the child of parents who fled Vietnam in 1975 to escape the Communists. If anyone needs proof that a new Vietnam has emerged, this surely was it – the union of the Vietnamese communist daughter and the American-backed venture capitalist. There were 200 guests at the celebration, the most the hotel can accommodate – though this was later ascribed to the couple's choice for a 'small' wedding. Apart from a tiny article in a Saigon paper, the wedding received no official coverage in Vietnam. But in another sign of how the country is changing, it was quickly picked up by bloggers who discussed it as any western gossip column might.

What kind of society is 'The New Vietnam' becoming? It's still nominally communist but it certainly isn't communist in the way North Americans and Europeans usually think of the word. It's not drab or depressing – it's bright, exciting, fast-moving and colourful. Its leaders came to power fighting French colonialism, American imperialism and domestic capitalism, yet under their direction the country has opened its doors to corporations from France, the United States and every other country, and allowed private enterprise to flourish: the World Bank calls Vietnam a 'poster boy' for economic liberalisation. So, what has happened to the Party's socialist ideals? Many visitors, and even some commentators, see Vietnam's breathtaking transformation and assume that the country has opted wholeheartedly for capitalism and that any pretence to socialism is a vestige of a dying creed. The change has certainly been profound. In the course of a generation unpaved city streets have become neon-lit avenues of commerce, peasants have swapped buffalo ploughs for motorbikes, and paddy fields have become assembly lines. The sick have to pay for healthcare, parents have to pay for schooling and the unemployed are left to fend for themselves. But this is not the whole story.

Capitalism is highly visible but the froth of petty trading is distracting. Vietnam has not developed in the way it has – balancing rocketing economic growth with one of the most impressive reductions in poverty anywhere, ever – by completely liberalising the economy. Yes, restrictions on private enterprise have been lifted, markets have been allowed to flourish and foreign investment has been encouraged – but Vietnam's success is far from being a triumph of World Bank orthodoxy. Some might snigger at the official description of a 'socialist-oriented market economy' but it's not an empty slogan. Even today, the Communist Party retains control over most of the economy: either directly through the state-owned enterprises which monopolise key strategic sectors, through joint ventures between the state sector and foreign investors or, increasingly, through the elite networks which bind the Party to the new private sector.

More important to the Communist Party than economic dogma is self-preservation. Everything else: growth, poverty reduction, regional equality, media freedom, environmental protection – everything – is subordinate to that basic instinct. To survive, the Party knows it has to match a simple, but terrifying, figure: one million jobs a year. Every year Vietnam's schools produce a million new peasants and proletarians, the product of a huge post-war baby boom which is showing little sign of slowing down despite an intense 'two-child' policy. Growth is vital, but not at the expense of creating too much inequality. So is reducing poverty, but not at the expense of impeding growth too much. Over the past 30 years policy has swung back and forth, sometimes favouring growth, sometimes stability. The beneficiaries have been the peasants and proletarians. Vietnam's achievements in reducing poverty are impressive. In 1993, according to government figures, almost 60 per cent of the population lived below the poverty line. By 2004 that figure was down to 20 per cent. The country has met most of its Millennium Goals, the development targets set by the United Nations, early and escaped the ranks of the poorest countries to join the group of 'middle-income states'. People's living standards are soaring, their horizons are widening and their ambitions are growing. But there is danger in this success. 'The New Vietnam' is different to the old. The marriage of state control and liberalisation, of Party and private interest, is distorting the economy towards the wants of the few rather than the needs of the many. And these networks of 'crony socialism' are becoming a threat to Vietnam's future stability. Vietnam risks the fate of many of the World Bank's previous poster boys – boom followed by bust.

* * *

But is Vietnam really a poster boy for World Bank orthodoxy? The conventional explanation of Vietnam's economic success goes something like this: an economic crisis in the early 1980s forced a conscious choice to embrace market forces at the Sixth Communist Party Congress in December 1986, after which the economy was liberalised, with World Bank advice, until Vietnam eventually joined the World Trade Organisation in 2007. At best, that's only half the story. To understand the other half you have to start history earlier and change focus. A better explanation for Vietnam's success is that reform was begun to *protect* the state sector, not to dismantle it; that the state's involvement has remained consistently high throughout reform; and that, until recently, World Bank policy advice has been ignored, except where it fitted with the Communist Party's own priorities. To understand this fully we need a short detour into economic history.

United Vietnam's first economic crisis came just four years after Communist tanks crashed through the gates of the Presidential Palace in Saigon, ending both the 'American War' and two decades in which Vietnam had been divided into north and south. The rural economy was in ruins, the north had been bombed back to a pre-industrial age and the war had killed, wounded or displaced millions. Victory, however, seemed to prove the superiority of the communist model: it had beaten the capitalists and their American backers. But triumph didn't last; Vietnamese state socialism couldn't deliver. By 1979 heavy industry was swallowing resources without much effect on output, light industry was contracting and agriculture stagnating, as peasants in the newly communist south resisted attempts to collectivise them. The country was forced to import 200,000 tonnes of rice just to prevent starvation. To cap it all Vietnam invaded Cambodia, and China attacked Vietnam and cut off all economic aid. Those parts of the economy dependent on Chinese imports fell into crisis. Something had to be done. The decision which the Communist Party leadership took in August 1979 was intended to preserve the communist economy they'd spent a quarter of a century building but ultimately would unravel it. Centralised economic planning and the allocation of resources by the state – all this dogma would eventually dissipate. The leadership called for production to 'explode'. State-owned enterprises still had to meet their commitments to the central plan – but they were now allowed to buy and sell any surplus independently. Farmers could also sell any rice they had left over once they'd supplied their allotted quota to the state.[1] In 1979, before China and the Soviet Union opened the door to industrial capitalism, Vietnam's communists had already started experimenting with it.

The purpose of the policy was not to abandon socialist planning, but to try to save it. Some State Owned Enterprises (SOEs) were already trading informally, and some even doing business with foreigners, just to pay the bills. By tacitly approving these informal transactions the Party leadership hoped to control them and gradually rein them in. Instead the opposite happened. Illegal trading doubled from 20 per cent of the market in 1980 to 40 per cent two years later.[2] This became known as *pha rao* – fence-breaking – the bending of rules to get things done.[3] In January 1981, the leadership tried to get tough. It issued Decree 25–CP, ordering all state firms to register their market trading. It was an attempt to control the black market but at the same time it allowed SOEs to 'self-balance' – to buy and sell independently – once they had fulfilled their commitments to the official Economic Plan. It was the real beginning of economic reform. Provincial bosses in the south pushed things even further. At the end of 1985 Ho Chi Minh City's authorities ignored national law and unilaterally allowed firms to use 'new methods' of management. Economic liberalisation was well under way long before the 'official' start of reform in 1986.

And in that year a lot of things happened at once. Growth fell, as did food output, and inflation hit almost 500 per cent.[4] Le Duan, the Stalinist Party boss who'd formally led the country since Ho Chi Minh's death in 1969 (and informally for at least a decade before that), died. The Party called a national Congress and all the pressures that had been building up inside it for a decade exploded. The driving force was partly a group of economic reformers within the Party, but mainly the bosses of the state enterprises who were now enjoying the fruits of their fence-breaking and wanted to legitimise their freedom to trade. They forced the Party leadership to abandon central planning and let the market have greater influence – the process now known as *doi moi*: literally 'change to something new', but more usually translated as 'renovation'. Gradually the parallel 'free' market became dominant, allowing a transition away from old-style central planning far gentler than in any other state socialist country. A vast land reform programme gave farmers control over their fields, agricultural output (which still accounted for 40 per cent of the economy)[5] boomed, Vietnam pulled its troops out of Cambodia and restored relations with China, which in turn allowed cheap imports to resume across the northern border.[6] Peace allowed big reductions in military spending and the fall in Soviet aid forced bigger cuts in public spending generally. By 1991, inflation had fallen to manageable levels.

But if the transition was gentle, it was also slow, confused and contradictory. It's ironic that Vietnam is frequently held up as a shining example of economic liberalisation. The reality is in some ways the opposite. Vietnam's transition was marked by rising state involvement in the economy, by strong efforts to direct the economy from the centre and the Communist Party's determination to take an independent path, regardless of the advice of the World Bank, the International Monetary Fund and other advocates of *laissez-faire* capitalism. At every crisis and juncture the Party's priority has been its own survival. The needs to buy off dissent, spread the benefits of growth and mitigate regional disparities have always trumped calls for too-great liberalisation, deregulation or the singular pursuit of economic growth. The result has, so far, been a combination of economic growth, poverty reduction and political stability unmatched by any other developing country. In the words of Ho Chi Minh, it has been 'success, success, great success'.

When Communism collapsed in Europe, it was foreign capitalists and international donors who maintained Communist Party control in Vietnam. In 1981, aid from the Soviet Union funded about 40 per cent of the Vietnamese state budget. In 1991, it was cut off completely. The Party declared Vietnam open for foreign investment and the combination of low wages, under-used factories and a great geographical location was too tempting for overseas corporations to miss. But even at this point, the state remained in control, and foreign investment was directed into joint ventures with state firms. In every other communist country that has embarked on economic transition, the proportion of the economy controlled by the state has fallen. In Vietnam it actually rose: from 39 per cent in 1992 to 41 per cent in 2003 – and these figures exclude foreign-invested firms, which were usually joint ventures with SOEs.[7] But unlike many other countries, state control did not mean economic torpor – growth rocketed to 8 per cent a year. The boom was particularly strong in the south. By the end of the decade, state firms in Ho Chi Minh City contributed about half of the national state budget. In effect Saigon and its surroundings had taken over the role performed by the Soviet Union two decades earlier.

In almost every other country where the state's share of the economy has risen, the consequences have been stagnation, fiscal crisis and hyper-inflation. Vietnam was different because its state enterprises operated largely without state support; so much so that their 'owners' – government ministries, provincial authorities, Party structures and so on – treated them as, in effect, private companies, albeit ones with privileged access to borrowing from state banks and protection by state agencies. Adam Fforde, a leading economic analyst of Vietnam, calls them 'virtual share companies'. They made profits, they expanded and diversified: Vietnam's exports increased fourfold between 1990 and 1996.[8] Their managers made deals, paid off their protectors and prospered. It was easy for those with the right connections to shut down competition from rivals, imports or newly arrived foreigners. Corruption became endemic, state banks lent money with abandon and some of the firms tried to turn themselves into mini-empires – to the extent, in some cases, that they formed unofficial joint ventures with secretive investors well beyond the scrutiny of the state which was supposed to own them. In the worst cases some of these corporations became outright criminals.

This was not what international donors had been pushing for. Ever since 1993, when the end of the US embargo allowed the World Bank to resume lending to Vietnam, it – and the IMF – had been attempting to persuade the government to follow its traditional recipe of economic liberalisation. In 1996 the Bank, the government and the IMF had even agreed a joint Policy Framework Paper setting out the steps which would be undertaken. It was never implemented. There were plenty in the Party who objected to any attempt to undermine the position of SOEs or to open up the economy to excessive foreign influence. Trying to do so in 1997, when previous World Bank poster boys like Indonesia were in economic meltdown, reinforced the difficulty. The Bank offered $300 million in Structural Adjustment Credits. Vietnam simply turned it down. The country had very little debt and was making enough money from exports and commercial foreign investment not to need the cash. The World Bank, not used to being given the brush-off, walked away with its tail between its legs.

By late 1998 the Bank was back. It and other donors offered Vietnam $500 million in extra assistance (on top of $2.2 billion in unconditional funding) if it agreed to implement a timetable to sell off the remaining SOEs, restructure the state banking sector and introduce a trade reform programme. The government agreed to the deal but then took no action to implement it. The demands were too much for the mainstream of the Party to accept. In December 1999 the donors pledged even more – $700 million – if the country followed its recommendations. The response was uncompromising. Minister of Planning and Investment, Tran Xuan Gia, told journalists, 'You cannot buy reforms with money . . . no one is going to bombard Vietnam into acting.'[9] There could hardly be a clearer demonstration of the Party's priorities. Over the course of three years it turned down a total of $1.5 billion because it placed political stability ahead of the promises of economic liberalisation. Although the Bank continued to lend large sums of ordinary aid which came without strings attached, it failed to enforce its conditions. Vietnam had gone eyeball-to-eyeball with the mighty institution from Washington and won. The Bank came to the conclusion that it was easier to work with the Party rather than against it.

But while the battle with the Bank was raging, the Party began to realise that, even with foreign investment, the state sector wasn't going to be able to provide the necessary million jobs a year. It took an historic decision: to let private industry flourish. In May 1999 a new Enterprise Law was passed, abolishing most of the cumbersome bureaucracy which had prevented private companies from formally registering themselves. The impact, once it came into effect on 1 January 2000, was almost instantaneous: over the following five years 160,000 enterprises were registered. Most of these were existing businesses which had been operating without licences and took advantage of the new law to register. However, the law meant the private sector had finally arrived in Vietnam – 20 years after the start of economic reform. With hindsight, perhaps the long build-up gave these small 'mom and pop' enterprises the time to build up capital and experience before the rude shock of unrestrained market forces steamrollered them into the ground. Vietnam has done much better in this regard than many other 'transition' economies.

Having unleashed the private sector, the final big fight in the Party was about how wide to open the doors to international commerce. It crystallised around whether to sign a Bilateral Trade Agreement with the United States. Talks had begun in 1995, been terminated by Hanoi in 1997, but later resumed. After nine long rounds of negotiations – the final session in July 1999 lasting 17 hours – the two sides agreed what was described as the most complex trade deal in American history, 100 pages long. A key figure on the Vietnamese side was the then Deputy Prime Minister, Nguyen Tan Dung. Time and again when talks appeared to have reached an impasse the Americans spoke directly to him and the blockage was removed.[10] But Dung's deal didn't please those elements of the Party still hostile to foreign trade and the United States. A formal signing ceremony was arranged for that year's Asia-Pacific summit – but was cancelled at the last minute because key figures demanded the text be reviewed by the Party's policy-making body, the Central Committee. It took until July 2000 before the Committee would agree to sign. It was a momentous meeting. Not only did the Central Committee agree the BTA, it also approved the opening of a stock market in Ho Chi Minh City. From this point onwards growth in the private sector began to outstrip that of the state sector and has continued in the same direction ever since.[11] Vietnam was set on a path towards international economic integration which would culminate (after long negotiations) in its admission to the World Trade Organisation in January 2007. By then Nguyen Tan Dung, the man who had helped the Americans negotiate the BTA, was the country's Prime Minister and leading reformer and his daughter was an investment banker.

* * *

Looking at the teeming streets of big-city Vietnam – Hanoi, Danang, Haiphong and Ho Chi Minh City – it's easy to think that Vietnam is all market and no socialism. A riot of advertising overhead, a mêlée of traders below, every alleyway a potential noodle stall and every shady tree a possible barber's shop. Development is literally 'free wheeling'; borne on the back of care-worn motorbikes. But the frenetic activity exaggerates the importance of the indigenous private sector. It provides plenty of jobs and a lot of excitement but there are few private businesses of any size. From the peasant women who clog up junctions in the old quarter of Hanoi trying to sell fruit and vegetables to the shop owners who watch them with disdain, most private enterprises survive on low margins.

The history of Vietnam's private sector is literally built into one shop on the corner of Hang Chieu ('mat-selling street') and Nguyen Thien Thuat (named after an early resistance fighter against the French) in the Old Quarter. Above the efflorescence of consumer packaging, passers-by can see its heritage. The socialist stucco lettering over the front still declares the building a government store. This was where people once queued to buy the meagre rations of food available under the old state-subsidy system. Nguyen Quang Hao was one of the shop's administrators then and he remembers those days well. 'Under the subsidy system you could only buy your assigned portion,' he says. 'People brought their ration cards. They could only have 15 kilos of rice each per month.' Hao is now a relatively prosperous man, wearing a pair of designer spectacles to inspect the mountain of locally made and imported convenience foods piled up around his till. He took over the store in 1989 and now runs the place as the owner of a successful private business. Hao is very happy with economic reform. 'These days you can buy whatever you want, so long as you have the money,' he says with a grin.

There are bigger private firms but they're few in number. Although 350 companies are now listed on the country's two stock exchanges, 99 per cent of the country's businesses are still small or medium sized. In 2005 there were just 22 domestic privately owned firms among the top 200 companies and, as we'll see later, 'private' is a debatable term.[12] More important to the country at the moment is the international private sector. If you head due east from Hao's shop, over the Red River on the Chuong Duong Bridge and out to the city limits, you'll quickly understand the significance of foreign direct investment to Vietnam. The highway between Hanoi and Haiphong once ran through rice fields. Now the fields are mostly hidden behind a chain of industrial parks and manufacturing sheds stretching almost the entire 50 miles between the two cities. On the outskirts of Haiphong, one of those great sheds is home to the Taiwanese-owned Stella Shoe Factory. Within its massive compound 7,000 workers toil in four vast halls. Two or three long conveyor belts run the length of each hall under signs revealing who the footwear is being made for: boots for the American outdoor brands Timberland and Merrell, shoes for the British company Clarks and even designer-wear for a well-known Italian label. Clarks – one of Europe's biggest footwear brands – makes a third of its world output in Vietnam. Machines stamp and tenderise the leather, prepare the soles and finish the sealing but most of the other work is done by hand. Stretching the leather over the lath and precisely hammering in nails are tricky jobs. The noise is intense and the work unrelenting, but as shoe factories go, it's a nice one. It's bright, cool and the workers have access to a clinic and welfare services. Graeme Fiddler, the Vietnam Manager for Clarks has been to plenty of other shoe factories in Vietnam that his company would never work with. 'Clarks owners are Quakers, which means they try to live up to ethical standards,' he explains.

Graeme has watched the factory develop, literally, from a greenfield site in just a few years. Its first employees came straight out of the rice paddies and had to be trained from scratch. Many had never used a modern toilet before and would instead bring their own banana leaves to work. But they slowly acquired the skills necessary to make sports shoes and then, as their abilities improved, leather footwear. In mid-2006 each worker earned, on average, between $60 and $80 per month. In Europe and North America that would be below subsistence, but at the time it was double the minimum wage in Vietnam. It was also much more than any local farmer could earn. Vu Thi Tham, a worker on the children's shoes production line, didn't appear to be overjoyed with her job, but it paid better than being a peasant. 'Binh thuong,' she said in Vietnamese: 'It's OK. I'm working here because the income is stable. Before I was a farmer and my income depended on the weather. If it was good, I could make good money. But if it was bad, I couldn't. Even in good times I could only make $30 per month but working here I can make $60 or more if I do overtime.'

Low-skilled and labour-intensive industries like footwear are traditionally the first stop for any industrialising country. In Vietnam they have created hundreds of thousands of jobs and underpinned its boom. But to sustain growth the country needs to attract higher-skilled industries which pay better. Vietnam has been very lucky in that it opened its economy at just the time when multinational corporations began to doubt the wisdom of relying too much on China. Many have put huge amounts of investment into factories along China's southern and eastern coasts but are now making provision in case the situation there ever turns against them. This 'China+1' strategy has brought many big firms to Vietnam. The Japanese electronics giant Canon is one of them. It now makes more than half its computer printers in a complex of plants around the city of Bac Ninh, north-east of Hanoi. In 2005 it was the thirteenth-biggest company in Vietnam.[13] Beginning with relatively simple ink jet printers, it has now expanded output to include more sophisticated laser printers.

The factories are big, grey, windowless boxes. Security is a major concern; strangers aren't allowed inside lest they see the company's techno-logical secrets. Within, everything is highly disciplined. When the gates open early in the morning, hundreds of workers ride in on their bikes, change into their company overalls and stand in line to sing the company song. This is the way Vietnamese children start school every day, so it's been easy for Canon to find the right kind of worker. The company's General Director in Vietnam, Sachio Kageyama, is clear about why Canon chose to locate in Vietnam. 'Firstly there's a very stable political situation here, very stable economic growth and a very intelligent workforce. These are big advantages.' Most of Canon's workers in Vietnam only assemble compo-nents which are manufactured elsewhere. All day big trucks pull up at the factory gates bringing in parts from abroad. 'For the moment we import the vast majority of our parts from south-eastern China because industry in Vietnam is still immature,' explains Mr Kageyama. 'However, we are making efforts to raise the ratio of domestic parts and we are also making some key components inside our factory.' Potentially more significant for Vietnam than the big trucks at the gates are the few small ones bringing small quanti-ties of components from other manufacturers who've set up locally to supply Canon's assembly lines.

And Canon isn't alone. Vietnam is attracting more and more hi-tech companies. Samsung of South Korea is constructing a $700 million mobile phone plant nearby. The US chip-maker Intel has built a billion-dollar factory outside Ho Chi Minh City; Hon Hai, a Taiwanese company making iPods for Apple and computers for Dell and Hewlett-Packard, has opened a billion-dollar plant near Hanoi; and many others, including NEC, Foxconn, Brother and Matsushita have joined them. In 2006 Vietnam exported merchandise worth $40 billion – most of it from the foreign-invested sector.[14] The country is doing well.

But growth has exposed Vietnam's weaknesses. Manufacturers regularly complain that roads are falling to pieces and ports are too congested. More seriously, when Intel started to recruit staff it discovered that out of 2,000 applicants, just 40 were qualified to work in its factory, the lowest proportion of any country where it operates. Other foreign technology companies reported similar problems. Although Vietnam has been very successful in spreading literacy – official statistics show literacy levels of more than 90 per cent – university education has long suffered from corruption and over-emphasis on Marxist-Leninist studies and national defence training. The requirements for getting a degree from a Vietnamese state university typically include being able to sprint 100 metres and fire an AK-47. There's less emphasis on vocational skills. The Education Ministry says it plans to double the proportion of university lecturers with doctorates to 30 per cent by 2015. Whether that will solve the problem or simply make it worse by encouraging universities to hire staff with fake doctorates may not be discovered until it's too late.

Another major problem for foreign companies in Vietnam is the fragile state of the law, as the then twentieth largest bank in the world, the Dutch-owned ABN Amro, found out during 2006. The story began with a woman called Nguyen Thi Quynh Van. In March 2006, shortly before her 36th birthday, Van was arrested on suspicion of 'causing serious losses to the state' in her role as Deputy Head of Trade Financing at the Haiphong city branch of Vietnam's fourth largest bank, the state-owned Industrial and Commercial Bank of Vietnam: Incombank for short. She was alleged to have lost $5.4 million in a series of speculative currency deals with ABN Amro and at least two other foreign banks based in Vietnam. In most countries this would have been a relatively straightforward case of prosecuting a 'rogue trader'. But in Vietnam, losing state resources is a crime carrying the death penalty. Rather than focus on the alleged misdemeanours of its employee, Incombank chose to sue ABN Amro for the return of its money, insisting, in the words of one official, that 'Many kinds of currency have been illegally withdrawn and it is our policy that once someone has intentionally caused damage to our company, they have to be responsible for the return of what they have taken.' ABN Amro maintained that 'The trades were valid and all the trades were settled' and refused to pay. What ensued over the following eight months was a demonstration of the limits both of Vietnam's market economy and of the rule of law, as Incombank used the state and its security forces in what looked like a campaign of blackmail against ABN Amro. The trader and the bank clearly enjoyed the protection of what Vietnamese call an 'umbrella' – someone with power.

Six weeks after Van's arrest, police detained two of ABN Amro's local back office employees on the grounds that they had helped Van misappropriate the money. Its Country Executive, De Pham, a Vietnamese-American, was barred from leaving the country despite being pregnant and needing to travel for check-ups, as was another expatriate executive. In July, two more local ABN Amro employees were arrested, both of them currency traders, and a date was set for Incombank's case in the Hanoi court. At this point Incombank's case rested on a highly obscure piece of legislation: a directive issued by the State Bank of Vietnam (SBV) seven years before but not implemented until after the arrests had been made. Under Decision 101/QD–NHNN of 23 June 1999, foreign exchange dealers were obliged to register with the State Bank and, according to the Incombank official, 'The people involved at our branch weren't registered and persons at the other bank knew about this and still undertook transactions with them, so it's clear that they were wrong as well.' ABN Amro argued that the regulation was intended to apply to banks selling currency to the public – not to deals done between banks – and pointed out that the SBV had only asked banks to register their traders well after the case had become controversial. The SBV refused to explain its actions, despite being officially responsible for financial regulation. One very senior official would only say, 'The investigation is the responsibility of the Police Economic Crime Department. We have to wait for their results.'

The general assumption among businesspeople in Hanoi was that Van and Incombank were being protected by people with connections running deep into the Ministry of Public Security. The police simply barged the State Bank out of the way. What mattered was not the law but raw power. With six ABN Amro employees either in prison, under house arrest or barred from leaving the country, power was clearly in the hands of the Ministry of Public Security. But then came the first signs of a tussle. The foreign business community, which had been noticeably silent about the case, started to speak up. The Chairman of the American Chamber of Commerce Tom O'Dore said he was concerned by the 'criminalisation of normal business transactions, and the lack of involvement by the State Bank in legal proceedings involving financial institutions', and warned that this 'could freeze business in Vietnam and negatively impact Vietnam's financial markets in general and foreign exchange markets in particular'. The case began to receive coverage in the international media and the Prime Minister ordered an investigation. Shortly afterwards De Pham was allowed to fly abroad for medical treatment, on condition that she deposit $10,000 in bail and promise to return. But at the same time the Vietnamese media began to report that charges against her would be dropped, 'If the Dutch bank repaid the losses to the Vietnamese bank'. To foreign observers this looked extremely unsavoury. If the authorities believed a crime had been committed they should have pursued the allegation or dropped the charges. The position they adopted seemed more like extortion.

In September 2006 the Dutch government sent its Development Co-operation Minister to Hanoi to express its concern but the only response from the police was to widen the criminal investigation. Major-General Pham Quy Ngo, head of the investigation, tried to rebut allegations that the police were criminalising normal business operations but his comments in a news conference appeared to demonstrate that his team had little understanding of modern banking; he expressed surprise that '500 [foreign exchange] contracts were conducted without money changing hands'; the practice of 'netting off' profits against losses over a particular time period appeared to be unknown to him. However, he then introduced a new allegation: that some of the deals between Incombank and ABN Amro had been at rates outside the permitted bands for foreign exchange trading. This, he argued, 'was a new form of criminal activity'. At the time banks were only allowed to trade the US dollar and the Vietnamese dong within a band of 0.25 per cent either side of a rate set by the State Bank. (Nevertheless, it was widely understood in the financial community that trades regularly took place outside that band through the use of options and other financial instruments.) But, he again suggested, 'If ABN Amro repays the money, De Pham is not likely to be charged with any criminal offence.'

This seemed to be the killer move. The State Bank fell into line with the police, declaring at the end of October that its 'Inspection of the ABN Amro's Hanoi branch and an initial police investigation confirmed that ABN Amro's Hanoi branch seriously violated Vietnamese law and international practices.' There were also suggestions that the State Bank might start to investigate ABN Amro's transactions with another state-owned institution, the Bank for Agriculture and Rural Development, which was said to have lost over $18 million. ABN Amro began to see the writing on the wall. With the law so vague that it could not prove its innocence and with its staff still in various forms of detention, it gave in. At the end of November 2006 it announced it had transferred $4.5 million to a police custody account. Its only public comment was to say that it 'didn't wish to profit from illegal actions of others'. Shortly afterwards all the ABN Amro staff were freed from their various forms of detention and the Vietnamese government announced that the Incombank trader was not facing the death penalty. Things went quiet for a bit and then, seven months later, the Government Inspectorate announced the results of its investigation into the affair. It put the entire blame on the State Bank of Vietnam and its governor Le Duc Thuy, saying that the 'Discrepancies were due to a lack of proper regulations on trading foreign currencies among banks' – exactly what ABN Amro had been saying for the previous year. That seems to have been the end of the case, except that in April 2008 Incombank changed its name to Vietinbank. Businesspeople in Hanoi suggested it was partly because of the international notoriety it had earned during the case. On Christmas Day 2008 Vietinbank became the second state-owned bank to float on the stock exchange.

* * *

The foreign-invested sector is a highly visible part of the economy, employing millions of people and providing plenty of tax revenue, but it doesn't dominate the commanding heights. They are still, in theory at least, controlled by the state. In 2005, 122 of the 200 biggest firms in Vietnam were state-owned. The figure has changed only marginally since then, although some privately owned banks are now marching up the league. For the Party, a strong state sector is the way it can maintain national independence in an era of globalisation. It means the Party can still set the big goals – like its decision, in December 2006, to develop the country's 'maritime economy' – a catch-all concept covering everything from oil to fish and ships. It is also determined to maintain high degrees of state control over strategically important sectors such as natural resources, transport, finance, infrastructure, defence and communications.

The Party has learnt from the mistakes of the past: keeping state enterprises insulated from the outside world does the country no favours – to thrive they need new investment and modern technical and managerial skills. It's prepared to use all the tricks in the capitalist book to keep the socialist part of the economy sailing. Corporations have been free to form joint ventures with foreign partners and sell stakes to overseas investors, even to 'equitise' (the word 'privatise' is still politically suspect) – just so long as the management, as a whole, does the Party's bidding. In return, they get access to preferential government support. One of the best examples, although far from being the only one, is the Vietnam Shipbuilding Industry Group: VinaShin. VinaShin has benefited from an extraordinary amount of state support. When Vietnam issued its first sovereign bond worth $750 million in 2006, the proceeds didn't go to build roads or universities but to VinaShin. When Prime Minister Dung made an official visit to Germany in 2008 one tangible result was a $2 billion loan from Deutsche Bank – also for VinaShin.[15] The Swiss bank Credit Suisse lent the company another billion.

VinaShin has an ambitious goal: to make Vietnam the world's fourth-biggest shipbuilder by 2018. One of the ways it's doing this is by using that state financial support to build ships cheaper than anywhere else. One of the beneficiaries is a British company, Graig. Based in the Welsh capital, Cardiff, Graig specialises in commissioning bulk carriers and then contracting them out as workhorses of the international sea trade. Their 53,000 deadweight ton 'Diamond 53s' ships have been particularly successful. Most have been built in China, but in 2004 VinaShin won a contract to build 15 of them for a total price of $322 million. The deal would never have happened without state backing. VinaShin's facilities and skill levels were initially so poor that Graig needed a guarantee it would get its money back if the ships didn't float. But private banks wouldn't provide the guarantee and initially nor would the state-owned ones. It was only when the Prime Minister himself directly ordered the state banks to put up the guarantees, on the day before the deal was due to be signed, that it went ahead.

By April 2006 the first vessel was ready to launch at the Ha Long shipyard in the far north-eastern province of Quang Ninh. It was a huge occasion. The *Florence* was the largest ship ever built in Vietnam. On launch day its 190-metre-long black and red hull towered 30 metres over the assembled crowd. The workers who'd built the ship went quiet, the higher-ups who'd come to see the big day were all in place. It was a crucial moment for Vietnam's maritime industry. The order was given and the *Florence* slid down the slipway. Everyone cheered – for a while. But a few hours later the cheering was replaced by blushes. The *Florence* had sprung a leak – compartment four (of five) was half full of water. It wasn't the kind of publicity VinaShin wanted on the day that was supposed to mark Vietnam's entry into the shipbuilding big league. The press offered several explanations: that a block had fallen over during the launch and punctured a metre-long hole in the hull; that the slipway had been built too short and too steep so the hull cracked when it hit the water.[16] In spite of all the training and advice from Graig, VinaShin clearly had something to learn about building ships.

However, the hole was repaired and the *Florence* is now safely sailing the seas, along with several other Vietnam-built Diamond 53s. Since the unfortunate launch, Graig has expanded its contract with VinaShin to include 29 Diamond 53s and 10 smaller Diamond 34s – worth $1 billion in total. But the Harvard economist David Dapice wonders how Vietnam as a whole will benefit from the contract, given the amount of state funding being extended to VinaShin. He estimated the company could be losing up to $10 million on each of the first 15 ships that it's building for Graig and questioned whether this was the best way for a poor country to spend its money.[17] But other priorities are setting the agenda at the moment. VinaShin is a key part of the 'maritime economy' strategy so, for the time being at least, it has plenty of leeway to do what it wants – such as make a huge loss on a contract in order to build up the skills and experience it will need in the future. But this isn't the only thing that VinaShin has been doing with its cheap money. Like many of the other big state-owned corporations, VinaShin's attention has wandered from its primary mission and roamed into areas that potentially spell big trouble for Vietnam.

Some of the cheap money went into shipbuilding, but during 2007 VinaShin set up 154 subsidiary companies – one every one and a half days, excluding weekends.[18] Among its new investments were a brewery and a hotel complex in the province of Nam Dinh. It was far from alone. PetroVietnam, the state oil production monopoly, also moved into hotels, and other SOEs developed luxury housing. During 2007 and 2008 investments like these helped to inflate a huge property bubble. But more dangerous for the country as a whole is the way SOEs have moved into finance. Vietnam is heading down a familiar East Asian road. The biggest state corporations are setting up unaccountable funding channels to finance projects with minimal economic logic. By June 2008, 28 state-owned corporations had spent around $1.5 billion either establishing or buying controlling stakes in fund management companies, stockbrokerages, commercial banks and insurance firms. Three-quarters of Vietnam's finance companies are now owned by the biggest SOEs (those known as General Corporations). The cement, coal and rubber monopolies all own at least one. Under Vietnamese law a 'finance company' is almost the same as a bank, except it can't settle payments. But some General Corporations (GCs) now have stakes in banks too. VinaShin owns part of Hanoi Building Bank (Habubank) and there are several other examples. Many also have bought securities companies dealing in shares.

Add all this together and several of Vietnam's biggest General Corporations have the potential to become self-financing 'black boxes'. Funding arrangements are opaque. In late 2008, for example, Electricity Viet Nam (EVN) owned 40 per cent of EVN Finance and 28 per cent of ABBank, which in turn owned 8 per cent of EVN Finance. Completing the circle, both ABBank and EVN owned securities firms which held stakes in EVN Finance. In the words of a recent report for the UN's Development Programme in Vietnam, 'The General Corporation can underwrite, purchase, trade, manipulate and profit from the equitisation of its member companies'.[19] The opportunities for unethical, criminal and nationally destabilising behaviour are plenty. GC bosses think they can make more money by dabbling in these areas than in their core business. As a senior official in the oil monopoly PetroVietnam told a newspaper, 'The most important thing for businesses is economic effectiveness. Over 40 per cent of income of our group comes from non-oil and gas industry. We know that we have to focus on the major fields of business but if investment in the major business fields is ineffective, why are we forced to invest in them?'[20] Despite benefiting from state largesse, company bosses often place greater emphasis on rewarding themselves than on being a national strategic asset.

The Communist Party leadership likes SOEs because they can implement its policies. The Party members who run them can be ordered to carry out Party policies. But many bosses like running SOEs because they provide plenty of opportunities for personal enrichment. Setting up a subsidiary company and appointing oneself to the board is an easy way to make money. Another is to set up a private company owned by a friend or relative and either sell its assets at cheap prices or award it lucrative contracts. With easy money around, it's not hard to bribe patrons, officials and regulators to turn a blind eye to breaches of the law. The Party members in charge of the SOE 'tail' end up wagging the Party policy 'dog'. But this isn't the whole story. What is remarkable about Vietnam is the way, at moments of crisis, the Communist Party can discipline its errant members.

To understand how this happens, it's worth looking at the way the Party operates. The Vietnamese Communist leadership wants to run the country along the lines of something which resembles Gaullism in France. Under 'Vietnamese-Gaullism' a behind-the-scenes elite (the Communist Party) is supposed to set the overall direction of policy and then delegate its implementation to the state (which is controlled by the Party). The government should then draw up the laws and use whatever resources are available to it – the state bureaucracy, SOEs, the private sector, foreign investors, international donors or whoever – to see the policy executed. And, behind the scenes, the Party should monitor, corral and press the various actors to make sure that its policy is followed. That, at least, is what the Party would like to happen. The reality is usually something different. Sometimes the Party acts as a cohesive force – taking a decision and enforcing it – and at others it breaks into factions, partly over ideology but increasingly around individuals and their patronage networks. No one gets elected to the CPV's leadership, the 15-person Politburo, without building up a network of supporters and delivering them benefits in return. Working out whether a particular decision is the result of ideology or patronage is often impossible. In most cases it's probably a bit of both.

Take the current President, for example – Nguyen Minh Triet. President Triet rose to power through the structures of Binh Duong province, just outside Ho Chi Minh City. He helped to turn it into an economic powerhouse, attracting huge amounts of foreign investment, providing hundreds of thousands of jobs and contributing a significant proportion of the national budget. He did so by bending the rules, *breaking fences*, to please investors. He cut through planning regulations to get industrial sites built, he did deals over taxation to attract foreign companies and gave state enterprises a helping hand when they needed it. The reward for his success was promotion within the Party, first to boss of Ho Chi Minh City and then to head of state. But his base is still Binh Duong province and it's now a family fiefdom. His nephew has taken over as the provincial boss and his family control many of its administrative structures. Vietnamese talk about being under someone's 'umbrella'. Triet's 'umbrella' shelters his family and network in Binh Duong just as his colleagues' umbrellas shelter theirs in other places. This shelter gives provinces, state-owned enterprises and, increasingly, the individuals in charge of them leeway to bend and break rules, knowing they are 'protected' from the law. But there are limits to how far any national leader can push the interests of their local networks. National interests eventually have to prevail. Policy must be the result of consensus: national, factional and local interests all have to be satisfied. But reaching consensus usually requires ferocious in-fighting.

In early 2008 the government realised that the property and stock market bubble had gone too far. The effects of wild times in the stock market were spilling over into the wider world. In 2006 the main share index, the VNI on the Ho Chi Minh City exchange, had risen 145 per cent. In the first two and a half months of 2007 it rose a further 50 per cent. The dealing floors of big-city brokerages were filled with people day-trading. Some brought in their savings to gamble on the market. The optimism was unrestrained. On 12 March 2007 the VNI hit a lifetime high of 1,170 points. It never went there again. It bumped around for a bit, ending the year still up about 20 per cent. But then, in 2008, it crashed. The index fell a full 70 per cent – wiping out many of those day traders and the families who'd gambled their savings. Inflation rose to 30 per cent, urban households couldn't make ends meet, factories suffered strikes and discontent grew. It started to look like the beginning of a threat to the Party's rule. It was time for the leadership to fight back.

In April 2008, Prime Minister Dung publicly urged SOEs to limit their non-core business to 30 per cent of their total capital.[21] The fact that the government was reduced to 'urging' SOEs to follow the law revealed the problems it was having in maintaining control. The SOEs didn't listen; behind the scenes in-fighting raged. The government was forced to try a different route. The central bank, which had been giving the GCs an easy ride with low interest rates and a generous money supply, was ordered into line. Rates were raised and the flow of cheap money reduced. Protective umbrellas had been put away; the leadership had been impelled to act in the national interest. It worked, the economy cooled down and the crisis abated.

The GCs were originally modelled along the lines of South Korea's *chaebols*. The *chaebols* had many failings but some, like Hyundai and Samsung, did become massive exporters. Vietnam's GCs have been far less successful: VinaShin has won orders by bidding below cost and PetroVietnam's oil deals in Cuba and Venezuela are more a product of government diplomacy than corporate ability. Most of the state-owned textile industry is unprofitable and steel is pretty backward too. But the state sector remains a pillar of the Party's control – both as a tool of economic policy and as a way to keep provincial supporters, trade unions and other interest groups happy. Though many SOEs are being sold off, the Party has made clear its determination to hold on to the 100–150 most important ones. They continue to benefit from the state's largesse. Although the days of the soft loan from a state bank are largely past, there are plenty of other ways to channel money to them. The state's Vietnam Development Bank (subsidised by aid from foreign governments) and its Social Insurance Fund (expected to become the biggest single investor in the country by 2015) seem to act as unaccountable 'slush funds' for the benefit of the state sector.[22] Clearly SOEs have a significant, if not necessarily bright, future ahead.

* * *

The intertwined networks of Party and business are not confined to the state sector. They dominate the private sector too. Many 'private' businesses are either former state-owned enterprises or still have some state ownership and are still run by Party members. Even truly private companies find it almost impossible to obtain licences, registrations, customs clearance and many other vital documents without good connections. Businesses that don't play the game quickly get into trouble. Surveys suggest that even privately owned banks prefer to lend to 'connected' people.[23] Most of the controllers of the commanding heights of the private sector are either Party appointees, their family or their friends. The Communist Party elite are turning Vietnamese capitalism into a family business. The new business elite are not separate from the Communist Party but members of it, or related to it.

One of Vietnam's richest men for example, Truong Gia Binh, is the Chief Executive of a company called FPT, which started out as the state-owned 'Corporation for Food Processing Technology' before evolving into the 'Corporation for Financing and Promoting Technology' and becoming the country's first IT firm. He's also the only man in Vietnam commonly referred to with the prefix 'former son-in-law' because he was once married to a daughter of Vo Nguyen Giap – war hero, ex-army commander and one-time Deputy Prime Minister. During the 1990s, if a business needed contacts with the army's extensive array of companies or in construction or communications, then General Giap was the man to see. A useful connection for a company selling software and mobile phones. Binh now has other connections: among the investors in his companies are US venture capital firms Intel Capital and Texas Pacific Group.

There are many, many more examples. So many, in fact, that the Vietnamese now have special phrases to describe them: 'COCC' and '5C'. COCC is the junior tier of the new Party-business elite – the provincial bosses and lower-level national Party and government officials. It stands for *Con Ong Chau Cha* – literally 'son of father, grandson of grandfather' but the meaning is obvious to anyone familiar with the traditions of Vietnamese families – the young offer loyalty, the old offer protection. Those under the umbrella of COCC can get away with almost anything, for their patrons outrank the police and the courts. The real elite is known as 5C: they can get away with absolutely anything. It's even alleged that one 5C son murdered another one, but the whole thing was hushed up. 5C stands for *Con Chau Cac Cu Ca* – literally 'all children and grandchildren of the great grandfather'. *Cu* is the most exalted position in the Vietnamese family and every national President and Communist Party General Secretary is eventually given the title. The umbrella of the 5C spreads wide – beyond direct descendants to include more or less the whole family.

In Vietnam such relationships have a cash value. Companies – both domestic and foreign – are prepared to pay large fees for introductions and access to decision-makers. Those who already have access – through family connections – have a big advantage. A good introduction to a key official can be worth as much as $100,000. The money doesn't usually go directly to the politician, it goes to the facilitator – often a relative. Sometimes it's not money but a gift, even a free apartment, which is why state employees on nominal salaries of $100 per month can enjoy a standard of living equivalent to that of a successful business leader. Vietnamese talk of having 'one leg inside and one leg outside' the system. A family member with a low-paid job somewhere in the bureaucracy is a useful way to keep the connections alive while wives, brothers and cousins fish for business outside. Official jobs now also have a value. Heads of departments can charge several thousand dollars for a junior position which offers opportunities and connections.

But making introductions is just one way to make money. Family members of senior officials have found niches all over the business world.

From the beginning of economic reform the Party elite have sent their children abroad to study and allowed them to leverage their position into business advantage. These children have returned home well qualified and ready to take jobs with foreign investors and the new private sector. In the early 1990s, when the World Bank wanted to stimulate private sector development in Vietnam, it awarded many scholarships to young people, including one to a woman called Dinh Thi Hoa who became socialist Vietnam's first Harvard MBA. On her return she founded a company called Galaxy which now incorporates a PR agency, most of the good Western-style restaurant chains in the country, a big cinema in Ho Chi Minh City and a film production company. In many ways it's a model of private sector success. But Galaxy didn't just spring from nowhere. It's one of the many firms created by the children of the Party elite. The World Bank chose Hoa for the scholarship in part because her father was Deputy Foreign Minister. From the beginning reform has been encouraged by giving politicians a direct, tangible stake in it.

It's a common assumption among many observers of Vietnam that the coming of capitalism will create a new force in society, a new middle class with sources of income independent of the Communist Party and able to stand up and defend itself. This may come in time, but it seems a long way off. For the moment getting better off requires loyalty to the Party. The well connected are exploiting their connections to become rich, and the rich are exploiting their money to buy protection from the state. The result is widening inequality between rich and poor. Official figures don't reveal the problem but there are good reasons for that. Vietnam's Gini Coefficient, a widely used measure of inequality, rose from 0.33 to just 0.36 between 1993 and 2006 – about the same as most European countries. However, the data is based on small surveys – just 5,000 people in 1993 – and excludes many of the poorest: people such as low-wage migrants. It also uses out-of-date classifications of rural and urban districts – some once-rural districts are now part of towns – and so fails to fully capture the real inequalities between lifestyles in villages and in cities.[24] More grounded measurements of deprivation tell a different story. Poor families have benefited less from falls in infant mortality and malnutrition than better-off ones. A third of poor children are underweight, compared to just 5 per cent of better-off ones. Bear in mind that in Vietnam the 'poverty line' is around $15 per month. Anyone earning over that is not classified as 'poor'. A further problem is that most wealth in Vietnam is hidden from view, usually because it has been obtained through shadowy means. The gap between the top and the bottom of the pile is wide and getting wider.

Until recently, Vietnam had shared out the benefits of growth more equitably than any of its neighbours; the Party's socialist orientation still meant something. In the future though, redistribution will mean taking wealth away from those who are its biggest supporters. Does it have the ability to stand up to its own children and demand they hand over part of their wealth through taxation to benefit poorer people in faraway provinces? We shall see. On the edge of Hanoi the *Bao Son* – 'Paradise' – Company has built a theme park. The company, which grew out of the *Bao Son* Hotel in central Hanoi, owned by the family of a Party leader, features a re-creation of the streets of old Hanoi: single-storey houses, tiled roofs and cobbled streets. And there, for anyone who can afford the fee, it's possible to be pulled along in a rickshaw. The human rickshaw was seen as such a symbolic example of colonial exploitation by the early communist revolutionaries that they banned it after they seized power. Today, their children and grandchildren, Vietnam's nouveaux riches, are taking themselves for a ride. The question must be, 'Are they taking the country with them?'

2

Selling the fields

On 10 January 2007, the day before Vietnam joined the World Trade Organisation, Tran Thi Phu dug up her field in the northern province of Ha Tay and took it away in a wheelbarrow. Under a flat winter sky she and her cousin scraped away the topsoil with their hoes, piled it on top of old fertiliser bags and heaved it on to the barrow. The two then carted it into their village, Hoai Duc, several hundred metres away, to sell it to a neighbour who was expanding his fruit-growing business. Across the paddy fields behind them ran a line of low wooden marker posts. In a few weeks they would mark a boundary between the future and the past. Everything to their left would become part of a private housing development, while to the right barefooted women would continue to plant and transplant rice seedlings by hand. The day before, Mrs Phu had been told she would receive the equivalent of about five years' wages as a farmer for her land. But that hadn't made her happy. 'I don't know what to do with the money,' she said. 'Perhaps I'll invest it in something but I don't know what. I'm a farmer, I only know about growing rice and raising livestock. I don't know about business or buying or selling. I would prefer the government to build a big factory here so that we could go and work, it would be better than compensation – or apartments.'

To the right of the posts, life continued as normal. Despite being up to her calves in freezing grey water another farmer, Nguyen Thi Hang, was more than happy with her lot. She knew it was far better than it had ever been. 'Five years ago it took me most of the day to push my bike home from the market in Hanoi with the vegetables to feed the animals. Now I can get there and back in two hours if my husband takes me on his motorbike.' She was an advert for the new model peasant. 'It used to take six months to get a Vietnamese pig up to 60 kilos – now I can get a western breed up to that in just two months.' Her story is being repeated across the country; bad news for the traditional potbellied pig, which has almost died out in its home country, but a revolutionary advance for millions of Vietnamese farmers. She and her husband continued to work the land but her children had no intention of spending their lives bent double with fists full of muddy plants. Every day they motorbiked into Hanoi, the son to work for a computer company, the daughter in a clothes shop. Five years ago they would have been happy to ride a Chinese-made Honda Dream. Now they wouldn't be seen dead on such an old man's bike. Their consumption, whether of motorbikes or mobile phones, was intended to be conspicuous.

But in spite of all this, the family wasn't going to give up their land. Land remained their anchor. It was the loss of that anchor that, 100 metres away, Tran Thi Phu was mourning. For both women, indeed for any farmer over the age of 30, famine remains a vivid memory. For a time in the early 1980s the combination of war, sanctions and doctrinaire state socialism caused severe food shortages and hunger. The legacy of that period is written on the body of every Vietnamese whose growth was stunted by malnutrition. The fear that such a thing could happen again keeps peasants attached to their land: the belief that if the mobile phones ever stop ringing, they could still grow their own rice and survive. To lose land is to plunge into uncertainty.

These two women, Nguyen Thi Hang and Tran Thi Phu, are living proof of Vietnam's transformation. Life is vastly better now than 20 years ago. Most of the old vicissitudes of peasant life have been conquered. Malnutrition has fallen, infectious diseases have been contained and life expectancy lengthened. Land has been distributed widely and peasants have been empowered to farm what they want and sell it, in theory, to whomever they want. The results have been dramatic. In less than three decades the number of people living in poverty has plummeted, roads have been built, electricity lines connected, clinics, schools and sanitation systems constructed. But it's taking a long time to overcome the burdens of the past. Life as a farmer is still hard.

As the economy has industrialised, the share of agriculture in GDP has halved – from 40 per cent in the mid-1980s to about 20 per cent now. But the number of people working as farmers has fallen much more slowly – from three-quarters of the population in the 1980s to about half now. In other words farmers have shared out a smaller proportion of the gains of growth among a larger number of people. They've become better off, but significantly less better off than people working outside agriculture. Although some farmers are doing well, others are struggling to cope and they have a new set of problems to face. Ill winds still blow through the paddy fields in the form of land grabs, predatory local officials and swings in global commodity markets. The effects will be critical for the country's future because the countryside is still home to most Vietnamese – something around 70 per cent – although, as these two women were finding out, in many places 'rural area' exists more in the official classification than in the appearance of the land. Long after the Hoai Duc housing development is completed, the area is likely to remain classed as a 'rural area'.

The organisation tasked with defending farmers' interests is based in one of the many yellow-painted villas within the 'Party quarter' along Quan Thanh Street in Hanoi. Its meeting rooms have the regular trappings of every official institution: red velvet curtains, a brassy bust of Ho Chi Minh and a large golden motto insisting that 'The Communist Party of Vietnam will be glorious for ever'. The Farmers' Union is one of the Party's main 'mass organisations'. Its role is to be a 'transmission belt' representing farmers to the Party – but also instructing farmers about Party policy. Its leader in 2007, Vu Ngoc Ky, had an awesome task, but still spent his spare time writing and publishing poetry. On the day I met him he'd just finished another work – an ode in honour of his members. In it he called on farmers to make the country rich so that it can catch up with the rest of the world. 'Spring comes with many expectations, roses are fresh and we advance on tomorrow . . .' read one line. But he was well aware that for farmers on the margins of viability, spring brings foreboding rather than expectation. Will resources last until harvest time? How will ends meet?

Unlike farmers' leaders in most other countries Ky didn't see his job as defending his members' right to stay on the land. He was candid about what needed to be done. 'At the moment we have 32 million rural labourers and we can say around 10 million of them are underemployed.' His answer was not to demand greater subsidies for farmers to preserve their way of life. The Party had decided to industrialise the country, a large number of farmers needed to leave the land and, as head of the Farmers' Union, he would make sure it happened. Ky expected a third of the country's farmers to lose their jobs over the coming years as a result of agricultural modernisation and competition from imports. 'So the most important thing now is to provide training for them so they have better skills which will satisfy the requirements of the service industries,' he said. In other words, farmers needed to retrain as waiters and drivers. The union was already laying on classes to teach the skills it thinks will be demanded in the new economy.

* * *

Life – not just rural life: national life – depends upon rice. In spite of more than 20 years of economic liberalisation and rising living standards, the population still depends upon the paddy fields for the bulk of its daily calorific intake. Rice production contributes around two-thirds of the income of rural households. Rice is such an integral part of Vietnamese culture that the word for it – *com* – can also be used to mean both 'meal' and 'wife'. For some farmers rice is simply a means of survival. In the central region of Vietnam, where the mountains almost meet the sea and good land is in short supply, farmers sell, on average, just a third of what they harvest. The land is so poor, their farming so inefficient, that they barely grow enough to live on and only a very few are able to trade significant amounts. And yet they continue to cultivate it; it's a means of self-reliance and a form of insurance. If hard times fall at least there will be something to eat. For others rice is a commodity and a means of enrichment. In the northern Red River Delta, around the cities of Hanoi and Haiphong, farmers sell about two-thirds of their rice and in the Mekong Delta in the south even more, around three-quarters. Increasingly the Mekong River Delta both feeds the urban population and provides a steady source of export income. Despite the growth in manufacturing it still makes up around a fifth of the country's total export earnings.

The source of this bounty starts flowing almost 3,000 miles away in the mountains of Tibet. The Mekong River carries nutrients from China, Burma, Laos, Thailand and Cambodia to the paddy fields of *Cuu Long*, the nine-mouthed dragon of the Mekong Delta. Historically, the river's annual floods spread over the land, washing away the salt brought inland by sea tides and depositing in its place the silt of faraway lands. Farmers here don't have to scratch a living like their fellows in central Vietnam, nor do they fear the chronic uncertainty of drought and downpour like those in the north. Indochina's great fertilising river, with its predictable flows and its revitalising sediments, permits them to reap three crops a year from their paddy fields. But this bounty is not just the gift of the river. Without the ingenuity of its agriculturalists Vietnam's rice industry would be a shadow of its successful self. To see the difference they make, a visitor only has to drive up the holy mountain of Nui Sam outside the city of Chau Doc. From the summit (which used to be a secret military base until the army opened a business selling soft drinks and snacks to visiting pilgrims) a line snakes across the landscape: the border between Vietnam and Cambodia. On the southern side the fields are bright green, full of rice seedlings doing their bit for national development. Across the fence the fields are brown. Cambodia's farmers have harvested all they need and now they're taking a rest. Vietnam's success has been built upon the hard work of millions of peasants and some indefatigable scientists. One of the key figures was a man born within sight of Nui Sam mountain, Vo Tong Xuan.

Xuan was a city boy, the son of an office clerk, but trips to his uncle's house in the village bred in him an affection for Vietnam's farmers. He pitied the long hours they worked and tiny returns they received. Unable to afford an engineering degree, he studied agriculture in the Philippines and went into research at the International Rice Research Institute (IRRI) there, the birthplace of many new varieties of rice and techniques of farming – what became known as the 'green revolution'. In 1971 the University of Can Tho in his home province asked him to return and pass on what he had learnt. He'd been back just two months when he was drafted into the southern army, but thanks to string-pulling by the university president he was allowed to leave after basic training and return to teaching. Using manuals he translated himself, he preached the good news of the green revolution to farmers like his uncle. He quickly noticed the problems they were having with the brown plant-hopper, a tiny bug which literally sucks the life out of rice plants, and tried to introduce a resistant variety, known as IR25, which he'd seen developed at IRRI. The Mekong peasants weren't keen to risk the new grain, so Xuan took his message down to the local radio station, talked about the benefits of the new variety and offered any farmer who came to the station a kilo of free rice seed. The farmers were tempted and the plant-hoppers were beaten.

But despite successes like this, the situation in the Delta became more and more difficult as the fighting between Communist and government-backed forces intensified. Nonetheless, Xuan kept teaching and researching. In early 1975 he was completing his doctorate in Japan when he made a remarkable decision. He could easily have applied for asylum somewhere but, on 2 April, with the war in its final days and Communist forces closing on Saigon, he chose to return home once again and carry on his work with the farmers of the Delta. He and his colleagues guarded the department against looters and came to a working arrangement with the new management of the university. The Communist rector hadn't even graduated from high school but he allowed the staff to continue with their research and teaching. It was a fortunate decision. In 1976 a new strain of plant-hoppers returned, able to overcome IR25's defences. In response Xuan and his students promoted the virtues of another IRRI variety, IR36, and the problem was again contained. Despite this, things were getting worse for farmers in the Delta, though this time the problems were man-made. The plant-hoppers weren't the only invasion the farmers were facing. Emboldened by victory, Hanoi was moving quickly to try to enforce collective agriculture – in spite of having failed to make it a success in the north for the previous 20 years.

On collective farms peasants were generally organised into 'work brigades' and were paid – in food and sometimes in cash – on the basis of 'work points', broadly calculated on the amount of labour they contributed. But because farmers were paid on the basis of the whole brigade's achievements it was easy for idlers to let others take the strain and morale fell. Making things worse, the 'farm gate' price of rice was kept deliberately low in order to provide cheap food for the cities at the expense of low incomes for the farmers. In the end, peasants put more effort into the 5 per cent of the collective's land that they were allowed to farm privately than into the 95 per cent they were supposed to be working for the common good. Rice yields in the north fell from the early days of collectivisation in 1958 right to the early 1970s. When the Party tried to impose the system in the south the most productive farmers simply refused to join in. By 1986, ten years after unification, just 6 per cent of farmers in the Mekong Delta were in collectives. But rice yields still fell. They dropped by a quarter in the south in the four years after 1976 because the supply of inputs such as fertiliser had been put under the control of inefficient state-owned enterprises at prices set by the state. The response from the farmers was to sell more and more of their production outside state channels through unofficial markets. By the end of the 1970s, falling output, a lack of foreign aid, falling levels of state investment and a series of natural disasters meant the country was facing starvation: in 1979 it had to import 13 per cent of its basic subsistence needs.

Conceivably, the Party could have followed a path previously trodden by Joseph Stalin and the Khmer Rouge, sending the troops into the countryside, compelling peasants to work harder and liquidating those who resisted. But it didn't. Whether for reasons of principle or pragmatic politics it decided to pursue a different path. Two years after China had done the same thing, it moved away from collective farming and back towards household production. The 1980s was a decade of growth. In 1989 the country exported rice for the first time in many years. A decade after Hanoi had tried to impose northern-style land policies on the south, the Party had been forced to recognise their limitations. With farmers now responsible for the basic decisions about production, output has exploded – at least in the south. Vietnam is now the second biggest rice exporter in the world, after Thailand. (Not the second biggest *grower*: its output is dwarfed by China, India and, to a lesser extent, Indonesia.)

Not everything is rosy for the rice grower, though. The industry's success is based on quantity rather than quality. Vietnam's rice exports make up almost a fifth of the world total by volume but only 5 per cent by value. There's little incentive to improve the situation because most exports are arranged through government-to-government contracts with neighbours like the Philippines and Indonesia and old political allies such as Cuba and Iraq. These provide lucrative opportunities for officials in the Ministry of Trade and Industry and their subordinates to take a hefty cut. Although farmers could, in theory, sell to anyone, in reality they are tied to the people they know and who have the capital to buy. That usually means local agents of state-owned companies. These companies also provide farmers with their seeds and technical advice. Farmers are locked into the system. In 2008 this was the cause of a crisis right across the southern rice basket.

When fears of food shortages forced up global prices in the first months of the year, the government imposed tight export controls to try to preserve stocks at home. But that just pushed up international prices even more. By May the highest grade of rice was selling at over $1,000 per tonne on the international market – but Vietnamese farmers couldn't benefit because of the export ban. Instead local officials and agents of the state-owned food companies encouraged farmers to plant as much as they could of a high-yielding 'green revolution' variety of rice called IR50404 for the second crop of the year, hoping to reap the benefits in the autumn. But then it all went wrong. Global prices fell back very quickly. By September top-grade rice was shifting at just $600 a tonne. Prices for poorer-quality consignments (containing more broken grains) were significantly less. But what might have just been a bad year was turned into a catastrophic one for farmers in the Delta by the effects of corruption at the top. Professor Xuan would call it 'a bitter lesson'.[1]

Rice exports are managed by a very Vietnamese combination of a purportedly free market, corrupt officials and state-owned companies looking to leverage their monopoly positions into profits. The process is deliberately obscure. Although Vietnam officially abolished export quotas in May 2001 and allowed any local company, in theory, to trade rice, the state didn't give up its controlling influence. An official body, the Vietnam Food Association (VFA), still sets minimum prices for export, and rice can't be legally exported without its approval. In theory this protects farmers from exploitation by foreign traders. In practice it's a cumbersome means of maintaining corruption. Behind the scenes, the price is actually set by officials in the Ministry of Trade who control the big government-to-government contracts and share them out between the three big state-owned food companies (VinaFood 1 in the north, VinaFood 2 in the south and VinaFood 3 in the central region). Since international rice dealers aren't allowed to buy rice directly from farmers, and local private companies still rely on the VFA for export licences, the whole trade is, in effect, sewn up. The Trade Ministry officials get their commission from a few big deals, so they're not particularly interested in facilitating open-market trading by farmers with surplus production.

In mid-2008, despite the continuing fall in the global rice price, the VFA (on Trade Ministry instruction) held firm, insisting that top-grade rice should still be sold at $600 per tonne. In mid-August it went even further, raising the floor price to $650 a tonne. But with the global price significantly below that, no exporters were prepared to buy. None of this bothered the VFA or the Trade Ministry because their big deals were already agreed. The government then started issuing orders as if central planning had never gone away. The Prime Minister ordered the SBV, the central bank, to offer cheap loans to rice exporters and decreed that traders should buy rice at a price which gave farmers a profit of 40 per cent – but without defining what that price should be. By September the situation had turned into a crisis.

The Ministry of Agriculture calculated there were three million tonnes of rice sitting unsold in storage around the Delta. Farmers couldn't sell what they'd harvested in spring, and were expecting a bumper autumn crop very soon. There was no more storage capacity. Heaped up in damp piles, the grain started to rot on the farms. With the autumn rains and floods imminent, their whole harvest was at risk. Unable to sell their rice, some couldn't pay back the bank loans with which they'd bought their seeds and fertiliser. The situation burst into the national press and the Deputy Agriculture Minister, Diep Kinh Tan, admitted that he didn't know the VFA's floor price was higher than the market price. Farmers said they hadn't had it so tough for 20 years. They calculated they would make a loss of around $100 on each tonne they sold. But even those prepared to sell at such desperate prices couldn't find buyers. The problem stretched right down the supply chain. As the market price fell, traders left their stocks in storage hoping for the price to rise. One boatman, Tran Van Nam, had invested in a huge new rice barge at the beginning of the year, able to carry 20 tonnes at a time. But the price dropped so sharply that he was making a loss while he was sailing down the river. His load was worth $200 less when he arrived at the buyer's in the evening than when he'd set off from the farmer that morning. 'My wife and I have decided to quit and find another job after selling all the rice on this boat,' he told *Thanh Nien* newspaper.

In the first half of September prices crashed by a quarter. By the end of the month the Director of the Department of Agriculture and Rural Development in Hau Giang province, Nguyen Van Dong, was admitting that 'The situation is very tense'.[2] A farmer in the province, Nguyen Van Thanh, likened the situation to 'sitting on fire'.[3] The Deputy Minister, Nguyen Thanh Bien, openly admitted that half the Mekong Delta's output of IR50404 (probably a quarter of total production) could not find buyers because of its poor quality. Commercial traders were directing most of their criticism at the VFA, blaming its price regulation mechanism for choking off exports.[4] But the VFA was unrepentant. Its acting boss, Huynh Minh Hue, claimed the floor price was not 'preventively high and inflexible', maintaining, in spite of all the apparent evidence to the contrary, that it is 'aimed to protect the rights and interests of exporters and farmers.'[5] The government had run out of ideas. The Ministry of Trade banned reporters from a regular meeting about exports in October – the first time it had done so in ten years. In December the government was forced to admit that all its efforts at managing the market had failed and that it would buy a million tonnes of rice directly from the farmers. The prices weren't generous; farmers lost a lot of money. It also managed to offload a quarter of a million tonnes to a new customer: Nigeria. Given the developments during the previous year, this was probably the lowest-quality grain around.

The 2008 boom and bust have sped up the transformation of the Mekong Delta. Some of the farmers who borrowed beyond their means to try to increase production have fallen victim to suppliers, traders and bankers demanding land in exchange for payment. Many joined the ranks of hired labour or the lines of people heading to the cities in search of work. It's another example of the way economic reform has brought advancement for some but much greater insecurity for many others. Even the Asian Development Bank candidly admitted in a recent report: 'While trade liberalization in rice has had a substantial positive impact on the economy as a whole, the benefits have largely accrued to wealthier and land-rich households, while the poor have not reaped significant benefits.'[6] Those with resources can ride out the difficult years. Those without resources are vulnerable to the new economic storms.

* * *

The province of Thai Nguyen is famous in Vietnam for tea. There are dozens of varieties, from red-brown to bright green: tea for relaxation, tea for medicine and tea for socialising. Most of Thai Nguyen's tea cultivation has little in common with its Indian or Chinese counterparts with their great contouring estates of identical bushes tended by armies of contracted labour. Although some farmers work on contract to big industrial tea growers, most of Thai Nguyen's tea is cultivated by families on tiny fields at awkward angles, most without the benefit of irrigation. The dry earth is not the only difficulty they face. Vietnam is a significant exporter of tea – but its product is generally of low quality and historically its biggest market was Iraq, which took 40 per cent of the industry's exports. The US invasion in 2003 wasn't just a disaster for the people of that country; it badly hurt the livelihoods of tens of thousands of Vietnamese tea growers too.[7] Many of them, like Nguyen Thi Phuong, have a precarious existence. It takes two hours to pick five kilograms of leaf which produces just one kilo of dried tea. Depending on the market, this much tea will earn between 15,000 and 50,000 dong ($1–$3) from a trader – half the price of the product in the shops in the city.

Tea grows best between April and October. During those six happy months tea-picking families have enough cash to pay their bills. If they're lucky they can pay off their debts, and if they're especially fortunate they might be able to put some money by for the winter. But once the weather cools and the tea grows more slowly, life becomes harder and harder. After a few months Phuong's family has to go into debt simply to pay the two dollars a month that the village school charges them for each of their two children to attend. 'It's a struggle to get the money,' Phuong admits, 'but if the harvest fails or the price drops we will continue to send our children to school, and we'll have to borrow more money.' A few years ago the family home was a wooden shack thatched with palm leaves which leaked in the summer rains, blew away in the storms and demanded regular maintenance. Now it has a concrete floor and walls and a flat concrete roof. What made their improved standard of living possible was electricity, which arrived in 1998. The family have no radio or TV but they do own a rudimentary, hand-turned tea drier. With this heated basket the family can process their crop, adding some small value to it and cutting out one of the many middlemen standing between them and the city tea-shops. But they can't cut them all out. They don't have a motorbike to transport their leaves to market and they don't have the contacts to get a good price from the wholesalers. Without savings they have to sell as soon as their first harvest is ready, which is, of course, when all their neighbours want to sell too. The traders know this and screw down the prices. If the family had the resources to store their dried tea until prices rose in the winter they could double their money, but in the meantime they'd starve and their children would be kicked out of school.

The family have a simple ambition for their daughters: to get out of tea farming. 'We'd like them to be teachers – that's a good job. We don't mind if they stay here or if they move away. If they can't be teachers then farming is OK, but we don't want them growing tea – it's so time consuming and difficult.' They have no ambition to expand their farming, take over other plots and mechanise production. They don't have the skills to diversify into new forms of enterprise; they just want to earn a basic living doing what they know how to do. But things are unlikely to work out that way. The cost of living is getting more expensive, not cheaper. Since Vietnam joined the World Trade Organisation, their tea has had to compete with imports from abroad. Attempts to improve the quality and price of the national product will benefit bigger producers who can extract economies of scale and maintain consistent quality standards. At some point small-scale peasant production will finally dip below the margins of viability. Debts will become too great or aspirations too high and the family will be forced to change. Perhaps the family can hold on long enough, until their children get jobs and send remittances home from the city, or perhaps mother or father will follow in the bike tracks of many millions of other farmers who've abandoned the land.

Statistics on migration in Vietnam are sketchy. Like China, the state still tries to control movement with a residency permit system, the *ho khau* (see Chapter 4 for more on this). The lingering effects of the *ho khau* system mean that huge numbers of 'illegal' migrants are missed from the official surveys and even data about legal migrants is hard to interpret, but it's clear that millions are on the move. In the second half of the 1990s, 6.5 per cent of the population migrated and the number has certainly increased since then.[8] Back in the villages it's easy to tell which families have sent their children away. The houses are bigger, there's often a motorbike outside, and inside there's likely to be an ostentatiously large television set. Such conspicuous consumption advertises the benefits of migration to everyone else in the village, prompting more to make the journey. A survey by the international NGO Oxfam found that incomes in Ho Chi Minh City and Hanoi are – on average – more than five times higher than those of rural labourers.[9] The brutal truth is that the quickest way to escape poverty is to abandon farming. However, those who are poorest are usually the least able to be successful migrants. Without the resources to finance such a big risk, or the networks to guide them into good jobs, it's more difficult for them to find work in the booming assembly and manufacturing plants. Some work as petty traders, selling in markets or from the back of their bicycles on city streets. Plenty more work in construction.

Rural labour is powering the growth of Vietnam's industrial parks like the one in Bac Ninh on the new highway between Hanoi and the port of Haiphong. With a ready supply of cheap labour there is little need for building firms to spend money on expensive machinery. Factory foundations are dug with spades and the walls roughly mortared before they are rendered modern-looking with smooth coats of plaster. At Bac Ninh in early 2007 the barracks for this migrant army were rows of bamboo shacks erected by the construction company right on the site of the plastics factory they were building. It was a dormitory in the bleakest sense. A wooden platform ran the length of each shed. Some of the bed spaces were divided from each other by a sheet hanging from the ceiling. Scattered on the beds were the workers' small collections of possessions, mainly clothes. The platform kept them safe from the streams of waste water which ran across the site from the communal washing block in the corner. Here, a big concrete tank provided the water supply for the site and also a large open-air bath for the men who came off shift. The run-off, and any leakage from the toilet block, turned the workers' living area into a pungent swamp.

Beside the toilet block but out of the way of the run-off sat Pham Thi Dung, the site cook. It was her responsibility to keep the construction army fed and marching. Five roaring fires heated great vats of rice and *pho* noodle soup and filled her military surplus tent with smoke and steam. She didn't seem at all unhappy with the conditions either inside or outside the tent. She was quite happy to live in the squalid conditions on the site rather than back in her village. 'I've worked here for five or six years because my work is quite stable,' she said. 'I move with the company whenever they move to a new site. In the village my income was about 18,000 dong [just over a dollar] a day – but now it's double that. It's not much but it is stable, and I can support my family.' Her family were nowhere to be seen. They were back in the village, being kept on the land by the money Dung sent back each month.

* * *

The archetypal village in north and central Vietnam historically had a culture which helped to maintain a degree of equality between their inhabitants, or at least kept inequality within reasonable boundaries. Groups based upon family names, age, religion and trades functioned as a form of social insurance, providing aid if a member died leaving behind an impoverished family or when a natural disaster struck. Communal feasts and rituals demonstrated and reinforced the various hierarchies in the village, whether of age or wealth or learning – which is why the communists hated them. The Communist Party tried to co-opt the ethic of mutual aid through collectivisation but failed to do so, mainly because the state took the village output without providing enough in return. Nonetheless, 40 years of official socialism didn't undermine the tradition of communal solidarity. Many of the old groups still exist today, providing the basis for a strong ethic of mutual aid within the village, particularly at the most labour-intensive times of the year. Farmers provide help during sowing, transplanting and harvesting, knowing that they will receive help in return. Celebrations of weddings and funerals remain opportunities for resources to be transferred from rich to poor through gifts of money. Where these kinds of relationship survive they are helping to maintain village solidarity in the face of development. They're also, in many cases, the basis of resistance to it.

Things were, and are, different in the south. The stronger influence of French colonialism, the commercialisation of much more of the land, and the cultivation of crops such as rice and rubber explicitly for export, combined with a village culture that was significantly less corporate, laid the basis for a less equal and more profit-driven society.[10] Land holdings are bigger in the Mekong Delta – four hectares per household on average, as opposed to just a quarter-hectare in the north. Rather than mutual aid, farmers in the south tend to rely more on hired labour and those who need to earn money hire themselves out rather than working for reciprocal benefits. All these things explain why collectivisation failed so dismally in the Delta.

Collectivisation was not a total catastrophe. It failed to feed the country but it did bring the benefits of socialism deep into the countryside: health services, schools, public administration and so on. Literacy levels soared and disease rates fell. But economic liberalisation destroyed the state subsidy system. Central government now makes only limited contributions to such costs as teachers' wages, road building and water supplies. Local authorities have been obliged to turn to the people to make up the shortfall. As a result, some of the biggest financial pressures on the rural population now come from those who are supposed to be looking after them: the local authorities at the provincial, district and commune levels. A government survey in 1998 found that communes, the lowest level of government, raised about half their revenue from local taxes and a further 30 per cent from 'contributions' and 'donations'. Some of the income is collected as cash but some reflects more the realities of rural life since it's gathered in the form of work on local development projects or payments in kind.

While this might seem a necessary and pragmatic way to raise resources, the actual implementation is frequently oppressive and sometimes punitive for those at the bottom of the social scale. 'Taxes' are usually imposed on the basis of income or the size of land holdings, but 'contributions' can be assessed in ways that aren't transparent and are often demanded equally from everyone, regardless of their capacity to contribute. In 2005 the American anthropologist Pamela McElwee made a study of peasant villages in the north-central province of Ha Tinh.[11] She discovered that people there had to contribute in some way to at least 14 different local 'contribution' funds. There were state taxes on land and other resources, payments for services such as public works and disaster preparation measures, others for constructing new roads and public buildings and finally some that were regarded as voluntary but where there was strong social pressure to contribute, such as funds for flood relief or war veterans. In total some families said they were paying up to 40 per cent of their total household income in various kinds of tax and contribution. This was a vast increase. Four years earlier she had found the same families paying around just 5 per cent of their income. These 'contributions' are demanded of everyone but affect poor households more because they have less money to pay in the first place and also because they usually have larger families, so more is demanded of them. Quite apart from the fact that these fees are imposed without regard for the ability of people to pay, McElwee also found examples of oppressive implementation. A contribution to a road-building project was demanded of an elderly and infirm member of one household on the grounds that her funeral procession would have to pass over the new route.

Foreigners often think Vietnam is a monolithic state, where the centre issues orders which are implemented uniformly throughout the country. Equally they assume that what happens in the village must have been directly ordered from the top. Neither of these things is true. At each level of government, official policies and real-world actions are frequently quite different things and what actually happens depends upon the results of battles between competing interests – only one of which is the demands of Hanoi. At the local level the strongest pressure is usually the one to get rich and the easiest way to do that is to get into real estate. There are vast amounts of money to be made in converting agricultural land into housing or industrial sites, particularly those plots with direct access to major roads. The World Bank estimates that, every year, around 10,000 hectares of agricultural land on the margins of towns and cities is being taken for development. Given that the national average land holding is half a hectare and that supports an average family size of five people, around 100,000 people are likely to be losing their land through development alone each year: one million people in a decade. Some like Tran Thi Phu in Hoai Duc village resign themselves to their fate – but others fight it.

In August 2006 well over a thousand people from Hung Yen province, south-east of Hanoi, came to the capital and camped outside the National Assembly Office for several days. They were well organised, bringing mats to sit on, tarpaulins to keep off the rain and supplies of food and drink. They were so furious they blockaded the office's main gate and from time to time staged sit-ins on one of the capital's main streets. On paper they had no reason to be angry. Their land had been confiscated by a private company for a housing development and they had been offered the correct compensation – $1,200, equivalent to two years' wages. But that wasn't the point. The developers who'd taken the land had paid compensation according to the rates in force in June 2004. The date was crucial because two weeks later, on 1 July 2004, a new land law had come into force stipulating levels of compensation at the market value rather than the value of agricultural land. The farmers weren't bothered by legalities: they knew how much the difference in price was worth and regardless of the niceties of the law they were determined to get it. The demonstration appeared to resolve nothing – it was cleared away after a few days. But several weeks later the newspapers, who'd printed nothing about the initial demonstration, carried an article stating that the developers had agreed to increase the compensation. Behind the scenes arms had been twisted, deals made and a more satisfactory solution agreed.

Land disputes continue to be the hottest political issue in Vietnam, far more corrosive to the legitimacy of the Communist Party than calls for multi-party democracy. Dang Hung Vo was one of those attempting to resolve them. In early 2007, he was in the last few weeks of his term as Deputy Minister for Environment and Natural Resources and, as a result, was unusually open and candid for a senior government figure. He'd had four years in the job, after 18 years as Deputy Head of the National Land Administration, and was about to go into 'retirement' as the Director of the Land Administration Department at Hanoi University. His office, in a very spartan, very socialist, government-yellow office block on Nguyen Chi Thanh Road in the new western suburbs of Hanoi, was like that of a university professor with obsessive-compulsive disorder. It was as if his contribution to the environment was never to throw away any pieces of paper. That may have been because of the enormous range of issues his ministry was supposed to deal with: everything from land disputes to waste management and managing the country's coal industry. His ministry estimated then – it had no exact numbers – that there were at least 15,000 ongoing land disputes in the country. Of these, 'About 70 per cent are to do with compensation, 10 per cent relate to disputes about ownership, the next 10 per cent are the historic cases and 5 per cent are about corruption,' he said. He described the remaining 5 per cent as miscellaneous 'other cases'. In other words, the vast majority of officially registered complaints – around 10,000 – came from the seizure of land for development and arguments over compensation. 'In many villages the land managers use their power to make decisions to benefit certain people and other people disagree with those decisions,' he candidly admitted. 'This ministry's opinion is that we cannot avoid this situation, we have to face it and we have to fix what we have done wrong in the past and try to properly create the legal right of the people. Currently our ministry is issuing many measures to deal with the situation but the disputes are very large in both quantity and quality – things can be so tense.'

Corruption in local government has fuelled a large and growing number of rural protests in recent years. The most dramatic was in the province of Thai Binh in 1997 where something close to an uprising took place, requiring the deployment of large numbers of police and visits by delegations from the top Party leadership to both suppress and resolve the dispute. In the commune of An Ninh, villagers smashed up the local People's Committee building which had just been fitted out with $70,000 worth of chinaware and furniture and then trashed the houses of eight local officials. At one point 10,000 people gathered in the district capital to protest, before being dispersed by police and fire engines.[12] Another major dispute in Ha Tinh province in 2001 began when villagers in one district refused to do their compulsory service helping to repair the main north–south National Highway One in a protest against corruption. They later attacked government buildings, and managed to block the highway for several days.[13] Smaller disputes occur almost constantly, and increasingly farmers bring them to the streets of Hanoi or Ho Chi Minh City.

There's a saying in Vietnam: 'The emperor's rule stops at the village gate'. Historically, villages under Vietnamese rule (which in previous centuries largely meant villages in the north and centre) were largely self-governing and, so long as they paid allegiance and taxes to the king, they were left alone. The saying is still heard today, but it has come to symbolise the problems the Party leadership in Hanoi has in controlling what happens in the rest of the country. In places like Thai Binh province, local bosses have turned their positions into personal or family fiefdoms. Money and influence form a perfidious circle. The Party leadership is well aware of the problem and sees it as a clear threat to its legitimacy. Once people become unhappy with local leaders, it's only a short step to questioning the Party's entire right to rule. That was why, in 1988, it created the Farmers' Union. It realised that it needed a 'pressure group' in the villages to help individuals and households stand up to the old boys in the People's Committee and their network of friends. But now the Farmers' Union has been captured by the old boys, so the Party is looking for new ways to rectify the problem. Its answer has been some tentative steps towards democracy.

Prompted by the 1997 unrest in Thai Binh, the Party unveiled what's known in English as the Grassroots Democracy Decree. Its intent is frequently described by the official slogan: 'The people know, the people discuss, people do and people supervise.' This is not representative democracy with elections, but a form of direct democracy in which budgets are supposed to be transparent, some decisions are taken collectively and implementation of certain policies is overseen by everyone. Its powers, though, are very limited. The people only have the right to *know* about central and provincial government policies – not to discuss them. They have the right to both know and express their opinions about the *implementation* of government policies but it's only when it comes to the management of local infrastructure and social affairs within the village that they have the right to decide anything. The big problem for the Party leadership in Hanoi is that in many places their local cadres are either indifferent or actively hostile to the will or supervision of 'the people'. In many areas it's fallen to international NGOs to educate villages about their new rights and to teach them how to assert them. The fact that foreign organisations have been allowed to conduct this relatively sensitive work shows that the central government is serious about its implementation. The countervailing fact that the NGOs usually have to disguise their intentions amid more general development work shows the difficulties of persuading provincial, district and commune authorities to get on board.

There are lots of interesting battles going on in villages around the country. In some places the whole Grassroots Democracy Decree process has been taken over by the officials it's meant to hold to account. Where 'community development boards' have been set up so that the 'community' can manage a project, they have tended to be dominated by the existing commune officials who are automatically appointed to it. In other places, though, villagers are electing their own candidate as village head, in place of the candidate selected by the local Party officials from the commune. It's rarely discussed in public but things are quietly changing. In November 2008 the National Assembly came close to passing a law which would have allowed an experiment in more substantive democracy. The plan would have required the Chair of the People's Committee in almost 400 communes to be elected in 2009. But Assembly members found too many gaps in the legislation; it was unclear who would select the candidates, for example. The vote was postponed and the terms of incumbent People's Committee bosses were extended by two years. But the process now seems to be developing its own momentum. A form of 'managed democracy' seems to be coming to Vietnam's villages.

* * *

What does the future hold for Vietnam's farmers? The answer is going to be different in different parts of the country. In the Red River Delta around Hanoi, most farmers cling to their land, even though, in a strictly economic sense, there is little point – their farms are just too small and provide too little income. The profit from growing rice on the average-sized plot still leaves a four-person household below the official poverty line. Nevertheless, village culture holds them tight – even among the poorest 20 per cent of the population, just 7 per cent are classified as landless. In the central region, where productivity is low, relatively little produce is sold commercially and Party control remains firm, rural change will be slow, and households are likely to depend on migration for survival. In the south, landlessness is on the rise. In the Mekong Delta region the transition to capitalist farming is almost complete. Large numbers of people have left the land – either through choice or by force – and most of the remaining land has been incorporated into large farms which are managed with mechanised equipment and hired labour.

Migration to the cities is gathering pace but so far Vietnam has largely prevented the development of the kind of vast shanty towns typically found on the outskirts of most Asian cities. The *ho khau* system is partly responsible, but the government long ago recognised that bureaucracy wouldn't be enough to prevent the cities becoming swamped with migrants. Farming households needed to be given alternative sources of employment near their homes. Across the Red River Delta the government has sponsored the development of at least a thousand 'craft villages' directly employing around a million people.[14] Villages around Hanoi have specialised in particular crafts for centuries. The difference is that now their crafts range from the traditional (such as conical hat making, silk weaving or noodle production) to the industrial – such as Da Hoi in Bac Ninh province which specialises in scrap metal smelting. Duyen Truong specialises in the mass production of lacquerware. They have replaced the ancient skill of polishing objects with layers of tree sap by a quick spray with a can of car paint. Another, Son Dong, even specialises in the making of antiques: the craftspeople have a range of techniques to pre-age the products so they will look authentically ancient. It may be that, as these villages develop, the fate of the Red River Delta is to become a vast industrial conurbation stretching from Hanoi to Haiphong.

The Communist Party is playing a very ambiguous role in all this. It's most important economic priorities are economic growth and the creation of jobs for a swelling population. But these are always trumped by its desire to remain in power. On one hand the Party is pushing policies that disrupt, and in some cases destroy, rural life. On the other it's trying to implement policies that it hopes will dissipate local anger and resentment. The evident downside is that in doing so these development policies are provoking land grabs, corruption and new stresses in the lives of the people they're intended to help. As Tran Thi Phu and Nguyen Thi Hang, the two women from the village of Hoai Duc, were finding out, development is both enriching people and tearing apart the old structures which gave them security and gave their lives meaning and purpose. Vietnam's rural transformation has been remarkable, and on the surface things look fine, but there's still plenty of potential for disruption.

3

★

Living on the streets

In 24 hours Nguyen Quy Duc Street would be a pile of rubble but at midday on 27 December 2006 everything seemed normal – 130 shops were still doing business. Nguyen Quy Duc wasn't a pretty street but neither was it significantly uglier than many others in modern Hanoi. This area, the south-west, had exploded out of the old city boundaries long before. The city planners had had grand ambitions – punching a four-lane highway through the fields and lining it with new university campuses, factories and Soviet-inspired housing projects. In between the concrete blocks they had left plenty of spaces, spaces which uninvited people had colonised: spaces like Nguyen Quy Duc Street.

Their story was that of migrants the world over. They had moved to the city in search of work, money and shelter; found a patch of land and put up shacks, each about three metres wide and a couple of metres deep. As the economy liberalised they prospered. They sold the basics of life – street food, clothes, fruit and vegetables – earning enough in the process to turn their shacks into ramshackle concrete houses. Some had even been able to add a floor, or at least a mezzanine, on top to house their extended families. The northern side of the street had become a jumble of grey concrete, corrugated iron roofs, striped awnings and plastic hoardings advertising footwear and Vietnamese German sausage. The buildings were both shops and homes. Meals were cooked over a charcoal stove out front and eaten on plastic stools among the stock. Once the customers were gone, the family beds were rolled out on the floor. In total over a thousand people lived in the 130 shops.

The inhabitants were undoubtedly squatters, but they were squatters who'd been living on their patches for around 20 years, in some cases even paying rent to the local authorities. The buildings were illegal but they were also the livelihood and the future hope of the people who built them. Now they have been told to move out – to make way for what the local authorities were calling a beautification project. Their homes were to be replaced by trees. Rumours that the end was coming had begun to circulate among the residents about three weeks before. Two weeks after that, they were formally told their houses were going to be demolished – and then they were given five days' notice of the actual date. Different people had been offered widely varying amounts of compensation depending, according to some of the shopkeepers, on how good a relationship they had with the officials of the People's Committee of Thanh Xuan district, the local authority.

Most had been offered three million dong in compensation (about $200 at the time) – the equivalent of just one month's income and far less than they'd all invested in their shops. A woman who owned a frozen food store had been offered more – 20 million dong: a fraction of the cost of the freezers and stock she was about to lose. One distraught middle-aged woman, her thin jacket failing to warm her against the damp cold air, her neat appearance defying the imminent destruction, cried out her story. During the day Mrs Hoa sold *pho* – noodle soup – and during the night her home sheltered 14 people, including her deaf son. She'd been offered compensation – she said around $100, the equivalent for her of two months' income – but she said she wasn't going to accept it. She just sat on the pavement and cried. Another woman, Lan, had lived in the street since she was three. The family home was a clothes shop which had clearly been reasonably successful; a good range of stock was hidden behind metal shutters. She had nowhere else to go and once her home was gone, expected to sleep on the street. She would be one of the few who would resist to the bitter end.

Within 24 hours, 22 years of construction on Nguyen Quy Duc Street had been destroyed. It was a textbook demonstration of the way the Vietnamese state can get things done when it needs to: a highly effective mix of persuasion, bribery, leverage and intimidation. The short notice gave the inhabitants little time to get organised, People's Committee officials exhorted them to do their duty, Communist Party members were ordered to set a good example and flatten their own houses early and those with connections were paid large amounts to do the same. The remainder were given a stark choice: demolish your own homes – and salvage the materials – or let the bulldozers do it. Most chose the DIY option. By six o'clock the following morning, well before the heavy machinery arrived, the street was already half demolished. A few, including Lan, left their doors and shutters defiantly locked but they barely hindered the bulldozers. The home made houses didn't offer much more resistance than their bamboo predecessors might have done. As the diggers worked their way along the street, crushing each building in turn, the inhabitants were scattered across the city: squeezing in with other relatives or setting up new illegal houses.

There wasn't much that was special about Nguyen Quy Duc Street. The destruction is being repeated in streets like it every week across the urban areas of Vietnam as their rulers try to transform them from the proletarian cities they once were into the bourgeois cities they want them to become. The residents of Nguyen Quy Duc were peasants who had brought their rural ways into the city: some becoming shopkeepers, others part of the industrial workforce. All were swept aside in the effort to make the district beautiful. No matter that the result would be far from the conventional idea of beauty – just grey concrete and untended desolation. For the district authorities, the dispersal of the disorderly poor would be sufficient proof that their part of the city had become modern. Through demolitions like this Vietnam's cities are being remade – both physically and socially. It's a Herculean battle. Every day city authorities attempt to cleanse their own Augean stables: for every piece of disorder they erase, another appears.

Waves of migrants are moving in, roads are jamming up, electricity is rationed and frequently cut, sanitation ranges from the barely adequate to the non-existent. Hanoi, Ho Chi Minh City, Danang and all the others are strained to breaking point. Tons of untreated industrial waste are being dumped every day, houses are collapsing because so much ground water has been extracted, the rivers around Ho Chi Minh City are biologically dead and air pollution in Hanoi is way above internationally accepted levels. But none of this deters the thousands who move to the cities each day, for whom migration is by far the easiest way to escape rural poverty. Nor does it prevent those already in the cities from seizing the fruits of economic growth – buying new things to fill their houses and expanding their houses to accommodate the new things. The cities teem with life and the enthusiasm of a young country on the move; regenerating, copying and inventing urban culture in the process.

* * *

Modern Hanoi has always been overcrowded. When the French left in 1954 the Communists inherited a capital with more than a quarter of its housing stock destroyed or badly damaged by fighting.[1] Bloated by refugees, the population had swelled to 300,000. A third of them were crammed into the old centre and many of the rest in slums and shanty towns around the city fringes. The answer seemed obvious. The property of departed colonial administrators and the old Vietnamese elite was seized and reallocated to those the Communist Party wanted to reward. In Hanoi they gave the best villas to themselves. The yellow-painted houses along the avenues north of Ba Dinh Square still house the leadership, the ex-leadership, their think-tanks, state agencies and ministries. Elsewhere in the city, properties were allocated to the people. All houses larger than a single room were nationalised. The new rulers simply partitioned the grand houses and apportioned them out. The original inhabitants were given just one room, which they had to rent from the state for a nominal sum. Other rooms were then allocated to other families by Party cadres. In some houses this was forced upon the inhabitants. But others who could see what was coming divided up their own houses and invited in relatives and friends, rather than have the state impose strangers upon them.

At that time, Nguyen Mink Hoa's* grandfather was asked to look after a house on Hang Gai (now better known as Silk Street) by a friend of his who fled to the south. He took two rooms on the first floor for himself and his two young sons and invited the original owner's relatives and friends to occupy the other five. The ground-floor room next to the street wasn't wanted so it was 'donated' to the city authorities. The maternal side of Hoa's family owned a large house on Ma May Street. They too decided to divide it up themselves. They kept the first floor, invited a brother's family to take the downstairs rooms at the back and gave the rooms looking on to the streets to a more distant relative. Both these streets lie within the Old Quarter of Hanoi, the triangular maze known as the '36 streets'[2] where roads were named after the items they specialised in selling: paper, silver,

* This name has been changed

baskets and so on. The traditional houses which lined them were long thin 'tube houses' – three or four metres wide but 30, sometimes 50 metres long. In the middle would be a private courtyard. Air rising from the yard would pull a refreshing draught through the house. Rooms nearest the courtyard were much more comfortable, particularly those on the first floor: cooler and further from the noise and dirt of the streets.

Privacy barely existed in these shared houses; cooking and washing facilities were communal and moving around often meant passing through other families' rooms. This might have been just about bearable when numbers were small and all the occupants came from one extended family. But in collective households which had been pushed together by the state, relations were frequently difficult, and as the city's population began to rise, so did overcrowding. Life spilled out on to the streets. The streets weren't being used for very much else – there was little trade taking place (most private business activity then was illegal) and precious little entertainment. Looking at the mayhem in Vietnamese cities today, it's almost impossible to imagine them without shops or motorbikes, without street traders, televisions or karaoke and often without tarmac or electric lights. But as recently as 20 years ago city streets would be quiet most of the day and night. Life was turned inside out; the streets became 'private' places where domestic life could take place. Women cooked meals on the pavements and in the alleyways families would wash hair, clothes and children. To some extent this was a reflection of the 'ruralisation' of the city. Peasants who'd migrated to Hanoi retained many of their village ways – such as doing things outdoors.[3] But for long-time urbanites too, living on the street became a necessity.

Even the new 'socialist' housing, which the government started to build after 1965 with Russian help, ended up reproducing the overcrowding and communal living of the Old Quarter. Soviet-style apartment blocks were built on the outskirts of the city, with shared cooking and washing facilities. They rapidly became over-populated too. Sanctions and American bombing made construction difficult and the supply of homes never kept up with demand. Even relatively senior officials and their families, the recipients of these modern apartments, found themselves conducting the basics of life in public. Everyone bar the top elite lived in overcrowded, undermaintained accommodation. The gap between rich and poor was measured by a couple of square metres, and that was the way life remained for most of Hanoi's population until relatively recently.

From the mid-1980s, however, once the market began to take over from the state-subsidy economy, city residents took matters into their own hands, illegally expanding their homes upwards or outwards with precarious cantilevered balconies. It also became much easier for people from rural areas to set up home and shop in places like Nguyen Quy Duc Street. Petty trading both allowed households to survive beyond the state and freed the state from the obligation to provide for households. The houses and livelihoods were illegal, but if the state had enforced the law the result would have been mass destitution and instability. Instead, households and state reached a compromise which was both pragmatic and tasty. In 1989, as state-owned enterprises and the military laid off a million and a half people, the streets were 'opened' and Vietnam's street-food revolution began. Women led the way. They took control of the means of production: a charcoal burner, a large pot and a few wooden (later plastic) stools, and began to support themselves and their families by selling tea, *pho* noodle soup, *bun cha* mini kebabs on noodles, *lau* stew and all the other homemade delights for which Vietnamese food has now become justly famous. Previously petty trading like this would have been quickly, and literally, stamped out. Now, a change in police behaviour made it obvious that they'd been told to leave the women alone.

And where soup stalls led the way, a riot of other informal enterprises followed: vegetable sellers, clothing shops, portable speak-your-weight machines, pineapple peelers, roadside barbers and bicycle repair men. These were the pioneers of petty capitalism and they asserted their moral right to survive over any regulation which tried to limit them. Some, like the demobilised soldiers who fixed punctures for a fee, were city dwellers, but most were migrants. Many of them stayed and swelled the ranks of the urban poor: collecting cardboard for recycling, selling newspapers or labouring in the markets while living in shanty housing and unofficial dormitories. They became the city's lumpenproletariat, its reserve army of labour, willing to do the most menial of tasks for the smallest of rewards because, no matter how bad things got, 'It is better to be poor in the city than rich in the village', as the Vietnamese saying goes. For a brief period after the start of *doi moi* the cities were theirs. They provided the muscle to get the economy moving. But 20 years on, the city doesn't want them around, or at least not visibly.

City authorities now want their streets to look 'civilised', and that means clearing away the old street life. Things began to change in late 2003 when an official campaign to promote *van minh* – 'civilised living' – really began.

Vietnam was about to host its first big international occasion: the Southeast Asia Games. In an attempt to demonstrate to visitors how 'modern' the country was becoming, orders went out to clear away 'unsightly' food stalls and street businesses. In Ho Chi Minh City they were mostly successful, but not in Hanoi. The battles still go backwards and forwards. Periodic attempts to clean up the streets, particularly when the city is hosting a large international event, are swiftly reversed once the campaigns are over. White Hyundai police pick-up trucks patrol the streets carting away whatever they can find there: plastic stools, peasants' bamboo baskets piled with fruit, and even tailors' dummies. Informal shopping streets are now known as 'frog markets' because of the way the traders leap up and carry away their merchandise at the sight of a policeman.

In its efforts to clean up the streets, the Communist Party is attempting not only to clean up the city but also to remake its relationships with the inhabitants – forming a new alliance with the owners of private property.[4] In effect, the Party is trying to replace the cities' disorderly proletarian and peasant characters and replace them with something more respectable. The vanguard of the working-class revolution is now trying to make the masses respect middle-class values. Urban beautification projects and street-clearing campaigns are just two of the ways the Party is redefining what it means by 'the people'. Campaigns like these are launched under the banner of *van minh* – and who can oppose civilisation? But in practice civilisation means prioritising the interests of property, of foreign investors and of middle-class shoppers over the interests of the poor. It is truly the end of communism as a political principle – although it's entirely compatible with the continuing rule of a Communist Party which needs to shore up its support from the most powerful sections of Vietnam's new society.

The transition has gone full circle. Now one of the smartest places to eat in Vietnamese cities is a chain of restaurants called Quan An Ngon, literally 'delicious food stall'. The restaurants are attractively designed, often making use of old villas, comfortable and sanitary. Inside, the middle-class clientele dine on proper tables rather than plastic footstools and around the courtyard women who once cooked in alleyways now serve up their street food specialities under stylised 'rural' thatched roofs. What was once nothing more than a way to survive has been transformed into a new piece of Vietnam's heritage. And delicious it is too.

This isn't the only way the 'civilising' campaign is changing the city. Recreation is being transformed too. After work has stopped and things get a little cooler, Hanoi's sidewalks turn into the world's most democratic badminton club. The pitches are already marked out in white paint on the paving slabs and tarmac; all the players have to do is bring along their racquets and shuttlecock, tie their net between the trees and serve. The courts are squeezed in wherever possible. In some cases the court markings go up over the corner of a flowerbed and down the other side. All along the former colonial boulevards convivial groups of sprightly men and women in white chat and play, oblivious to the traffic rushing past them. There's no shame in sweating on the street, no concern about the recklessness of swinging a racquet close to the noses of pedestrians and motorcyclists. But street badminton players are noticeably middle-aged and older. It's not a sport for the new middle classes. The nouveaux riches don't want to exercise in public. They choose instead to play their sports behind closed doors where they can only be observed by people of equal social standing. The new game in town is tennis. Clubs have sprouted up in the gardens of former villas and anywhere that a court can be laid out away from public view. Private clubs must also have changing rooms for modesty and spaces to network with business clients. And if tennis is not exclusive enough, a better option might be the golf course. Out of town locations lure players even further from the city crowds.

* * *

In the new civilised city, streets are less and less places for living, and more and more places for consuming. The basic necessities of life are moving indoors, and outdoors is becoming a place for frippery and display. The previous order of things has been up-ended. Before *doi moi*, street-front property was the least valued: now street frontage is the most valuable part of any building. Those who previously found themselves at the bottom of the housing allocation have in many cases found themselves sitting on top of a fortune, particularly if they were lucky enough to live in a part of town which has become a main shopping street. When *doi moi* came along they simply converted their living rooms into shops, tore down the front walls and replaced them with windows and shutters. They pay little rent and can sell directly to the passing trade. Capitalism has inverted the Party's original preferences: those who were last then are now coming first.

Sitting in his photo shop, Phong is typical of those clinging on to their toehold in Hanoi's Old Quarter. All he has is about a metre and a half of street frontage and a room above. But it's on Ma May, a street lined with tourist hostels and travel agents. Phong has been offered large amounts of money to sell up but he isn't going anywhere. Property (strictly speaking, the right to occupy state-owned property) in his street sells for up to $7,000 per square metre. That would value a typical Old Quarter plot at between half a million and a million dollars. Rich people from outside Hanoi want to buy property in the city as investments. 'They don't like putting it in the bank. If you put money in the bank they own you, if you put it in your house, you own it,' Phong says. This is the economic reason why many people in his street like to stay put, but they also like to remain because it was once their ancestors' property and they like to live with their spirits. More than half the people on Ma May choose to live upstairs and rent out the ground floor to shops and other businesses.

The overcrowding and confusion of ownership in the centre of Hanoi means that 'civilisation' will be impossible to achieve without either a great deal of money or considerable hardship. These days an easy way to tell how many families live in a building is to count the number of electricity meters on the wall outside. In one extreme example, a house on the corner of Ly Quoc Su and Sam Cam Street near the Catholic Cathedral has twelve. The once-beautiful old villa is now falling to pieces because its inhabitants can't agree who owns what and who should pay for repairs. However, disputes like these are a good thing for the old city's heritage. In almost all other cases where families reached agreement on ownership and compensation the result has been the demolition of the old house and the construction of a new one in the multi-storeyed, pilastered, balconied, Graeco-Roman, colonial-revival style – sometimes known locally as 'Towers of Pisa' – in which old Hanoi's residents have chosen to rebuild the city. Most of its historic buildings have gone for ever. Just two of the old 'tube houses' have been preserved in their original state, both with the help of foreign aid – the rest are either suffering from a lack of maintenance or have made way for Towers of Pisa, housing as many as six families in each.

Things are quite different down south. Although properties were nationalised and redistributed in Saigon after unification, there was, by then, more housing and it was better constructed. Under *doi moi* the Ho Chi Minh City authorities have been more ruthless in evicting people in the name of progress, resolving property disputes and facilitating the emergence of the new proper-tied class. Civilising the city is, in effect, a process of expropriating informally owned property from the poor and giving it formally to the rich. Those with property are lauded as the vanguard of the new civilised city. They're encour-aged to see themselves as more civilised than their fellow citizens who, without right to property, are condemned to a marginal existence in the interstices of the new urban order. Shopkeepers and professionals look down on the street traders and the itinerant workers, deride them for their rural ways, call them *nha que* (country bumpkin) and support the state's campaigns to keep them off the street. The result is stronger middle-class support for what the city author-ities are trying to do. The process is more or less complete in Ho Chi Minh City but is still being contested in Hanoi and other places where the poor are more numerous and property rights less straight-forward, and where capitalism has not yet created as much social differentiation.

The campaign for civilised living extends beyond property to a more general assault on 'uncivilised' behaviour. As controls on street life were formally lifted, or enforcement was relaxed, it became possible to do a great many new things in the city. Trading was just one part of it: the opportuni-ties for entertainment, shopping, drinking and relaxation mushroomed. Economic liberalisation brought social liberalisation in its wake. The subsidy economy had depended upon surveillance. Police and neighbourhood authorities watched to ensure no private trading or subversive activity took place, neighbours could see and hear almost everything in overcrowded housing and under-employed parents had plenty of time to monitor their children. Between them they created a system dedicated, in effect, to the prevention of pleasure. Control was everything, frivolity was frowned upon. The Party viewed religious and social rituals as a burden on society that the poor could not afford and rules were laid out for the celebration of weddings and other family occasions. Only on official holidays and at Tet, lunar new year, were festivities allowed: state food shops received extra rations at those times. But *doi moi* has changed all of this. For the new generation with some level of disposable income, money has bought freedom: bigger living space, privacy, and money to bribe the bureaucracy. Urban life is now marked by conspicuous consumption, ostentatious celebration and reinvented rituals.

'Civilised living' demands that the basics of life be taken indoors. Whether families are living as extended groups in self-built multi-storey houses or as nuclear units in apartment blocks, they now cook, eat, wash and gossip out of public view. The street is less and less a venue for the basics of life and more and more a venue for the celebration of it. And as the city has expanded, become wealthier and filled with strangers, control has become more difficult. The effectiveness of the state's all-knowing surveillance system has been reduced, along with families' ability to watch over their children. The street is now a place of excitement and danger, where the authorities' need for control battles youthful desires for pleasure. Unsurprisingly the struggles crystallise around the perennial issues of sex, drugs and rock and roll.

* * *

For teenagers growing up under the constant gaze of their extended families, perhaps sharing communal living and sleeping rooms, freedom has most palpably come in the form of a motorbike. Saturday night is best spent cruising around the streets – boyfriend driving girlfriend, even if it's her bike. Tens of thousands of preened riders while away the hours astride their polished chargers in a sinuous display of brashness. Alone in their crowd of like-minded thrill-seekers they can enjoy the freedom to cuddle – well away from disapproving eyes. The days of girls with long black hair riding bicycles in their *ao dai* are long gone. Girls cut their hair short, dye it purple or highlight it with peroxide. The only time they wear their *ao dai* is on family or formal occasions or if they work in some part of the hospitality industry, and only the poorest teenager would be seen on a push-bike on a Saturday night. A more typical Saturday night in Hanoi begins at the ride-in ice-cream parlour. All evening, bikes pull into the alley off Trang Tien Street, the once-grand promenade between the opera house and Hoan Kiem Lake, and park in the covered courtyard behind. Part of the pleasure is the ice-cream, though its cheap consistency harks back to the days before *doi moi*. Most of the fun is just sitting on the bike watching and being watched.

Looking at the scrubbed-up teenagers perched between conformity and rebellion, the overwhelming impression is of having travelled back to 1950s California – as if we're expecting James Dean to ride in and set everyone's pulses racing. But if Dean's generation rebelled against materialism, Vietnam's teenagers are rebelling against years of communist austerity. The boys and girls who catch the stares are those with money and matching accessories: shiny, brightly coloured, dent-free bikes; crisp designer shirts and Korean-inspired hairstyles. To be cool is to have disposable income and to be able to make a noise. Motorbike culture makes possible spontaneous celebration: a contrast and a riposte to the officially sanctioned restraint and moderation. Celebration ranges from the formulaic to the bizarre, from football victory celebrations to the stampede of Santa-hatted youth riding around the city on Christmas Eve.

The motorbike also makes possible the first furtive forays into sex, allowing journeys across town to the few public spaces which allow some intimacy – the Botanic Gardens are a popular spot, as is the causeway between Truc Bach Lake (the patch of water into which John McCain parachuted when he was shot down in 1967) and West Lake. The next step is often a trip around one of the lakes in a swan-shaped pedalo. In January 2007, Hanoi-based artist Nguyen Quang Huy took one of these swan boats out of the water, cleaned it, lovingly redecorated it with traditional shades of lacquer like a devotional object in a pagoda and exhibited it under the title 'Temple of Love', calling it: 'A symbol of love for all those living today in a cramped and dusty Hanoi'. For those at a more advanced stage of their relationship the main roads of every city offer a huge number of *nha nghi* – literally 'rest houses'. While some people do use *nha nghi* to rest, most don't. Rooms can be rented by the hour, without the usual formalities of leaving an identity card at reception. They are frequently the place for pre-marital and extra-marital affairs of one kind or another and also for married couples unable to find intimacy in overcrowded housing.

In Ho Chi Minh City youth culture has moved further. The memory of raunchier times before 1975 lived on, even though the American money which sustained them disappeared. As money has come back into the city, from American and other foreign investors, night-life has returned. If Hanoi's youth culture is just reaching the late 1950s then Ho Chi Minh City's is well into the 1960s. Trends and styles are more advanced and differentiated, and the higher incomes in the city mean foreign clothes and accessories are more affordable. But perhaps because of the higher standard of living, southerners tend to be less concerned about the appearance of status and, with less to prove, fashion is less obviously flash; there's less cool in riding a brand new motorbike than in Hanoi. Given the experience of forcible redistribution after unification in 1975, there's also greater wariness about displaying wealth in public. Life in the central cities of Danang and Hue tends to be slower. Less exposed to outside influences than either Ho Chi Minh City or Hanoi, the pace of change is gentler.

But regardless of region, for the time being the desires of most urban young people seem to be quite compatible with those of their parents. Parents want their children to be successful, to avoid the privations of their own youth, and their children want the same – the tangible benefits of a rising standard of living. Surveys suggest that the more educated the children, the more concerned they are to obtain a good job. They're prepared to study hard and work to achieve material success. Their horizons are wide and their hopes are high. In the mainstream of teenage and young adult life there's very little cynicism or defiance of parental wishes. Traditional values of respect for elders and a sense of community responsibility are still strongly inculcated by parents and schools and the vast majority of children still expect their parents to have a strong influence over how they live their lives. For these young people, 'youth' is a period of temporary independence between the demands of childhood and the new demands of a different kind of family life which will begin with early marriage.

Even among Vietnam's newly emerging 'subcultures', rebellion is more about questions of rhythm than rejecting parental values. Breakdancing, skateboarding and all the other 'scenes' which are starting to appear in Hanoi and Ho Chi Minh City are visible – because the kids tend to congregate in the few available public spaces – but the scenes are very small and composed of those with the means to buy the necessary accessories. Their regular evening meetings for dance-offs and boarding sessions are rarely interfered with, suggesting that whoever makes the rules sees them as less threatening to social order than peasants with shoulder poles. After they've had enough they go home like the good sons and daughters they are and study for their exams. Each scene is more an expression of individualism and a vehicle for self-advancement – perhaps as professional dancers or musicians – than a means of rebellion against the established order.

This, of course, fits quite nicely with the official idea of what the country's youth should be striving for. Youth television programmes are full of eager, bespectacled, fresh faces competing in some kind of educational quiz or another. The Vietnamese word for youth – *thanh nien* – means, literally, 'green years' with all the associated values of growth, development and enthusiasm. The Communist Party has put great effort into cultivating support from the younger generation: billboards along roadsides proclaim, in large letters: 'The children of today are the world of tomorrow', and images of Uncle Ho surrounded by children are ubiquitous. It's not hard for cultural monitors and state TV producers to co-opt hip-hop as a form of modernity and positive self-expression while jettisoning the unsavoury baggage associated with it in the West. It's no longer even regarded as an American import. The influences upon organised dance groups with names like Big Toe, Blue Toe and Cold Crew come as much from Japanese, Korean and Thai hip-hoppers as they do from the US. In fact this more 'clean-cut' hip-hop is much easier to assimilate than its loud-mouthed parent. And so long as it remains the preserve of youth with disposable income rather than of itinerant construction workers, domestic servants and others in the urban poor, it's likely to stay that way.

But in spite of this burgeoning market of young consumers, Hanoi has very little night-life, particularly in comparison with Ho Chi Minh City and other cities in the south. Until April 2007 it had one mega-club, the New Century. A cavernous venue, with a capacity of 2,000, it became a legend. As flash as any nightspot in Europe or North America, it regularly hosted stars from the south, international DJs and singers from Vietnamese communities abroad. It was well 'connected'. The security guards were said to be local police officers, and visiting VIPs had *carte blanche* to use the grounds of the National Library opposite as a car park. For eight years it had led a charmed life. No matter that the place was notorious for drug use, prostitution and even a few killings, the club remained open and won awards from the Hanoi city authorities for 'contributing to the fight against drugs'. The reason was simple: it was owned by a friend of the son of the Prime Minister, Phan Van Khai. But after Khai retired in mid-2006, the days of the club were numbered. Less than a year later, in the early hours of Sunday, 29 April, the place was permanently closed down in what looked like a military operation.

Five hundred armed and helmeted officers from special units were used because the Hanoi police couldn't be trusted to co-operate; they weren't even told the raid was happening. The police said they found 200 packets of drugs, seven couples having sex in private rooms and 'many used condoms' inside the club. The manager and the chief accountant were charged with harbouring drug users. More significantly, after a police investigation 17 Hanoi officials and 12 police officers were demoted or reprimanded, including the head of the city's Department of Culture who had allowed the club to go on operating without a licence. But even this action wasn't enough to quell the rumours about the club. The city gossip suggested that it wasn't raided because of the drug use but simply because some influential people were cut out of the profits being made there. It's typical of city dwellers' distrust of the authorities that even when they take what they call 'anti-crime' measures many people still assume the motives are criminal.

The gap between the official doctrine of 'civilised living' and the reality of city life gets wider each day. Prostitution is now so integral to male life in Vietnamese cities that it seems ridiculous even to try to eradicate it. An official report from 2001 estimated that at least half a million women were working as prostitutes – more than 1 per cent of the female population – and the number has probably grown since then. The civilised living campaign obliges city authorities to at least appear to be making some effort to stop it. From time to time people at the top order crackdowns, but implementation at the local level is usually half-hearted. Local police take orders both from their own officers and from the local political authority, the People's Committee. The confused lines of communication are frequently an excuse for inaction when a senior official might have been persuaded by some means not to enforce the crackdown in a particular street at a particular moment.[5]

For several years the focus of the state's efforts has been karaoke bars. Japanese-style sing-alongs are hugely popular in Vietnam but the availability of private rooms, music, alcohol and hostesses means many karaoke bars are just brothels in disguise. In July 2006 a new law came into force to make it more difficult for the sex trade. Bars are now banned from selling drinks stronger than beer, only one waitress can work in each room, doors have to have large windows in them and lights must be kept on so managers can see what's going on inside. But the fines are small compared to the money that can be made from sex. The largest fine is $600 – huge in terms of the income of a policeman, for example – but not much for the sex trade. In a virtual admission of the difficulty of ending prostitution in karaoke bars, this fine is reserved for bar owners who install an alarm system to warn customers of the arrival of the police.

The range of establishments where sex can be bought stretches from karaoke shops to the smartest hotels. The trade is much less conspicuous than in many other Asian cities, but that doesn't mean it's any less widespread. On certain streets prostitutes and pimps assertively tout for business. A Hanoi journalist's exposé of conditions in one parlour on Thai Thinh Street in the western suburbs described a business based on turnover rather than margins. One room 10 metres square accommodated five dirty beds, separated by flowery curtains. The busiest period was between eight and ten in the evening; at times queues formed on the stairs. The establishment made a small pretence of being a legitimate massage parlour. Clients paid 30,000 dong (about two US dollars) to the owner and a 5,000 dong (about 30 US cents) fee to the girls. But once behind the curtains private deals were made for which the girls expected to receive around 50,000 more in tips. For a poor girl from a rural area that's the equivalent of several days' income earned in a few minutes. At more expensive hotels the rate can be up to ten times as much. Some hotels have an entire floor dedicated to 'massage'. The extra money buys privacy, clean sheets and a less hurried encounter. In exchange the girls can earn 10 million dong – $600 – a month, a huge sum in Vietnam.

Paying for sex is, for the most part, a communal experience. Groups of friends go out together. In Hanoi, they call them *ban choi* – literally 'playmates' – but the same phenomenon is found across the country. The evening usually begins with food and *bia hoi* (fresh-brewed weak beer) in a noisy bar. Many places double as entertainment venues and brothels, in particular *bia om* – literally 'cuddle beer' – bars where men can have a glass in one hand and a girl in the other. The evening progresses through the international male bonding rituals of jokes, stories and more alcohol – leading, almost inevitably, to sex. The communal spirit is often reinforced by the group pooling their money to buy the services of a few prostitutes whom they will share. While it may be possible for a member of the group to excuse himself from sex if he can think of a good reason, it's almost impossible if he is with his boss or a business partner. In these cases paid-for sex is a respected way to form bonds of trust and friendship and thus an essential part of doing business. Deals will often be lubricated and celebrated with the assistance of a cohort of sex workers.

Illicit sex is, more or less, a staple of mainstream male life in Vietnam but so long as it's done discreetly it's unlikely to incur the wrath of the authorities. It's only when the authorities' rule is directly challenged by ostentatious rule breaking that crackdowns get serious. When the notoriety of the New Century club became too great, when karaoke bars became the stuff of public gossip and when illegal motorbike races around the streets started to attract large crowds, the authorities were obliged to act to maintain their credibility. It's not so much the behaviour that is targeted as the public disregard of authority. Prostitutes working indoors are unlikely to be targeted, whereas those working the streets will be. Clubbers taking cocaine can get away with their drug use, but heroin users shooting up in alleyways can't. Migrant children working in sweatshops are usually ignored, those begging on the streets are not.

* * *

The official response to public prostitution, public drug use and public vagrancy is the same: first of all try to persuade the offender to change their uncivilised lifestyle and then, if they fail to reform, remove them from the city. Control of what the authorities still call 'social evil' falls, not to the police, but to the local People's Committee. Party cadres will visit uncivilised households, Women's Union activists will try to persuade prostitutes to give up their trade and local neighbourhood wardens will try to organise neighbours to fight antisocial behaviour. But if they fail then the People's Committee – not the court – will order detention. The campaign to promote civilised living has co-opted the old ways of dealing with social problems: exclusion and re-education.

From political dissidents in the 1950s, to army officers from the defeated south in the 1970s, to prostitutes and drug users now, the Party has long treated 'deviants' on the premise that it can change their minds and make them 'better' citizens. Re-education is an unsettling combination of liberalism and totalitarianism. On the one hand the regime believes that most of those with unacceptable behaviour can be 'reformed', but on the other it has a very rigid definition of acceptable behaviour. In practice, re-education has been far from liberal. Hundreds, perhaps thousands, of former southern soldiers, officials and dissidents died from abuse and neglect in re-education camps after the war and these days the centres set up to reform cases of 'social evil' more often harm their inmates than help them.

Male drug users are sent to '06 centres'. Female sex workers, who may also be drug users, are sent to '05 centres' and street children to social protection centres. These are usually in remote places and although they are managed by the Ministry of Labour, Invalids and Social Affairs (MoLISA) rather than the Ministry of Public Security, in practice they are run like prisons. There are more than 80 state-run 06 centres in the country, each holding around a thousand inmates. There are few, if any, trained drugs counsellors or social workers in the centres; staff are simply allocated to work there by the Ministry. Inmates are all treated the same; little attempt is made to understand individuals or why they might have become involved with drugs or sex work. Re-education isn't exactly stimulating. Half the day is spent memorising Party positions and the laws on crime, and chanting slogans such as: 'The whole nation condemns social evil'. The rest is spent performing manual labour. The inmates wear blue striped pyjamas, conditions are hard and they are frequently beaten.

Unsurprisingly, the centres usually fail. They keep people off the streets for two or three years but then return them to the same neighbourhood and the same social problems, and the result is almost always the same. They're then likely to be picked up again and sent away for another spell in the camp. While the centres may give the authorities the impression that they're in control of the problem, in many ways they've made it worse. Surveys suggest that 60 per cent of the inmates of 06 centres are now HIV-positive. Though the authorities deny it, intravenous drug use is rampant and there is plenty of unsafe sex between inmates. Given that neither problem is supposed to exist, MoLISA refuses to provide them with clean needles or condoms. Maintaining the Party line has failed to change inmates' behaviour. Instead it's just increased the prevalence of HIV.

Party experts and government officials are struggling to find new ideas for ways to cope with the problems of the new society they are building. The top of the hierarchy clings to the utopian idea that socialism can solve everything. Theoreticians still argue over the legacies of social thinkers like Karl Marx, Max Weber and Émile Durkheim and their implications for solving the country's problems. The lower levels try to cope using whatever resources are to hand. Social work – once abolished on the grounds that it was unnecessary under socialism – is being encouraged again. Religious groups, including the Catholic Church, are being allowed to provide social care; 'empathy groups' of families of people with HIV are being allowed to organise autonomously of the Party; and international experts from the UN and other agencies are being invited to advise on new strategies. Western-trained practitioners are turning local NGOs into agencies to try to treat the problems directly.

The problems are tying the Party's ideologues up in ideological knots. For decades they argued that social evils were the result of foreign and capitalist influence, starting under the French and continuing under the Americans. Trying to explain why they have surged now, under Party leadership, has pitted theorists who hold the line that socialism has the answers against practitioners who work on the assumption that it hasn't. It seems unlikely that the old line can be held for much longer but it still has powerful supporters. They don't understand the new world they have created – they still announce strategies calling for a 90 per cent reduction in crime, for example – and for the time being it's easier to fall back on traditional ideas than seek out new ones. Other arguments are familiar from other countries. Why should money be spent on those who've abused the Party, state and nation's generosity when loyal citizens get by with less? Many people, addicts' families included, see the re-education camps as a good solution to the problem. Families have been known to imprison their own children at home or bribe the army to send them to bases on remote islands to prevent them using drugs – why should they be opposed to sending them away to an 06 centre?

Similar dilemmas exist over street children. There are few sights which offend urbanites – Vietnamese and foreign – more than seeing children living on the street. Compared with most cities in Asia, the number of visible street children in Vietnam is relatively small, but that doesn't mean they don't exist. The authorities in the two big cities take dramatically contrasting approaches. Hanoi tends to be more hard line, regularly rounding up apparently vagrant children. In Ho Chi Minh City they are more tolerant. In Hanoi shoe-shine boys have learnt not to carry the tools of their trade openly. Instead they buy a school uniform and carry the brushes and polish in a rucksack so that the police don't spot them. They also take less visible jobs, working in the markets rather than selling postcards in the tourist areas. In Ho Chi Minh City, tolerance has allowed well-organised trafficking rings to flourish. They 'rent' children from poor families, particularly in the centre of the country, promising to take care of their accommodation and employment. They tell the families the children will be trained and well looked after but the kids are usually put to work as cheap labour; selling flowers, cutting cloth and working in restaurants or as domestic servants. Sixteen-hour days, minimal wages and Dickensian accommodation are the norm.

In Hanoi, street children are detained in institutions, especially when big events roll into town. In November 2006, in the run-up to the Asia-Pacific summit, the local security forces in the centre of the city were given orders to arrest any they found. One quite candidly admitted to me, 'The problem with the street children shining shoes and selling books is that they normally follow foreigners and tourists. We will put them in the social protection centre so they will be taken care of by the state.' The children he and his fellow officers detained were taken to what's called Social Protection Centre Number 1, in the village of Dong Dau a few miles east of the city. From the outside it looks more like a prison than a children's home. Set back from the road in a landscape of paddy fields and encircled by a barbed-wire-topped wall, it could easily be a textile plant except that it's painted government yellow.

The thinking behind the centre is the same as that for drug users and street prostitutes: clear away the evidence and the problem will disappear. Former inmates say its purpose is to scare children away from a life on the streets. The first sentence is usually just 15 days. Children are locked in a room with ten others and let out twice a day for 30 minutes at a time. They complain that the guards beat them, that food is insufficient and hygiene poor. The European Union has been funding improvements to the centre and training staff to help unite the children with their families. It's hard to get an accurate picture of the realities of life inside. Inspection visits are arranged well in advance so everything can look nice for the funders.

Which is the better solution to the problem? Although some of these children have run away from home, most are in the city with their families' consent. Statistics aren't reliable, but there's evidence that most child workers actually come to the cities with their families. Child labour is a fact of life in Vietnam. The average two-adult, three-child rural household relies on the children to do at least a third of the work and families generally regard it as not only necessary for survival but good for their children's development. Sending them away to work is simply an extension of what they would do at home. Fishing communities on the coast of Thanh Hoa province, for example, frequently send their children to Hanoi to earn money to help their families pay off the loans they've taken out to buy their boats. Networks exist to find the children jobs and remit the money they earn back to their parents. When the children are old enough they leave the city, return to the village and become fishermen or start a family. Wherever the family is from, if the child's income is part of the household budget then losing it might force the whole family into poverty or cause all of them, rather than just mother and son, to migrate to the city.

* * *

The pressures on the city are becoming greater every day. Migration without official permission and registration is illegal, and that has helped keep urban populations low. But hundreds of thousands of people are now moving every year, regardless. Some migrants have family and friends they can live with while they find work. Others have to start at the bottom. Shanty housing is becoming more obvious in Vietnamese cities, though for the time being it's largely hidden from public view. On many city streets a handwritten sign 'cho thue' – for rent – reveals that what looks like a garage or a storage shed is in fact an illegal dormitory for migrant workers. The dream of each of these migrants is to make it in the city, for their children to have an education and to enjoy a better life than they had.

This was what the inhabitants of Nguyen Quy Duc Street were striving for. Their children wanted the things which mark success in the new consumer society: the clothes, motorbike and hairstyles that they see in the new glossy magazines. The question is whether Party policies are making that process easier or more difficult. The Party's priority is political survival and that requires both control over the population and the creation of alliances with the new middle and elite classes. The result is policies which defend the advantages of propertied urbanites over the claims of migrants and the poor. The Party does have both a rhetorical commitment to, and a demonstrable track record of, sharing out the benefits of economic growth to all. But is that commitment fading in the face of its new alliance with the wealthy?

Outsiders have to be careful not to subject Vietnam to criticism that we wouldn't impose on ourselves. Baron Haussman had to destroy the old Paris to make the city that the world now adores. Few Americans would think of setting up a food stall on a busy shopping street without some kind of licence, nor would they tolerate the sight of shoe-shine boys skipping school. 'Something' would have to be done. It's refreshing, in a world that has largely abandoned the dream of 'solving' social problems and talks of merely 'managing' them, that the Communist Party still thinks it can find clear answers. But the current combination of old socialist ideas mixed with appeals for what one might loosely call a Confucian-based respect for authority seems unlikely to provide them. On the surface it appears that Vietnam is managing its social problems reasonably well. Poverty has fallen dramatically, the cities aren't surrounded by shanty towns, levels of drug use and HIV appear to be manageable. But in contrast to most other countries in the region, Vietnam is still at the beginning of its transition. In the next few years its urban population is likely to double and then, ultimately, triple.

Vietnam is a poor country and is already struggling to manage the pressures of economic transition. Its current structures won't be able to cope.

No one denies that things have to change in Vietnam's cities; the question is how that change is managed and whether its outcome is in the interests of the majority or simply the elite. Two weeks after their house in Nguyen Quy Duc Street was demolished, I tracked down one of the families, now living in another semi-legal, one-storey, two-roomed construction on the new outskirts of the city. Out of their window they could see paddy fields just as they could from Nguyen Quy Duc Street 20 years before. They'd lost a lot of money when their shop was destroyed and they hadn't been able to do any work since – they had no street frontage from which to sell anything. They told me they wanted the People's Committee to pay proper compensation or provide them with a pitch so they could make a living from another shop. But they wanted something more: 'We want respect. They don't respect our rights and we don't have the freedom to say that we don't agree with this policy.' One of them was wearing an American-style baseball jacket with 'US Army' on the chest. As he was an older man I joked about him wearing the uniform of his former enemy but he made a heartfelt point in return. 'I was a soldier. For ten years I fought the aircraft bombing Hanoi. But I like the American and the French people. They have all the rights that we don't have.' It was, perhaps, the bitter sentiment of someone who had lost everything but it was also a warning that those whom the state treats so callously carry their resentment with them. There may come a time when they get their own back.

★

4

Grandfather is watching you

Each January, Nguyen Hai's work begins anew. From the bleakly modern interior of his small office on one of the main tourist shopping streets in Hanoi's Old Quarter, he and his team rejoin the battle to improve the lifestyles of the city's inhabitants. Mr Hai's instructions will cascade down to every district, ward, neighbourhood, and eventually to every home. By the time the process is complete, each household in Hanoi will have been asked to account for its behaviour and submit itself for judgement by its neighbours. Stories of disputes and squabbles will have been retold, allegations made and refuted and the intimacies of family life anatomised. And the reward for this public exposure? A yellow certificate which can be proudly displayed on the wall. Framed and mounted, the certificate is official recognition that the household has achieved the status of *Gia Dinh Van Hoa* – a 'cultured family'.

Mr Hai is in charge of what's called 'The Office of Civilised Living and Cultured Families' for Hanoi City People's Committee. Part of his work is to manage the civilised living campaign described in Chapter 3. The rest is to bring culture to the backward. But culture, for the city authorities, is not a question of reading books or appreciating opera. The official booklet specifying the requirements for the certificate is concerned with a very different kind of culture. It sets out 22 criteria under four headings: 'Having a harmonious and progressive family'; 'Improving the material and spiritual life of the family'; 'Strengthening mutual assistance within the neighbourhood'; and 'Fully implementing citizens' responsibilities'. For 'culture', read 'model citizen'. Under the each heading are such specific requirements as: having 'harmonious and faithful relations between husband and wife'; 'legitimate income'; 'reasonable and thrifty consumption'; 'basic audio and visual equipment to get access to public news and information'; and 'no third child'. There are also requirements to take part in community activities and consent to rules such as: 'implement the community's conventions'; 'fully implement the Party and state's guidelines, policies, regulations and laws; fully implement citizens' responsibilities (such as military service and payment of taxes) and obey regulation of all authority levels'; and 'participate in protecting political security and social safety and order'. In effect, Mr Hai is the Hanoi representative of a national system of social control.

But Mr Hai doesn't see it that way. He is at pains to make clear that the whole campaign is voluntary and that there is no punishment for anyone who doesn't take part. On the face of it, that's true; but, as he points out, Vietnamese take family honour very seriously and people will 'feel shame if they don't live up to their commitments'. There might be other consequences if, for example, the family ever needed help from local officials. Each neighbourhood in the country, about 60–80 households – a unit Vietnamese call a *to dan pho* – has a 'neighbourhood warden'; most wardens are retired officials from some part of the Party or state. Their role is to monitor the activities of residents and visitors. The system seems totally Orwellian to westerners, but it is generally accepted in Vietnam because of the way it has been spliced into the traditional social order. The wardens are not simply spies; they also advise, mediate and persuade, try to keep the local peace and help resolve disputes. They are answerable to the Ministry of Public Security but they also 'belong' to the community: they are local and they are usually elected by the neighbourhood for four-year terms. They also tend to be older, grandfatherly (sometimes grandmotherly) figures, with all that implies for respect and honour. It's a very flexible form of very local control.

There are many reasons why Vietnam has been able to maintain both growth and stability far better than most of its neighbours. Some of them can be found in the long development of its communal culture and others in very modern techniques of political control. Uniting them is the way Vietnam's rulers have successfully grafted Leninism – in particular the idea that the Communist Party should take the leading role in society – on to Confucianism with its traditions of respect for elders. More precisely, the Party has tried to co-opt traditional extended family structures into its vast state surveillance system.

Every January, each warden, sometimes accompanied by officials from the People's Committee of the ward (*phuong* in Vietnamese, the lowest level of local government), is supposed to visit the families in their neighbourhood and discuss which of the 22 criteria they wish to achieve. Each criterion is given a mark and the household has to achieve 80 out of a possible 100 to be given its 'Cultured Family' certificate. At the end of the year the family is given a form so they can assess themselves. Then the fireworks can begin. On the appointed night, the heads of every household in the neighbourhood are invited to a formal meeting to pass judgement on their neighbours. Most meetings will go smoothly but in others arguments will be rehashed and old scores settled. After all this, the warden will decide whether each household deserves the status of a 'cultured family'. If they do, the certificate is presented to the head of the extended family, usually the grandfather, who is then responsible for ensuring his household lives up to its commitments, using all the power that traditional Vietnamese society confers upon him. If he fails, the certificate will be publicly taken away. In effect, the campaign tries to turn grandfathers into the state's enforcers. As a tool of discipline in a close-knit society it has no equal.

Mr Hai insists that the certificate does not affect residents' entitlement to help from the state. That's not, however, supported by the evidence from the street. Since each neighbourhood and village can also be awarded 'Cultured' status and one of the criteria is that 80 per cent of households within it are also regarded as 'Cultured', there's every incentive for neighbourhood wardens and Party officials to use all the leverage at their disposal to ensure they reach their target. So if the family thinks that it's likely to require help or permission for something – whether it's a building permit or a licence to set up a tea stand – the pressure to conform to the local authority's requirements will be intense.

The campaign can be rolled out for other purposes too. During major international events the neighbourhood wardens are sent out to remind citizens of the need to behave well and perhaps refrain from driving their motorbikes near the event venues. For those living near the Sheraton Hotel in November 2006, the neighbourhood advice included a warning not to venture out on to their roof terraces to hang out their washing in case it unnerved the security team of visiting US President George Bush. In the run-up to the South East Asian Games in Hanoi in 2003 there was an added incentive to sign up to the rules of good behaviour: all the completed pledges were to be entered into a lottery where the first prize was a modern apartment and others included a TV, refrigerator and washing machine. The Games were a success and passed off without disorder and, even better for the city authorities, they didn't have to give away a flat because the winner of the lottery, a resident of Dong Da district according to Mr Hai, had unfortunately lost the winning form to the incisors of a rodent. The winner may have been cultured, but was also infested.

Since the 1990s, the 'Cultured Families' campaign has become more prominent, mainly because of the failure of a more heavy-handed system. From the earliest days of communist Vietnam, the cornerstone of social control was a system of household registration called the *ho khau*. It still exists. Every person has to be registered in a specific place at birth. If they want to move, they need the consent of the authorities both where they're registered and where they want to go. Borrowed from China, the system was initially intended to control anti-communist resistance. Over subsequent decades, even though the central state lacked the resources to ensure it was fully implemented everywhere, it became the basis for economic planning, the provision of social services and the distribution of food and goods.[1]

As the economy liberalised, however, it became easier for people to evade the system. The distribution of state-supplied jobs, food and housing had once been largely dependent on holding a valid *ho khau*, but as more goods and services became available on the open market, its power was reduced. Villagers left their villages without permission, unregistered housing sprang up in the cities and illegal traders tramped the streets. Daily life could, to a larger extent, bypass the authorities. (Hence the need to augment the *ho khau* with the 'Cultured Families' campaign.) The *ho khau* survives, however, because it continues to be a useful tool for the state: it reduces migration, provides useful economic data and, above all, helps the police to keep tabs on people. It's another lever in the official tool kit. Anyone without a valid *ho khau* is permanently at the authorities' mercy. Unregistered households have to build a life's worth of corrupt relationships simply to keep living and working in a particular place. If they misbehave, life can get very difficult.

The consequence for the unregistered can be severe. If an unregistered couple wants to get married, register the birth of their child or even be buried in the cemetery they will find it difficult, sometimes even impossible. They could return to the place where their official *ho khau* was registered, but if they have been absent for more than six months, they may find that their name has been removed from the register. As a result they will be officially beyond the law. Often the only way to survive is through bribery – paying local officials either to grant them a *ho khau* or to turn a blind eye whenever they need to do something which requires it. Their births won't be registered or their marriages licensed, their housing will be illegal and their living conditions precarious. They're not included in population statistics, poverty calculations or social services provision. More than a quarter of the babies born in 2000 weren't registered.[2] In just one year that implies 250,000 undocumented children. As a result, the government was forced to adjust the rules to fit reality. New laws and regulations were introduced from 2004 allowing children to be registered where they are born, not where their parents' *ho khau* was issued. But local authorities are reluctant to regularise so many new inhabitants whom they would then be obliged to take care of. Consequently communities are growing up across Vietnam, perhaps a few million people in all, who do not officially exist.

In spite of this, and other, clear evidence of the failure of the *ho khau* system, there's no sign of it being abandoned. In part, this is because it continues to perform its original function, allowing surveillance of the population. In addition to its more general roles in controlling movement and guiding economic planning, the *ho khau* is the basis of the Public Security Ministry's system of political records, known as the *ly lich*. The *ly lich* has a long history. In its original incarnation, in the 1950s, individuals were obliged to write their life histories for the police. Those who had worked for the French, been members of non-communist political parties or were part of the landlord class, or whose parents or grandparents did so, could then be kept out of important positions or pushed down the queue for goods and services.

Today the legacies of those old *ly lich* continue to blight the lives of descendants, particularly among former officials of the old Saigon regime and their children. And new *ly lich* are still being written. The essay format continues to be used for most people applying for jobs in the public sector and for anyone wanting to join the Communist Party. But the police also compile their own *ly lich* on those they consider subversive or worth watching – journalists, foreigners, those who have contact with journalists and foreigners, and so on. It may no longer be a universal requirement and it's no longer such a public procedure but it continues to exist in the processes of the Ministry of Public Security. From secret police files and residency permits to neighbourhood wardens and cultured family campaigns, Vietnam has built a low-tech but effective system of near-total surveillance.

* * *

Vietnam, and the international community, had reason to be grateful for the system's draconian powers when Severe Acute Respiratory Syndrome (SARS) struck Hanoi at the end of February 2003. What could conceivably have been a major national epidemic, with the possibility of a global pandemic, was stopped in its tracks. Although it took persistent lobbying by the local office of the World Health Organisation to persuade the government to take the issue seriously, once it did so all the stops were pulled out. The WHO's statement on the control measures taken at the time said simply: 'Mobile teams from the Ministry of Health continue to visit the homes of hospitalised SARS cases on a daily basis to check household members for possible symptoms of the disease' along with carrying out 'other infection control measures'. But people living in Hanoi at the time remember a much more impressive security operation. Uniformed and plain clothes security personnel appeared around the homes of every infected person, whole city wards were closed off and access to them severely restricted. It worked. Just over a month later, the WHO declared the disease 'contained' in Vietnam.

At times like these Vietnam has no problem with finding the manpower to take action. Carl Thayer of the Australian Defence Force Academy, probably the Western world's most authoritative observer of the Vietnamese military, has estimated the size of Vietnam's various security forces as at least 6.7 million. Given that the country's total working population is around 43 million this suggests that one person in six works either full or part time for a security force. And given the lack of published data, even this figure is probably a significant underestimate of the total size of the internal security apparatus.

But the paradox of Vietnam's internal security situation is that, although the Party-state has huge resources at its disposal, its ability to use them is limited. It can wield enormous coercive power over limited areas or short time spans but it could not sustain rigid discipline across the whole country in the style of North Korea or Burma in any circumstances short of national emergency. There simply isn't the political will inside the Party to reimpose Stalinism; it failed the first time. The Party leadership has to tread carefully, actively courting support from leaders lower down the hierarchy and from different interest groups within Vietnamese society. The loyalty of bosses of state-owned enterprises or city or provincial authorities can't simply be assumed by those at the top; it must be won. No significant decision can be taken at any level of government without a sufficient level of consensus among intra-party networks, elements of government, the military, business and other key interests.

Even after the decisions are taken at the top, the chances of them being implemented on the ground exactly as planned are slim. The Party-state leadership has trouble enough getting local officials to control karaoke bars or enforce building regulations, let alone maintain totalitarianism. Whenever officials have to choose between national instructions and local demands, it's usually the local that wins. Local officials answer to local bosses, so local 'relationships', influence and bribery tend to be more effective than central policy. State salaries are so low that officials depend upon the benevolence of those they are supposed to regulate to make ends meet. As the economy grows, those with the money to buy connections and influence can pay less heed to what local officials think. The legacy of fence-breaking is still strong. The centre is fighting a constant battle to prevent the system crumbling away at the edges.

The 'Cultured Families' campaign is suffering from this crumbling. Those who work in the private sector and have less need for official 'permissions' can be more independent of the state and its minions. In other places, officials aren't as zealous in their enforcement as they are supposed to be. In one Hanoi district, the onomatopoeic Phuc Xa, officials are fighting a losing battle against what other Hanoians regard as a tide of immorality. Wedged between the Red River and the dyke which protects the rest of the city from flooding, the area has long attracted migrants, those without *ho khau*, the poor and others on society's margins. As a result, Phuc Xa is a priority for social improvement. Several neighbourhoods proudly display an arched sign over the entrance to their street advertising their 'cultured' status – something which only serves to undermine the concept in the minds of the rest of the city. One Phuc Xa resident described the hollowing out of the assessment process. 'The warden simply draws up a list of the people he thinks deserve the certificate and then reads it out to the meeting. They get the certificate but they can't even control their children.' The formal campaign is adhered to but there's much less discussion, much less community censure, which in effect destroys the very foundation of the campaign.

The Hanoi City People's Committee has begun to notice, complaining that too many households are getting cultured status and demanding more rigorous enforcement of the criteria.

To try to counteract the crumbling, the system demands near-constant mobilisation from its cadres and officials to try to keep them loyal and active. Mobilisation comes in many forms, of which one is the 'Cultured Families' campaign. Another consists of the public address systems found on the corner of almost every street. Twice a day, at 6.30 a.m. and 4.30 p.m., the loudspeakers blare out news and views to the citizens. Production qualities are basic. It's an extraordinary throwback to the days when a radio was a rare and prized possession and it continues despite the ubiquity of radios and televisions today and the Party's monopoly of the airwaves. But the loudspeakers have something broadcasting lacks – local character. Each system is managed by the district People's Committee and provides a mixture of national propaganda and local information. A typical address might include news of the latest decision by the Party Central Committee and a reminder that the post office will be closed the following afternoon. They're increasingly ignored by a population with access to MP3 players and other distractions but they remain an important tool. At the very least people can't say they haven't been warned about the latest mobilisation when questioned about it by a local Party cadre.

It might seem strange, given the system's surveillance and security networks, but the Communist Party is wary of high-profile law enforcement campaigns. Failure would be worse than embarrassing for a party which is supposed to represent the people's will. Such campaigns are only ever risked at times and in ways which demonstrate the Party's continuing hold on power. But when such a moment arrives, the Party has the capacity to mix propaganda, persuasion and punishment with impressive efficiency. One such campaign was fought in late 2007, over a new law to force motorbike riders, which means almost everyone in the country, to wear helmets. Although it had been compulsory for some time to wear helmets on highways, it was almost unheard of within towns and cities. Everyone agreed helmets were too hot and cumbersome to wear and women complained that they messed up their hair. However, with an average of 30 people being killed on the roads each day, and an estimate from the Asian Development Bank that casualties were costing the country around $885 million each year in lost earnings and health bills, the Party decided something needed to be done.

The campaign was a classic of its kind, combining co-option and coercion, propaganda and punishment. It began by obliging those over whom the state had direct leverage to set a good example: government employees were required to wear reinforced helmets from 15 September, as were people in rural areas. This gave the authorities three months to work on the cities before the ban came into force there on 15 December. But even in mid-October it was easy to find riders asserting that the law was unworkable. Yet on the day the ban actually came into force there was near-total observance. For many it was compliance in name only: some strapped kitchen pots to their heads, others wore their helmets without straps and children continued to travel unprotected. As a result, the effect of the law on human health was less dramatic than hoped. A year later, road deaths had fallen just 10 per cent.[3] Wearing helmets doesn't prevent speeding, drink-driving, ignoring traffic signals or carrying insane loads. Nonetheless the Party had achieved what some thought impossible: getting the population to observe the helmet law. It had laid its credibility on the line and demonstrated its ability to enforce its rule.

* * *

For two decades the Party has been working out how to stay in charge as the basis of its control shrinks. The end of central planning, the influx of foreign investment and the rise of the private sector have all brought new dangers. The basic reflex of the security establishment is still to try to control everything, but that's proving increasingly difficult as society becomes more sophisticated. Controlling the internet is a case in point. Vietnam only connected to the internet on 19 November 1997, after six years of cautious experimentation with more basic forms of electronic communication. Some in the Party could see clear benefits for the country but when the then Minister of Post and Telecommunications, Do Trung Ta, presented the idea to the Party's Central Committee in late 1996 most of the discussion was devoted to ways of 'preventing bad influences'. Great importance was placed on having a national firewall.[4] Since then, internet use has exploded in Vietnam, but the urge to control is just as strong.

The national firewall was easy to install since the gateways to the outside world were controlled by three companies owned by government ministries: VNPT, owned by the Telecoms Ministry; FPT, owned by the Science

Ministry, and Viettel, owned by the Ministry of Defence. With just 3,000 subscribers in the first months and the cost unaffordable for most, the net was easy to monitor. But not for long. By the end of 2001 the number of subscribers was estimated at around 165,000, and a year later, after a cut in prices, well over a million. By the end of 2007 it stood at 18 million[5] – but the three original firms still controlled 98 per cent of the market.[6] With computers beyond the pocket of most families the vast majority of users still do their surfing in cybercafés. Every city neighbourhood can boast at least one and some streets are lined with dozens. From mountain towns in the far north-west to islands in the Mekong Delta, a generation of pasty-faced schoolchildren is developing hunched shoulders and repetitive strain injury from playing online games like the spectacularly popular Vo Lam Truyen Ky – Swordsman Online – based on ancient Chinese epic tales, or discussing the latest celebrity sex tape in chat rooms and on instant messenger sites.

Vietnam is far from alone in wanting to control its citizens' access to harmful content on the internet. It's just that its definition of what is harmful and the lengths to which it is prepared to go to control it have landed it on the list of 13 'Enemies of the Internet' compiled by the media freedom organisation Reporters Sans Frontières. 'Politics and religion are taboo,' says RSF. 'Almost 2,000 sites deemed politically or morally "dangerous" are filtered [and] authorities target foreign news and human rights sites created by the large Vietnamese community overseas.' The government's response is dismissive: 'Our policy is to prevent youngsters from accessing unhealthy sites. We do not apply any measures for any political goals,' the official spokesman told his press conference.[7] But the opposite is true. Research by the OpenNet Initiative, a collaborative project of four British and North American universities[8] published in summer 2006, discovered that, 'While [Vietnam] doesn't block any of the pornographic sites ONI tested, it filters a significant fraction – in some cases the great majority of – sites with politically or religiously sensitive material.'[9] In other words the Vietnamese firewall allows youngsters to consume plenty of porn but not Amnesty International reports.

Privately owned internet service providers can only have connections with state-controlled 'internet exchange points', which in turn connect directly to the internet. Private ISPs aren't allowed to connect with one another directly, nor with the web. So all content has to pass through a limited number of state-controlled access points – making it much easier to filter. And just to make sure, rules issued in July 2005 order internet cafés to install software to record which sites its users visit, whether they use email or chat and how long they stay online. They're also supposed to register the name, address and ID card number of each user. However, the authorities have had considerable trouble enforcing the law; the deadline for the installation of the snooping software was repeatedly delayed. And internet cafés find it too onerous to record their users' details. In cities, it almost never happens and café owners and users have tried to dodge or resist the regulations.

So instead the state is trying to get the ISPs to act as their enforcers – just as it tries to get grandfathers to perform this role within families. They're responsible for ensuring that internet shops use their connections in accordance with the law: they even have to develop their own software to monitor their customers. And delegation of responsibility goes a step further. If a user finds any illegal content online they are obliged to report it to the local authorities. Again, this hardly ever happens. However, as monitoring technology improves it may become easier for the state to take action against specific internet shops and users that break the law.

In the meantime, just as useful for the state is the pervasive sense of fear that has been instilled into most Vietnamese about having contact with anything which might seem subversive. Even the researchers for the OpenNet Initiative found this. They had carried out similar research in countries such as China and Iran and hired local assistants to help them, but they found it impossible to find anyone in Vietnam willing to take the risk. Even a simple and uncontroversial request to put up a blog about sport was thought to be too dangerous.[10] Similarly, postgraduate students in the Social Sciences Faculty of the Vietnam National University being taught by a British lecturer were warned by the Party representative in their class not to access the websites of overseas Social Sciences associations and were surprised that it was even possible to view them from within the country. They had simply assumed that they would be blocked.

* * *

Another consequence of the retreat from state socialism in Vietnam has been the rise of the non-governmental organisation. Up until the late 1980s there were no NGOs: the state provided all forms of social assistance, and the mass organisations (particularly the Women's Union, Youth Union, Trade Union and Farmers' Union) under the Party's umbrella organisation, the

Vietnam Fatherland Front (for which see Chapter 5, pp. 98–103) took charge of mobilising society. It was the loss of Soviet aid to Vietnam in 1991 that forced a change of direction. Faced with a funding crisis, the Party saw a way to move many of its costs off its books by getting foreigners to pay for social services. It was typical of the far-sightedness of the Party that they came up with a system that allows considerable day-to-day autonomy while ensuring that everything remains under its thumb. The Party has been able to enjoy the benefits of international assistance while minimising the danger of an 'Orange Revolution' led by NGOs.

In the first place the bosses of the new 'non-governmental' organisations were mainly former government employees. Some of them even continued to be part-time public servants, supplementing their meagre official salaries with aid dollars. Many of them, and their staff, were also Party members, so it wasn't hard for their former bosses to keep an eye on them. Another layer of oversight came through the system of 'belonging'. There is minimal room in the Vietnamese system for such a dangerous thing as an autonomous organisation. Apart from some very local groups (such as village lineage societies based upon shared surnames) every organisation – from a chess club upwards – is supposed to 'belong' somewhere. 'Belonging' – *thuoc* or *cua* in Vietnamese – is crucial.

Every formal organisation must be linked by a chain of official ties to the Central Committee of the Communist Party. So, sports clubs must be registered with their province's Department of Sport and, for example, Catholic believers with the official Patriotic Catholic organisation which 'belongs' to the Vietnam Fatherland Front (VFF) – the umbrella organisation through which the Party tries to control everything which in other countries might be considered 'civil society'. The chain is crucial because it means that if anyone ever steps out of line there is always, at least on paper, a personal contact from a higher level who can step in and have a quiet (or not so quiet) word and sort things out. There are officially no truly 'non-governmental' organisations in Vietnam; everything is (formally at least) part of either a Party or a state structure. In reality, though, the Party is struggling to stay in control.

Some Vietnamese non-governmental organisations (VNGOs) fall under the wing of their former ministry or another government department or a university.[11] Many departments regard their former colleagues as performing the same duties as they used to, but in a different building with better funding. VNGOs are also highly dependent on overseas money: one major survey, carried out in 2000, discovered they were 80 per cent dependent on foreign cash.[12] But this, in the opinion of at least one long-standing international development worker in Vietnam, is quite deliberate. With a regular supply of foreign cash there's little need for most VNGOs to develop indigenous sources of funding which might one day allow them some autonomy. By ensuring that VNGOs are dependent on foreigners, both can be kept on a tight leash. If the government, for any reason, wants the foreign organisation to leave the country then they know that its partners inside the country will collapse. This places a moral obligation on the international NGO not to do anything that might put its partner at risk and also gives the state an easy way to nip any signs of subversion in the bud.

On a day-to-day level the staff of both local and international organisations have considerable autonomy in that they can get their work done in the way they wish, and can wheel and deal and act in the best interests of those they're trying to serve: 52 per cent of the groups in the civic organisations survey mentioned above said they worked independently. But when it comes to things the Party finds important, everything is kept on a tight leash. Surveillance works both formally and informally. Formally the activities of all organisations are monitored by the system of 'chops'. Every organisation must have a 'chop' – a stamp which guarantees any document and proves that it is officially sanctioned rather than simply the act of an errant official. A signature on its own, whether from a government office or a private organisation, has no weight without the proper 'chop'. The registration of chops is tightly controlled; an organisation can't simply get one made up in a back-street. It may be possible for an organisation to escape the rules for a short time, but when something requires official approval, things will get difficult. There are additional controls too. Foreign NGO workers are routinely followed and spied upon, and local NGO workers are routinely questioned to make sure their international partners are not breaking the rules.

In addition to the usual controls one might expect on implementing development projects, every publication must be officially approved and every speech vetted by local authorities. Even calling for an end to poverty can be too controversial. In October 2006 one large international NGO had to cancel an event for the international 'White Wristband Day' (organised by the Global Call to Action against Poverty – the Make Poverty History campaign) because local authorities were suspicious of the organisers' possible hidden agenda. Events that were safely under the control of the VFF, however, were allowed to take place. This rigorous monitoring means international NGO representatives rarely speak publicly on controversial issues without first seeking approval from their partner organisation and local authorities. As a result there is no public criticism of governmental policies or priorities from those who know most about it. All comment has to be channelled through Party-controlled structures. The INGOs have been safely tamed. They believe that it's a price worth paying because the quid pro quo is that they are embedded in the development planning structures and guaranteed an input into policy formulation. The overall effect, however, is that evidence of failures, mistakes and bad policy or even disinterested analysis of the situation on the ground isn't available to outside observers.

* * *

In the past few years though, Vietnamese NGOs have become more confident of their position and begun to assert themselves. The Party leadership is, very slowly, being obliged to respond to the voices of some people outside the formal political system. It began with elite groups operating inside the corridors of power but in their wake new organisations are now testing the limits of what the Party will tolerate. The urban middle class is starting to get organised. An early example of such pressure group activity which came to public attention pitted one of the country's most prestigious national projects against the preservation of one of its most important ancient sites. In December 2002 a small team of Vietnamese archaeologists dug a trench in the garden behind the National Assembly in the centre of Hanoi. They were there because the site had been designated as the home for a new and much enlarged National Assembly building and a prestigious new National Convention Centre, and this was their last chance to save what they believed was underneath. The treasures they eventually found would excite historians around the world and dazzle the few visitors allowed to see them: jewels, weapons, ancient coins, terracotta phoenixes and stone dragons. They would also provoke a five-year-long fight at the highest political level over what some regarded as the nation's historic soul.

Throughout 2003 the archaeologists' trowels turned up millions of objects, evidence that five different cultures, from the sixth-century Chinese Sui Dynasty right up to the last Vietnamese monarchy, had occupied the site. The discoveries confirmed the diggers' initial supposition that the area

was once part of the ancient Citadel of Thang Long, which had ruled the
'Vietnamese' kingdom for most of the period from 1010 until the capital was
moved to Hue in 1802. Most of the Citadel had been destroyed in the nineteenth century, particularly after French colonists captured Hanoi in 1873.
Since then it had been neglected but in the summer of 2003 rumours of the
riches on the site began to circulate in Hanoi, and in September the first articles about them appeared in the press. Behind the scenes the archaeologists
were mobilising.

The construction project had some powerful backers – notably the
General Secretary of the Party, Nong Duc Manh, and his supporters and
people connected to the project's managers in the Ministry of Construction.
In the conservation corner was a bunch of grey-haired academics: two
venerable members of the Association of Vietnamese Historians, Phan Huy
Le and the late Tran Quoc Vuong, along with the influential President of the
Vietnam Academy of Social Sciences, Professor Do Hoai Nam, a member
of the Party's Central Committee, started working the corridors of power.
They had one huge factor in their favour: many of the key people they
sought to influence had been their students at Hanoi National University.
They had contacts and seniority on their side. Along with Tong Trung Tin,
the Deputy Director of the Institute of Archaeology, they built up a formi-
dable coalition of allies. They briefed newspapers about their discoveries
and gave important people tours of the site. They were careful, however, not
to directly attack the construction project or its backers. Private criticism
and lobbying is tolerated but public criticism of leaders by outsiders remains
politically unacceptable.

A deadline was approaching: the government had set 1 October as the
date for the ground-breaking ceremony for the Assembly. The discussion
went right to the very top, and the deadline was missed. Then, in early
November 2003, the Politburo itself (the Party's highest body) announced
that construction of the new National Assembly had been halted pending
further consultation. Equally importantly, it declared that the proposed
National Convention Centre would now be built in the city's south-western
suburbs. Round one to the historians. But a tougher battle was just getting
going. Nong Duc Manh and the supporters of the new Assembly building
gathered their forces. In response, the archaeologists organised a national
tour for a small but high-profile exhibition about the discoveries on the
Thang Long site. The exhibition was particularly well received in the south,

where politicians like former Prime Minister Vo Van Kiet showed much more interest in preserving the historic remains than their northern counterparts.

Apart from the prestige and the kickbacks involved in the construction project there were some other, more surprising, factors in its favour. Despite their professed atheism and campaigns against 'backwardism', parts of the Party leadership seem to have been strongly influenced by two pieces of what they usually call 'superstition'. One was the site's auspicious geomancy: the interpretation of landscape features around the capital which placed the old Citadel in the 'belly of the dragon' – a place laden with power. The second was the belief that the removal of the seat of government from Thang Long on two previous occasions (in 1397 and in 1802) had precipitated foreign invasion. Whatever the reason, Nong Duc Manh's supporters were determined to keep the Assembly on its original hallowed site. The government set about trying to find a compromise. In August 2004, after a week-long series of workshops, the archaeologists put forward their proposal – to ban new construction, preserve the entire site and leave the National Assembly in its existing 1950s building.

In March 2005 the then Prime Minister Phan Van Khai announced what appeared to be the happy ending. The new National Assembly would not be built on the proposed site. The archaeologists started preparing papers for submission to UNESCO so the Citadel could be declared a World Heritage Site in time for its 1,000th anniversary in 2010. Foreign governments delegated advisers and funding to help with the project. But there was an epilogue to the story. The pressure to construct a new Assembly building had not dissipated. In September 2007 it was announced that the project would go ahead after all. The new building was to be constructed on the site of the old one and on the adjoining Ba Dinh Club – the French-built swimming pool and leisure complex, membership of which was one of the perks of being a Party cadre. The excavations already uncovered would be preserved – but no new areas were to be incorporated into the conservation site.

Archaeologists decided there was little point pressing on with the campaign. They had won a significant victory already. The most important areas, of the Citadel had been saved; the area to be redeveloped had probably lost most of the significant remains during the construction of the original Assembly and the club anyway. And now the Politburo had reached a final agreement, any dissent would have been regarded as disloyalty.

Round two had gone to the construction lobby. The debate now focused on the best choice of design for the new building. There was one small point of resistance, though. Former general and national hero Vo Nguyen Giap wrote a letter to the press calling for the old Assembly building to be retained as part of the country's communist heritage. Editors were instructed not to print it. All obeyed except for *Dai Doan Ket* (Great Solidarity), the mouthpiece of the Vietnam Fatherland Front (VFF), which put the letter on its front page in November 2007. A year later, after two other controversies, both the paper's editor-in-chief and his deputy were fired. By then the old Assembly building had been demolished.

* * *

The main defenders of the old Citadel were academic experts, carrying out a role which the Party had, in fact, asked them to perform. Their associations were (and are) members of VUSTA, the Vietnam Union of Science and Technology Associations which, in 2002, was formally given the legal right to critique and evaluate the projects of government ministries, agencies and provincial and city authorities. VUSTA is a part of the Party-state, and falls under the 'umbrella' of the VFF. Its Chairman is Professor Vu Tuyen Hoang. An outspoken man, Professor Hoang openly talks of the need for democracy, freedom of speech and freedom of association in Vietnam and has a touching faith in the reforming and liberating power of science. He embodies Enlightenment hopes that politics might become a contest between ideas and that democracy will allow the people 'to select the leaders in each field based on their professional knowledge'. One can't help feeling that if democracy ever came to Vietnam it would disappoint Professor Hoang.

Saving the Citadel site is one of Professor Hoang's greatest achievements; 'There are the remains of 13 centuries there, they had to be protected.' He's also very pleased with VUSTA's successful efforts to reduce the impact of the vast Son La Dam in the north-west of the country, the biggest hydro-electric project in Vietnam and one of the biggest in Southeast Asia. VUSTA successfully lobbied to have the height of the dam reduced by 50 metres because of the danger of earthquakes. It also pointed out where the project failed to meet the government's own standards for environmental protection and resettling the mostly ethnic minority people being displaced by the development. 'The current dam is being implemented according to the VUSTA plan,' he says proudly. That was a technocratic battle: bringing down scientific firepower on a badly designed project being implemented by one part of the state where the impacts could clearly be demonstrated to be potentially harmful to the state as a whole. This was exactly the role which VUSTA was asked to undertake by the government.

But VUSTA has had a more difficult time trying to open up further space for the development of 'civil society' in Vietnam. The most crucial battle of recent years has been fought over what's known as the Law on Associations. The advocates of a stronger role for civil society, backed by international aid donors, have been pushing for a new way to regulate the thousands of organisations which have sprung up to provide sports facilities, entertainment, social services and advocacy for local communities and national interest groups. The only comprehensive legal document on the regulation of VNGOs remains a decree issued by Ho Chi Minh back in 1957.[13] A government directive in 1989 first allowed the creation of 'popular associations' but in 1998 the Politburo called for a new law to replace the old decree. The battle has now raged for more than a decade and still the Law on Associations seems as far from the statute books as ever.

Foreign embassies saw this law as a key step towards the emergence of a truly autonomous civil society. For several years it would appear on the list of legislation to be approved in the next session of the National Assembly, but each time it would be withdrawn. Things reached a crescendo during 2005–6: international NGOs sponsored conferences on the draft law, aid was provided to Vietnamese associations that were lobbying for change and lots of people were sent on study tours to learn from the examples of other civil society organisations in other countries. But then, in October 2006 with the law then in its 13th draft, the head of the National Assembly Office candidly admitted at his pre-session press conference that: 'There remain a lot of issues to be resolved so the law will not be enacted during this session.' And that was as far as the Law on Associations ever got.

No agreement could be reached between the progressives in VUSTA and the conservatives in the Public Security Ministry and the VFF. All the millions of dollars and euros, all the hundreds of hours of conferences and the thousands of study-tour air miles spent on promoting the idea amounted to nothing in the face of the Politburo's opposition. The law is not formally dead, just awaiting further discussion; but its return isn't expected for a few years.[14] In the meantime, organisations like VUSTA and its constituents are steadily building up their organising and lobbying capacity, stretching the law up to and beyond its limits. In this, as in many other areas of life in Vietnam, the law will probably end up as an *ex post facto* recognition of the realities of life rather than a conscious policy-driven attempt to set the agenda. Change is coming through people's day-to-day actions and the current ambiguities of state law and Party policy suit most people very well.

For the time being, associations are pushing their agendas and the Party is pushing back when things go too far: everything is a haze of creative uncertainty. In 2007 a group of the country's leading intellectuals set up the pro-market Viet Nam Institute of Development Studies (VNIDS) as a private organisation, unaffiliated to any Party or state body. They argued that the provisions of the Law on Science and Technology gave them the right to do this since they were an 'institute' not an 'association'. They registered the Institute with the Hanoi City Department of Science and Technology and organised weekly seminars about economic and social development, many of which criticised government policy. Things went smoothly until they were featured on a programme of the US-funded broadcaster Radio Free Asia at which point the Politburo suddenly took notice. Hanoi gossip suggested the Party General-Secretary Nong Duc Manh himself ordered an investigation. The order was given for the VNIDS to close.

The Institute's directors (all but one of whom was a Party member) stood firm, saying they had acted within the law. Each was then approached informally by Party officials to persuade them to close the Institute voluntarily. When they didn't give in, things got a bit tougher. The Ministry of Public Security and the army's Department Two sent agents to the weekly seminars to keep an eye on the discussions. The government ordered the ministries of Home Affairs and Science and Technology to dissolve the Institute but they refused, saying they had no legal basis on which to do this. Instead, on 24 July 2009, Prime Minister Nguyen Tan Dung issued Decree 97 limiting private research organisations to a list of 317 topics which excluded macroeconomics and views 'opposing the line, objectives and policies of the Party and state'. On 14 September 2009, the day before the Decree came into effect, the Institute finally gave in and announced its dissolution. Even though they saw themselves as loyal Party members, their independence had been too much for the leadership to tolerate. Significantly though, the Decree seems to have simultaneously created a space for other private groups to research less controversial topics.

As a result of these pioneering efforts by insiders it's now become possible for a wider range of groups to try to influence the actions of government. One of the forces pushing this new openness has been the country's incipient HIV epidemic. The sense of emergency has forced the Party to try new ways to tackle a problem it couldn't control in the old ways. The local office of UNAIDS, the United Nations body in charge of co-ordinating the campaign against HIV/AIDS, had wanted to set up a network of 'empathy groups', to link up people with experience of the disease. One such group gathered five women in a People's Committee building in south-western Hanoi. When I met them in July 2006 they didn't look like the kind of people who could shake a one-party state. But the debate about whether to allow their meeting to take place had reached all the way up to the Politburo. The women were all either HIV-positive or mothers of children with HIV: the result of an epidemic of injecting drug use in the city suburbs. This 'empathy group' just wanted to sit and talk together and share experiences and offer moral support to each other. But they wanted to do so in their own way – not under the umbrella of an official body. In 2006, after much internal debate within the Party, UNAIDS was led to understand that networks might now be permitted. For the first time 'ordinary people' were to be allowed to organise outside Party structures.

Other groups are getting together to work on other issues. They have even adopted the English word 'lobby' to describe what they do. The key to 'lobbying' is to find some part of the state which supports the group's agenda and then work through it. This way any 'political' activity appears to be entirely loyal and unthreatening to the system. One early example was the way an informal network of activists lobbied to preserve a miraculous oasis of green space in the centre of Hanoi, Reunification Park (better known by the name it bore between 1980 and 2003, Lenin Park), from commercial development. Early in 2007, the city's People's Committee approved plans for two private companies to spend $45 million turning almost all of the Park's 50 hectares into an entertainment venue with, among other 'attractions', a five-level underground car park and shopping area, 3D theatre and nightclub.[15]

Gradually, as spring turned into summer, a few independent 'experts' began to criticise the plans in the only public space available to them: the internet. The first to break the silence was an architect, Hai Nguyen, who wrote an article entitled, 'Let's save the park! Let's save our city!' on dothi.net, a website devoted to city issues owned by the online news provider, VNExpress. Other architects, retired central government officials, journalists and individuals joined in, and the online news site VietNamNet started to print their concerns. Behind the scenes, quiet lobbying was also taking place. Supporters worked their connections, finding a sympathetic ear from one highly placed official in the People's Committee. They also co-opted an official body, the Vietnam Urban Planners' Association to take up the cause and built links with useful journalists. In early August a Canadian NGO, HealthBridge, sponsored a conference on the 'System of Green Public Space in Hanoi' with invited contributions from the Prime Minister's Office (which by now had let it be known that it opposed the development) and the City's Department of Construction which ended with a call to 'save green space in Hanoi'. It provoked an avalanche of media coverage and comment in the press – the vast majority of it in favour of preserving the Park. Two weeks later the city indefinitely suspended the construction plans. By leveraging the power of central government against the city authorities and, for the first time in communist Vietnam, mobilising large amounts of public opinion in their support, the campaigners won the day.

* * *

None of this is meant to suggest that the Communist Party is struggling to keep the lid on a pressure cooker of political frustration. Although unhappiness with land seizures provokes frequent protests and economic problems provoke periodic grumbling, only a very few are prepared to challenge the right of the Party to rule the country (see Chapter 6 for more about political dissidents). The vast majority of the population is happy with their – gradually improving – lot. The political system remains firmly Leninist (in the words of one analyst, 'very, very Leninist')[16] – the Party's right to lead the people can't be challenged. More and more, however, people are seeking to organise their own activities independently of the Party and the state. Unwilling to crack down on these otherwise loyal citizens, the Party is grudgingly giving them more space in which to do so.

But in parallel with these small liberalising steps, the Ministry of Public Security is taking precautions in case the experiments go too far. Two blocks south of Hoan Kiem Lake on Hang Bai Street, in the centre of Hanoi, is a raggle-taggle complex of Ministry buildings. One of them administers visa extensions for foreigners and passport applications. Another is home to the Truck and its occupants. After a few months in Hanoi a journalist learns to look for the Truck. Whenever there is any kind of protest, the Truck is parked nearby, sometimes out of sight but never far away. The Truck is the kind of green canvas-covered troop carrier used by armies all over the world but it has government licence plates: white on blue rather than the military's white on red. Hanging out of the front and back like rangy hounds is usually a pack of lean young men, all in plain clothes, the muscle from the Ministry. Once the men from Public Security feel that a demonstration has outstayed its welcome, it's a simple matter to make sure it disperses in a timely fashion.

The Ministry is looking for more sophisticated methods. At the end of January 2007, the Chairman of the Belarus Ministry of Internal Affairs, Vladimir Naumov, visited Hanoi. Like most senior Belarus officials Naumov was banned from visiting European Union countries because of his alleged role in repressing opposition activists. But that didn't concern the authorities in Hanoi. On his return to Minsk he told Belarus's official news agency that Vietnam was interested in acquiring what he called 'special technical materials'. That's a phrase used by the Belarus security services to describe crowd control equipment such as truncheons, tear gas, electric-shock weapons and personal armour.[17] The Belarus Ministry is the successor to the Soviet secret police, the KGB. Belarus-based journalists say it is 'feared by opposition activists for its agents' ability to penetrate anti-government groups and to monitor their communications using wire taps and secret telephone monitoring'. Naumov told the news agency that this would also be something which 'experts from both sides will be studying'.

There's little doubt that any serious challenge to the Party's rule would be met by determined force. Under the constitution the army has the duty to defend, not just the country, but socialism itself. The state could put millions of soldiers and police on the streets at very short notice. Could it ever come to that? In the current circumstances it seems highly unlikely that there could be a generalised uprising against the Communist Party. Most people are happy with their lot and the state's vast surveillance networks give ample warning of any incipient threats. The 'Cultured Families' campaign, the sophistication of its internet controls and the management of pressure groups all suggest the Party is looking ahead to future challenges. It's also trying a different approach. Where once the Party squared up to potential challengers – from the Catholic Church to critical intellectuals – now it's finding ways to co-opt its critics so that, perhaps even against their own will, they end up supporting its position. Opposition has been brought inside the 'big tent' and tamed.

The Party still labours night and day to ensure that it, and only it, is the focus of political and economic life – both the driver of change and the guarantor of stability. Yet there's plenty of evidence that many of the structures which sustained the Party's rule are either crumbling at the edges or decaying from within. If the Party's leadership were ever to lose control of its lower echelons or if corruption caused them to lose legitimacy, if the public and parts of the state lost their belief that the system was delivering, then – and only then – the result could be fracture and crisis. The Party's most important battle is the one to preserve its position, as we'll see in the next chapter.

★

5

'Greet the Party, Greet Spring!'

Ba Dinh Square, the epicentre of political life in Vietnam, was designed for parades. The great boulevard along its western side can accommodate hundreds of military vehicles, the tiered reviewing stands and the lawns opposite have space for thousands of cheering spectators and Ho Chi Minh's grey marble mausoleum has a terrace from which Communist Party leadership can wave at the masses. Except the masses don't come any more – not even for Uncle Ho's birthday. Once upon a time, before about 1998, Ba Dinh Square would be filled on national occasions. No longer. The party of the masses no longer trusts crowds and the crowds have got better things to do than act out the role of the masses.[1] The peasantry aren't bussed in to sing and cheer, the flag-waving proletariat don't line the streets; even the tourists get cleared away. The audience for Uncle Ho's birthday is virtual: images of the occasion are conveyed to the masses by television. The masses themselves aren't allowed to intrude, for fear that some piece of disorder might upset the celebration and – more importantly – be seen to upset it on the screens of the nation.

In May 2008 the birthday celebration took place inside the National Assembly building, on the eastern side of the square opposite the Mausoleum. It was a variety show of song, dance and rhetoric watched by, in the words of the Party newspaper, 'more than 800 people from all walks of life including intellectuals, religious people and armed forces'. The stage was decorated only with bouquets of flowers, a bust of Uncle Ho and, behind the singers, dancers and rhetoricians, a large, oval-shaped painting of Karl Marx and Vladimir Lenin. Once it was over, a small group of men and women in suits, the Communist Party leadership, made their way across the empty square to lay an enormous wreath at the Mausoleum. All around them, indeed all around the country, red banners hung from lamp posts bearing simply the gold-printed numbers '19–5'. Nothing else was needed: everyone knew the significance of the date.

The spectacle of Ho Chi Minh's birthday is a public display of the primacy of the Communist Party but also of the adjustments it has been forced to make as a result of economic liberalisation. Its leaders no longer expect mass devotion. All they require is acknowledgement that they are the sole political force in the country and that their procession across Ba Dinh Square is noted, respected and uninterrupted. Yet, in one key respect the Party is exactly the same as it was at its foundation in 1930. It is a vanguard organisation, straight out of Lenin's textbook. Its self-appointed, self-confident role is to lead the whole of society towards modernity and development. It guards this role jealously. What *has* changed is the way it leads. In wartime and austerity the Party could control most areas of day-to-day life through its near-monopoly of the distribution of goods and services. But the more anarchic society unleashed by the *doi moi* liberalisation can't be managed in the same way. State-owned industries have carved out their own niches, local and provincial governments have turned themselves into money-making fiefdoms, the private sector has grown and the Party leadership has often found itself struggling to control its subordinates.

Many people see Vietnam as a classic one-party state, directed by a mono-lithic power whose writ rules across the country. This is also the image of itself the Communist Party of Vietnam likes to project. The reality is that the Party leadership's hold over events can be partial and fragile. Most of the problems which the country faces, from corruption to environmental degradation, are the result of a *lack* of central control, not a surfeit of it. The Party leadership's attempts to reassert control in the past two decades have led it in several directions – to try to co-opt powerful new interest groups, to broaden the range of voices it listens to and, in particular, to develop a system of law with which to discipline its unruly minions and force powerful private interests into line. It has been the leadership's good fortune that it's done so at a time when interna-tional development organisations have focused on questions of what they call 'good governance' and, as a result, the World Bank, the United Nations Development Programme and most overseas aid providers have advised and subsidised the Party's efforts to find new ways to solidify one-party rule.

In the old days the law was largely meaningless. The Ministry of Justice was actually abolished between 1960 and 1981. There was no need for it: political decisions made by local Party officials sufficed. Now, the Party leadership thinks the law will perform two functions: forcing local officials to follow central instructions, and simultaneously getting officials off the backs of entrepreneurs and investors, enabling them to create jobs. The leadership has come to understand that it cannot foster economic growth or meet the material and creative aspirations of the people if it tries to control everything. Instead, the Party leadership wants 'a law-based state' – a Vietnam in which rules are consistent across the country and the people have a measure of freedom. This fits very nicely with the well-funded international vogue for 'good governance' but it would be a mistake to think that the Party is bowing out of politics. Far from it. It's taking a step back, allowing more flexibility in the way it rules the country but not letting go. It wants to use the state to retain its control over the country and, in the process, turn itself into an elite which will direct the state from behind the scenes.

The reality behind the 'law-based state' can be seen in a short walk around Ba Dinh Square, the capital of Vietnamese political life for most of the past millennium. At the northern end are two sets of buildings divided by Hung Vuong Road, the broad triumphal boulevard named after the mythical first king of ancient Vietnam. On the eastern side is the old French school, the Lycée Albert Sarraut. It's now the offices of the Central Committee, the main decision-making body of the Communist Party. On the western side, in a space carved out of the Botanic Gardens, is the former French Governor-General's residence, now the Presidential Palace, and behind it, hidden in the trees, the Prime Minister's Office. If political transformation truly was taking place in Vietnam it should be a one-way transfer of power across Hung Vuong Road from the Party buildings on one side to the government buildings on the other. It's not that simple.

If interior design is any marker of status, then it's not hard to see where power really lies. Inside the President's Palace the décor is still French Colonial overlaid with a strong whiff of socialist austerity. The Prime Minister's office is a slice of Soviet Chic. But across the road, the Central Committee building is all New Chinese opulent: enormous wooden doors, echoing marble corridors and gilded meeting rooms full of throne-like chairs for visiting delegations. The old Lycée buildings have been given a modern frontage, and a giant hammer and sickle now dominates the ornate gardens.

Whoever designed it didn't think it was going to be abandoned any time soon. The Party may be changing but it's not going away. On Ho Chi Minh's birthday, the wreath-laying procession across the Square demonstrated the real order of political power in Vietnam. In most countries, national commemorations are led by state officials. Not in Vietnam. The birthday celebration, like the country, is led by the Communist Party. The state and the government follow on behind. The man at the head of the procession was the Party General Secretary, Nong Duc Manh, and next to him was his predecessor Le Kha Phieu. Only in the second row came the leaders of the state, President Nguyen Minh Triet and Prime Minister Nguyen Tan Dung. In spite of expectations to the contrary, this is the way things are likely to stay.

* * *

Adjacent to the Central Committee building, opposite the Mausoleum and partly surrounded by the vestiges of the thousand-year-old Thang Long Citadel, stands a building which demonstrates how this behind-the-scenes power works (although at the time of writing, the building is being rebuilt. See Chapter 4, pp. 81–5). The National Assembly is, according to Vietnam's Constitution, the country's supreme authority. There is no separation of powers. As well as approving laws and holding ministers to account, the National Assembly selects the President and Prime Minister, manages the Supreme Court and the legal system, amends the Constitution and adjudicates conflicts between the Constitution and legislation. In reality, however, the Assembly is not the all-powerful body the Constitution makes it out to be because, like the rest of the state, it is a tool of the Party. Almost every law passed by the Assembly carries a preamble stating which piece of Party policy it is based upon, and its internal elections are everything that one might expect in a one-party state.

The elections of the current President and Prime Minister, in late June 2006, were a case in point. They came in the final week of the National Assembly session, the international press were invited and every member of the Assembly wore their finest: hundreds of besuited men, army officers in crisp uniforms, women in their most beautiful *ao dai*, ethnic minorities in traditional dress and Buddhist monks in saffron robes and woolly hats. The vote for each post was a piece of theatre. The single candidate (who had been selected by a meeting of the Party's Central Committee a few weeks earlier) was formally announced and gave a speech. Each member of the Assembly was given a voting paper printed with a single name and a question: 'Do you vote in favour or against?' Then, at the given moment, they all trooped up on to the stage to deposit their papers in a large transparent ballot box. They did the same for each position and then had tea while the results were calculated. They were, unsurprisingly, almost unanimous – 92 per cent for Prime Minister Dung and 94 per cent for President Triet.

Because of spectacles like this, it's tempting to dismiss the National Assembly as a joke parliament. Of its current delegates, 91 per cent are members of the Communist Party. The remaining 9 per cent had to pass a stringent Party-controlled nomination process. The candidates it elects to state posts are all chosen in advance by the Party and the legislation it passes follows the Party's agenda. And yet, as Prime Minister Dung discovered just a day after being elected, that is not the whole story.

That day, the Assembly was asked to approve the resignation of the previous government. Many delegates though, were irate that the Transport Minister, Dao Dinh Binh, was being allowed to retire honourably along with his colleagues. Two weeks previously, Binh had been savaged by members of the Assembly, live on television, for failing to stop the country's biggest corruption scandal, known as the PMU18 affair (see Chapter 7 for more on the scandal). Mr Binh resigned from office and escaped formal punishment but many delegates wanted to make an example of him. Dung, however, wanted him to be treated the same as other outgoing members of the government. When it came to a vote, almost half the Assembly failed to support the Prime Minister: 44 per cent either voted against or abstained. It was a radical intervention for an organisation which had been a rubber stamp for the previous half-century.

How did this come about? Why did an assembly so dominated by the Party end up delivering such a rebuke to the national leadership? The answer lies in the role the Party has deliberately developed for the Assembly as a buttress to its rule. Part of this is theatre – the Assembly is presented to the public and the outside world as a genuine parliament, with elections and the power to make laws and confirm appointments, even though, in all these areas, its independence is firmly circumscribed. But part of it is reality. The American legal scholar Mark Sidel, who has monitored the development of the National Assembly for many years, argues that it has both allowed different points of view to be represented within a Party-controlled framework and also helped bind some of the Party's critics within the elite.[2] And as Dr Frankenstein found out, even an assemblage of automata can take on a life of its own, given a jolt of power. For the time being, however, the National Assembly remains stuck between its previous life as a Soviet-style rubber stamp for the Central Committee and the life many of its members want it to have as a proper legislature. One Assembly insider candidly admits the problem. 'We have violated the teachings of Lenin!' he says in mock horror. 'But we don't want to hurt him too much. It has to be step by step.'

Until the 2007 elections, Madame Ton Nu Thi Ninh was the National Assembly's international ambassador. Elegant, coiffed, assertive and poly-lingual, she travelled the world on its behalf and greeted its foreign visitors. 'She'll charm your socks off,' confided one British minister. The daughter of a mandarin of the former imperial court, Mme Ninh is not a democrat. 'I resist the idea that voters are always right,' she says. 'I know that there are in any country enclaves of conservatism, and it's not by virtue of being a voter that you're always right. There are voters who are very conservative. Just remember in South Africa with apartheid. If you went to a white enclave their democratic answer would have been the status quo. What is right does not always coincide with majority rule. Democracy is more complex than just saying whatever the largest number says is right.' For Madame Ninh and her fellow thinkers in the Party, the role of the National Assembly is not to let the people rule but to widen the range of voices heard in the political main-stream. She once told a gathering of foreign ambassadors, 'In the end every-thing will come home to rest with the Party and we are happy with that.' She was proud that no one ever told her how to vote in the Assembly but this is hardly a demonstration of democracy. As a loyal member of the Communist Party she could be trusted to vote the right way without instruction.

Duong Trung Quoc is a reformer. He was elected to the Assembly by the voters of Dong Nai province (just north of Ho Chi Minh City), but more significantly he was selected by the Party to be chosen by the voters of Dong Nai because he is head of the Association of Vietnam Historians. Mr Quoc is a part-timer, receiving a third of his salary from the Assembly and spending a third of his time there. The rest of his work takes place in a small office at the back of the Museum of the Vietnamese Revolution in Hanoi where he's written several well-known books on the history of the country and now edits the magazine *Past and Present*. With silver hair and mous-tache and sporting a beret, collarless silk jacket and smart laptop bag, he looks like a Parisian intellectual. Now in his sixties he says he had wanted to slow down after one term in the Assembly but the combined pressure of the Historians' Association and his wife ('She's afraid that if I retire I'll spend all my time in karaoke bars') convinced him to stand again.

Although he was elected with Party backing, he's one of the few non-Party members in the Assembly and he calls the Party's 91 per cent monopoly of the Assembly 'unreasonable'. He says his views are shared by many Party members but that 'invisible barriers' stop them from speaking out. Mr Quoc is careful to couch his calls for reform within the tradition of Ho Chi Minh's political thought, using his official position as a national historian to buttress his political position. He argues that Uncle Ho's original 1946 Constitution guaranteed property rights, free voting and a 'proper' parliament, but that these rights were subordinated to the national struggle during the wars of 1946–75 and then to the wishes of the country's leaders after that. Now, according to Mr Quoc's reading of history, it's time to rediscover Uncle Ho's original intentions.

Mr Quoc could be called an advocate of bourgeois reform. He worries about the growing divide between the very rich and the poor and sees the expansion of a property-owning middle class as a good thing for democracy and for the country. 'Until we have owners, we can't have a market economy or a real democracy,' he says, and argues that having members of the Assembly who are owners – the bosses of enterprises, for example – helps to build democracy. But he's critical of those reformers who want to speed up the process of reform 'at any price', without regard to the consequences for social stability. 'That's why,' he says, 'I'm part of the compromise group.' He argues that the Assembly should follow wider political trends but not try to take the lead. When the current arrangements ultimately reach their limits new thinking will be required, he believes, and in time Vietnam will become 'normal'.

But the pace of change is slow, as the story of the 2007 National Assembly election demonstrates. From the day the election date was announced, in late January, the vote was stage-managed by the Party although not everything went according to plan. The election was set in motion by Politburo Directive 09–CT/TW which decreed that 'the consultation and nomination that help voters to select candidates with appropriate abilities and characters, who can be worthy representatives for the people in the body with highest state power, is a core duty for the entire party, the people and the army'. Three days later the National Assembly's Standing Committee set the election date for 20 May. And in a striking decision for those used to the rough and tumble of democratic politics it also agreed the number of existing members of the Assembly who should be re-elected: 160 of the 500 in total. In most elections setting a target for the number of sitting politicians to be re-elected would be pointless, but in Vietnam politics is just another area of life under central control, subject to the same kind of guidance as the economy.

This 'guidance' helps make the National Assembly one of the most socially representative parliaments in the world because the Party decides in advance who needs to be represented: how many women, how many members of ethnic minorities, how many delegates from different interest groups – the elderly, the military, the youth union, religious groups, etc – what proportion from government ministries, provincial authorities and so on. It does so through a peculiarly communist organisation: the Vietnam Fatherland Front. The VFF is a part of the state – its existence is mandated by the Constitution – but its job is to organise mass support for the Communist Party or, in the words of the Constitution, to 'Strengthen the people's unity of mind in political and spiritual matters'. From its offices in a big French villa set back from Trang Thi Street in central Hanoi it is responsible for managing most of what amounts to 'civil society' in Vietnam. Almost all the mass organisations in the country come under its umbrella: the Women's Union (with 12 million members), the Youth Union (with 3.5 million), the Farmers' Union, the Trades Union and so on. Constitutionally, the Communist Party (with just 3.1 million members) is itself a part of the VFF. In practice, of course, it's the Party which directs the Front.

In 2007 the Chairman of the VFF was Pham The Duyet whose avuncular manner belied his reputation as a bruiser. It was he who, ten years before, was sent by the Politburo to sort out Thai Binh province after the revolt (see Chapter 2). Silver-haired, bespectacled and sharp-suited he breezily batted away questions about why his organisation exists. 'The VFF is the home for all the mass organisations and gathers all the people in its work. The Party wants the VFF to unite the people. The VFF also works with social critics and improves the supervision work of the Party and local government to fight corruption and other social evils.' The VFF is a key instrument of Party rule – it's the organisation which keeps the National Assembly under Party control. Although any citizen can, in theory, stand for election to the

National Assembly, they first have to be vetted in a process managed by the VFF. The degree of control over the elections is revealed by the official targets set at the start of the election process. Apart from the number of re-elected NA members, the new Assembly was expected to comprise at least 150 women, 90 members of ethnic minorities and 50 people who weren't members of the Communist Party.

The process of getting elected is deliberately cumbersome. In 2007, as usual, it began with a convention organised by the Fatherland Front before and during which different parts of the Party-state jockeyed for their share of the members to be elected. After the haggling, central-level organisations were allowed to nominate 167 candidates, of whom the National Assembly Office was to nominate 81, the Fatherland Front 33, the government 24, the military 16 and the Party 11. The country's 64 provinces and cities nominated several hundred between them. Each organisation then had to decide who its representatives would be. Provinces tended to nominate senior figures within their own administrations. Members of the National Assembly (along with staff of the Assembly's administrative office) held a secret ballot to decide which of the outgoing members they wanted to re-elect. The VFF had to allocate its share between the Mass Organisations and smaller groups such as the Association of Vietnam Historians, the Union of the Elderly, the Writers' Association, religious groups and so on. It's a way of giving them more or less guaranteed representation in the Assembly.

Until the 1997 election all candidates had to be nominated by an official organisation – some part of either the Party or the state. But in that vote and since, individuals have been allowed to 'self-nominate'. In 2007 international observers and the local media took a great deal of interest in the number of people nominating themselves. Several well-known people put themselves forward. Some were businesspeople, some Party members who hadn't been included in the official selection process and others were complete outsiders. One folk hero who tried to run was Do Viet Khoa, a teacher from a village near Hanoi who became nationally famous in July 2006 for attempting to stop his pupils from cheating in their school exams. When his colleagues and head teacher refused to help him (because they'd been bribed by the children's parents) he videoed the pupils' cheating and sent the tape to national television. The broadcast caused a national scandal, and ultimately the replacement of the Education Minister. But national fame wasn't enough to get Khoa elected. By mid-April he'd been eliminated from the race.

Every prospective candidate has to be approved by two selection meetings: one in their workplace, the other in their neighbourhood. Khoa received three-quarters of the votes of his neighbourhood, from those who approved of his tough stance on corruption, but none at all from his teaching colleagues, who were furious that he'd cut off their source of 'side income'.[3] On the other hand, a businesswoman, Vu Thi Khanh Van, an exporter of rattan furniture, was approved by her workplace but not by her neighbours. 'Some people resented me for owning a car,' she said. Other, more popular, people were also excluded. Dang Hung Vo, the former Deputy Environment Minister and a noted campaigner against corruption, failed to make it on to the ballot paper, apparently after coming under pressure from his colleagues in the Party to withdraw his own nomination. Another high-profile person who also 'voluntarily' stood down described the kind of pressure he was put under. He was summoned to what he could only call 'a Maoist vetting session' at which eight strangers who could cite everything that he had ever published hurled accusations and criticism at him. Businesspeople fared particularly badly. Of 52 who nominated themselves in Ho Chi Minh City, just four made it to the ballot paper, and two of these were already Party members.[4]

But even if candidates get through this stage, they might not make it through the final vetting carried out by the VFF's local and national committees. These meetings can overturn earlier decisions to, for example, increase representation from the target groups or, more usually, reduce the amount of competition in any one constituency. By law there have to be at least two more candidates than seats available, so as to provide the semblance of a contest (most constituencies elect three or four delegates). But the law also states that, to win, a candidate must receive over 50 per cent of the vote, so the VFF won't allow too many candidates to stand in case the vote is spread too thinly. The VFF's final national meeting also decides which central candidate runs for which seat: candidates don't have to have any connection to the province which they notionally 'represent'. The Prime Minister, Nguyen Tan Dung, for example, represents the city of Haiphong where he has neither lived nor worked but still gets elected with 99 per cent of the vote. This allocation process is carefully done; indeed it's the centrepiece of the election management process. Centrally nominated candidates never run against each other and are usually placed in districts against much weaker local rivals. They're expected to win and go on to take high positions in the Assembly. However, provincial election boards decide which local candidates run in which districts, giving local politicians the power to ensure their favourite candidates get easier contests. Allocating candidates to seats demands considerable knowledge of local political scenes and is part of a tense negotiating process which tries to balance the interests of the central Party leadership with those of local Party bosses. Both must be guaranteed a fair degree of representation. Only then can the names go on the ballot.

By 25 April the list of candidates was complete: 877 people were running for 493 seats. And on 3 May, campaigning formally began. The election authorities claimed they spent $22 million on the process – a vast amount of money in a country with huge numbers of people still in poverty. Party members mobilised to turn out the vote, news programmes stressed the importance of a high turnout to demonstrate the nation's strength and street hoardings called upon everyone to do their patriotic duty. But the appearance of a campaign mattered more than the substance. Voters in one ward in central Hanoi said that, although local officials organised election meetings with the candidates, they went around the neighbourhood in the days before warning people not to ask any difficult or embarrassing questions. Self-nominated candidates complained that they couldn't talk about issues or their political programmes; voters' decisions seemed to be based mainly on the candidates' biographies.

In the run-up to Election Day, local party cells competed to see who could achieve the highest turnout. Heads of households, grandfathers and grandmothers, were strongly encouraged to ensure the whole family turned out. Members of the Mass Organisations, in particular the Women's Union, went from door to door asking people if they intended to vote. If the answer was 'no', they asked for the household's voter registration form so they could cast the vote on the household's behalf. The province of Vinh Long in the Mekong Delta actually managed a turnout of 100 per cent. Not a single person in the province was too ill, too lazy or too far from a polling station to vote, at least according to the official figures. The average national turnout was 99.6 per cent. These ludicrous figures are achieved partly by stuffing ballot boxes but mostly by proxy voting: heads of household cast the votes of the entire family. Although illegal it boosts turnout figures and makes the local officials look good. Everyone knows these figures are fictitious and some within the National Assembly go as far as to call them 'embarrassing' but they survive as part of the Party's general obsession with targets.

The international community, and also many reformists within Vietnam, had invested plenty of hope up until this point in the possibility that 2007 would widen the number of non-Party members elected to the National Assembly. They saw this as a way of gradually creating a body of independent politicians who could begin to act as a credible opposition. Some within the Party seemed to share that idea. Three months before the vote, Pham The Duyet, the VFF boss, told me his organisation was aiming to have 20 per cent of the seats won by independents. Some would be genuinely independent, self-nominated candidates while others would be non-Party members nominated by the Party. But it never happened. In fact the proportion of independents in the Assembly actually fell: from 10 per cent to 9 per cent. The self-nominated candidates fared even worse. Of the 236 individuals who nominated themselves, just 30 passed the approvals process and got on to the ballot paper and only one of them was actually elected – down from two in the previous Assembly. Despite all the talk of widening representation in the National Assembly, the actual results in 2007 were minimal. Just one of the 493 people elected to the Assembly was not nominated by the Communist Party.

Interestingly, the targeting process failed in other ways too. Only 127 women were elected instead of the 150 targeted. The ethnic minorities target came closer with 87 elected instead of 90. But most surprisingly, 12 of the centrally nominated candidates also failed to be elected – the highest number ever. This meant the number of re-elected Assembly members was also 12 short of the target, something bemoaned by several members who complained about the loss of expertise. All of this showed that not everything was under the control of the Party centre. Local interests were, in some places, able to capture the election process and defeat the central candidate. All 12 central nominee defeats took place in surplus provinces – the 11 provinces and cities of the 64 which are net donors to the national budget. (There's more on the significance of 'surplus provinces' in Chapter 10.) These local authorities have their own interests and income, and don't need to take as much notice of central instructions as those 'deficit provinces' which are dependent on Hanoi for subsidies. None of the latter rejected the centrally nominated candidates.[5] This is a clear point of concern for Hanoi. It's frightened that if wealthy provinces (which are mainly in the south) become more autonomous, regional grievances which it has success-fully buried since the end of the war could open up. The provincial bosses need to be kept in line.

* * *

One of the weapons the Party uses to keep the lower ranks in line is the ongoing campaign against corruption. The Party and the state are riddled with it. All along Dien Bien Phu Street in central Hanoi, the old French villas have been turned into consumer stores with extra plate glass, neon brand names and a procession of customers seeking the newest and shiniest digital devices. Even in a country where the average wage is $700 a year, there doesn't seem to be a shortage of people willing to pay eye-watering sums for ostentatious acces-sories. Mobiado is a Canadian company which makes mobile phones for people who like to stand out. Its phones are made with tropical hardwoods and decorated with precious stones. The shop at 14 Dien Bien Phu Street sells one model for $2,200 and there's no shortage of buyers, according to saleswoman Dao Diem Anh. 'We sell about ten of these a week – mostly to state officials and big business people,' she says. Few are bought for personal use – they are usually gifts to buy or reward favours. The fact that state officials, whose nominal salaries are usually a matter of $100 a month, can afford to give away such luxuries is easy evidence of the extent of corruption.

Almost every official transaction is likely to require some form of hidden payment: kindergarten teachers will have to bribe the boss to get hired, the children's parents will have to bribe the teacher to ensure their children get well treated, high school pupils will bribe their teachers to get good marks in exams and PhD students pay to get their theses written for them by their examiners' colleagues. The education system is not alone; extra payments are required to get good treatment in hospitals, to get electricity connections fixed and to get business. Corruption is systemic. Economic liberalisation and inflation, the rising cost of living and budget constraints in the state mean the entire administrative system now depends upon backhanders for its existence. A teacher is expected to live on $60 per month, for example; a university lecturer on $150. Even government ministers are supposed to get by on $200 per month.

The continual need to pay off officials is a cause for constant grumbling but over the past two decades bribery has been the way the system survived.

Without it, schools, universities and hospitals would have become bereft of teaching staff. Now that it is established, those who don't take bribes are regarded by their colleagues and superiors as potential whistleblowers who could undermine their position. Corruption is also a way of maintaining loyalty. Low pay keeps junior officials dependent upon senior ones for allocating them money and favours. But, perhaps most crucially, corruption allows, the system to bend rather than break. The whole structure of laws and regulations is so complex and rigid that if it weren't for graft it would have either broken or provoked so much resentment that there might have been active resistance to it. By allowing individuals to negotiate their way around its obstacles, corruption actually helps the system to fend off demands for wider reform.

The Party is well aware of the situation. Its own Internal Affairs Commission (supported by the Swedish development agency SIDA) interviewed 5,000 people across the country in 2005. Half said their bosses were involved in corruption and a third of public officials admitted to being willing to accept bribes.[6] (The remainder were presumably just unwilling to admit it.) The Party leadership has tolerated the situation, partly because choking off the flow of bribes would cause hardship for its lower-ranking cadres, partly because the leadership itself benefits from corruption and partly because its power to do anything about it is limited. Instead its response has been to try to contain it with, on one hand, high-profile but largely ineffective public relations campaigns to try to show it is taking the problem seriously, and, on the other, highly targeted crackdowns against certain individuals who've become too big for their boots.

On 2 February 2007 the stirring strains of the Internationale, the anthem of international communism, filled the National Assembly building, on this occasion the venue for a special meeting of the Communist Party. It was the launch of the Party campaign succinctly entitled 'Study, work and follow the moral guidance of Ho Chi Minh'. After a medley of revolutionary songs, paeans to Uncle Ho and a display by gymnasts dressed as workers and peasants, the business began. Nong Duc Manh, the head of the Communist Party, *primus inter pares* of the ruling elite, took the podium. Normally a good speaker, this sermon was below his best. Soberly dressed in a black business suit, rather than the khaki safari jacket he appears more comfortable in, he reminded his audience at length about the history of the Party, how Vietnam had faced challenges, defeated invaders and become the first democratic country in Southeast Asia. But then it got interesting.

Denouncing the 'large numbers of party members who have shown a decline in morality', he told the Party at large that 'Improving revolutionary morals must go along with giving up individualism. The reality of building the Party in the last 77 years has clearly shown that the deterioration in the morality and lifestyle of not-small numbers of government officials and Party members holding power – especially those who are heads of organisations – will paralyse the process of building the Party.' Campaigns like this are intended for public consumption – the event was broadcast live on national television. But the public at large are generally unimpressed, if the reaction in one street café was anything to go by. 'Why are you watching that rubbish?' asked a passer-by. It was Friday morning and they had better things to do than watch the launch of yet another campaign against corruption.

But the public does take an interest when the Party gets serious. Even fairly senior local Party leaders can be hung out to dry when it's necessary *pour encourager les autres*. A series of high-profile crackdowns since the mid-1990s have targeted high-level local officials in Ho Chi Minh City. The public was agog at the details of the cases – the 'disappearance' of millions of dollars, the gambling and the prostitution – all helpfully revealed by the police and published in full by the media. The British analyst Martin Gainsborough, who studied the cases, argues that they weren't simple prosecutions of bad behaviour but part of a systematic campaign to get the city's officials back under central control.[7] Where once its own internal methods of discipline might have sufficed to control its unruly subordinates they now appear to be insufficient. The Party needs other tools – in particular the rule of law and the powers of the state.

* * *

Trying to separate the Party from the state may be possible on paper but disentangling where one really stops and where the other begins is almost impossible. Within every state organisation there is a Party cell – the *ban can su dang*, literally the Party Affairs Committee – which receives the Party's edicts, and is supposed to ensure they are implemented. The *ban can su* acts as the Party's enforcer and intelligence gatherer. It oversees the hiring and (less often) the firing of state officials, and, particularly at the level of districts and communes, makes most of the key decisions about policy. It is almost always the case that the head of the People's Committee, the executive arm of local government, is the *deputy* head of the local Party unit. In other words, the local Party boss outranks them. The local heads of the Mass Organisations and the police also sit on the local Party branch executive.[8] Similar arrangements are found at each level of government. The Party directs the state. This means that using state institutions to control Party members can be fraught with difficulty.

Just as it did in the mandarinate of seventeenth-century Vietnam, success in the Party depends upon having a combination of three factors: talent, connections and money. Of the three, connections are the most important. Local bosses rise to the top by creating patronage machines, buying support and buying off opposition as necessary. Ambitious cadres will cultivate the support of business leaders, judges, police and their peers. If the Party leadership wanted to maintain rigid loyalty to central instructions it would have to replace local cadres with ones from other areas – but this would require a vast increase in resources, training and logistics, including proper salaries and other incentives for deployed cadres. It's much cheaper to use local staff, try to keep them in line and accept corruption as part of the price of rule. But if insubordination gets out of hand, disciplining local bosses demands the application of greater political force from above than they can muster in response. By giving more power to the institutions of the state – the courts, the police, government inspectorates and auditing agencies – the leadership in Hanoi has more mechanisms through which to try to enforce its will. District-level courts have become so completely captured by local politicians, for example, that the government is now setting up a system of regional courts which it hopes will take greater heed of central instructions than local ones.

Much of what the Party is trying to do with legal reform is being subsidised by foreign aid donors. Many of them are under the illusion that they are helping to build the 'rule of law' in Vietnam which will ultimately supplant the 'rule of the Party'. The Party leadership is, quite strategically, encouraging them to believe the illusion. In late May 2005, the Politburo passed Resolution 48, entitled the 'Strategy for Development and Improvement of the Legal System'. Eight days later it issued Resolution 49: the 'Strategy for Judicial Reform'. The similar-sounding names disguised profound differences between them. Legal development was tasked to the Ministry of Justice, which, with plenty of international advice and financial assistance, has focused on changing legislation to meet the requirements of an internationally integrated economy. In the era of national commerce and international trade, when the country has signed up to bilateral agreements with the United States and multilateral agreements with the World Trade Organisation, the old ways have to change.

Resolution 49, on the other hand, encapsulates the Party's new survival strategy – making sure that change isn't too drastic. Judicial reform remains under the control of the Party's internal structures without any significant foreign input. The Party is quite open about the fact that 'people-voted agencies' – for which read 'Party-controlled agencies' – will continue to supervise judicial operations. In 2002 the National Assembly passed the Law on the Organisation of the People's Courts, which increased courts' independence. But the Ministry of Justice then followed this up with Circular 05, which stipulated that judges still have to be approved by the local Party cell and must have 'Political Knowledge Credentials' – the term for the certificate awarded by the Party's training school, the Ho Chi Minh National Political Academy.

Any genuine separation of powers would rapidly undermine the Party's rule. If an independent Supreme Court started to strike down pieces of legislation which conflicted with the Constitution – for example, on limits to the freedom of the press – or if lower courts started to order the release of political prisoners held on trumped-up charges, or if independent prosecutors pursued allegations of corruption to the highest levels, then the Party's traditional techniques of rule would begin to collapse. What the Party needs now is something which looks like the rule of law and the separation of powers, but in fact isn't; something which appears to allow ever greater freedom and equality before the law but which perpetuates the Party's management of the country. It's the difference between 'rule of law,' – which has dangerous implications – and 'rule by law', which the Party believes is compatible with its own ambitions. The Party doesn't want a 'separation of powers' but a 'specialisation of powers' in which the various branches of government are assigned certain functions and overseen by proxy through the National Assembly. In the meantime, the cost of international legal training, new law schools, new computer systems and hundreds of thousands of hours of consultants' time is all being subsidised by foreign governments.

* * *

The Party's priority, above all else, is to remain in power. Although many of its members appear to be interested only in lining their own pockets, the

Party as a whole is clearly an 'intelligent' organisation pondering how to preserve its position as the country undergoes momentous change. The process is usually hidden behind the closed doors of the Ho Chi Minh Academy and the Party's various think tanks, but from time to time glimpses emerge. Cadres are sent to study in foreign universities; official delegations visit other parties, from the Kuomintang in Taiwan to the Social Democrats in Germany, to learn how they maintain themselves in power; and internal seminars debate ways to manage the media, civil society and the economy. Taken together, it looks as if the leadership wants the Party to evolve into a state-directing elite which maintains control over the commanding heights of society and the economy but reduces its role in the details of government. The Party would, if this strategy were successful, evolve into a 'socialist freemasonry' with its own rules and rituals, hidden from public view but with great influence through its formal and informal networks of power. Many other countries have some kind of equivalent – from Ivy League fraternities in the US to Oxbridge networks in the UK, or, perhaps the closest parallel, graduates of the École Normale d'Administration (the so-called ENArques) in France – but few have such a disciplined and formalised arrangement.

The Party has changed as the country it leads has changed and as battles within it have been resolved. Two of the most significant developments have been a shift in recruitment and the gerrymandering of elections. During the late 1990s the Party suffered a huge vote of no confidence from young people: during the last half of the decade just 7,000 students chose to join.[9] In response, it redefined what it offers to young people, abandoning its claim to fulfil their every revolutionary hope and instead offering them a path to personal advancement. Young Party members are frequently recruited explicitly on those terms, being told: 'If you want promotion you have to join'. Rather than burying selfish motives under a veneer of altruism and pious sentiments about wanting to help develop the country, it's now quite acceptable for a new Party member to tell their friends that they're doing it for personal gain. Indeed, it's embarrassingly uncool to admit wanting to build socialism or defend the revolution. It seems to have worked. The Party claimed that 60 per cent of the 170,000 people who joined it in 2005 were aged between 18 and 30.[10]

Most of the new members were recommended by the Party's main youth organisation, the Ho Chi Minh Youth Union.[11] The Union used to mobilise young people for revolutionary duty. During the war years its slogan was:

'Ready to fight; ready to join the armed forces; ready to go anywhere and do whatever the Fatherland requires'. Now its message is more careerist. Just like members of the Scout movement in other countries they're expected to join in organised community work, team sports and official celebrations, and to be patriotic and show respect for their elders and leaders.[12] The model is deliberately exclusive. Only about 15 per cent of young Vietnamese are members of the Youth Union – and the leadership tries to keep it that way. Members must come from a 'good family' and be hard-working students. The Union actively winnows its membership to exclude those who don't set a good enough example – members have to keep a book in which details of their family, school and personal behaviour are recorded. The Communist Party calls it a 'socialist school for youth'. Its purpose is not to mobilise large numbers of young people but to be a vanguard organisation whose members will lead their peers and from whose ranks subsequent generations of political and social leaders will emerge.

The effect on the outlook of the Party will be profound. Traditionally most Party cadres had rural backgrounds, came of age during wartime and drew their inspiration from the struggle for socialism. Younger members increasingly come from the urban middle classes and their priority is to deliver concrete benefits to an increasingly acquisitive society. The former base the Party's legitimacy on its historical success; the latter base it on present and future achievements. The Party is evolving into, to use Karl Marx's phrase, 'a committee for organising the interests of the bourgeoisie'. While that idea fills some parts of the Party with horror, others have actively expedited it. The American political scientist Eddy Malesky has shown how reformist politicians deliberately gerrymandered the country – dividing up certain provinces – in order to manufacture a pro-reform majority in the Central Committee and the National Assembly.

In 1996, following the defeat of his proposals to end preferential treatment of state-owned enterprises at the Eighth Party Congress, the then Prime Minister Vo Van Kiet set about marginalising the economic conservatives. Since their power base was in provinces dominated by state-owned enterprises, he engineered the splitting of eight of them in time for the elections the following year. He specifically ordered that the new boundaries should be drawn so as to ensure that the bulk of the state-owned industry ended up in one half of the province while the other half was dominated by the private sector. The most extreme example was in Vinh Phu province, north-west of

Hanoi. A tongue of land including the former state capital Viet Tri and its state-owned factories was included with the state-dominated half of the province, rather than in the more contiguous private sector half.

In this way (bearing in mind that one of the provinces was already dominated by the private sector) Kiet turned the voting of the eight provinces from being seven to one against further liberalisation into nine to seven in favour. Just to make sure that reluctant conservative local leaderships went along with the plans, Kiet bought them off by ensuring there was plenty of patronage and cash for the new provinces to hand around.[13] New provinces meant new leaders, new bureaucracies to staff and new facilities to construct – and all the associated kickbacks. Conservatives who might have opposed the division of their province on political grounds were reconciled to it through the provision of personal benefits. The end result has been a shift in voting power within the Party towards more economic openness. But that doesn't mean the end of politics within the Party: far from it.

Vietnam may be a one-party state, but it's not a dictatorship. The Party remains a Leninist institution: once policy is agreed it is defended by all. But the process of making policy contains all the alliance-building, plotting and back-stabbing that one would expect in a western democracy. The dynamics are complex and fluid. Loyalties and allegiances change. There are both reformers and conservatives and also cliques lining up behind key people in the hope of receiving the benefits of patronage.[14] These differences have crystallised into competition between factions. Some observers see this as the basis for a potential split within the Party at some point in the future but these factions don't necessarily have coherent positions across all issues. Economic reformers have clamped down just as hard on poltical dissent as the conservatives. Some economic conservatives are social liberals, and vice versa. For the time being, Party loyalty is stronger than any centrifugal forces within it. However, the result of factional rivalry is frequently political deadlock, with different groups able to use interlocking vetoes – their holds on different parts of the Party or state apparatus – to thwart the intentions of the other.

Gradually, however, the economic reformers have gained the upper hand. There are senior people in the Communist Party who talk of greater political liberalisation, of allowing more self-nominated candidates to win seats in the National Assembly, of giving the Assembly greater independence, even of allowing other parties to exist. For many 'reformers' though, greater democracy would be just a tactic, a way to bypass those opposed to

1 A woman selling chicks at a market in the central town of Hoi An. Petty-trading employs large numbers of people but the obvious vibrancy of the domestic private sector is not the whole story.

2 Nguyen Quang Hao inspects the vast mountain of stock on display in his shop, a former government store, in the Old Quarter of Hanoi, July 2006. 'These days you can buy whatever you want, so long as you have the money.'

3 One of the production lines at the Stella Shoe Factory outside Hai Phong. The factory makes footwear for well-known American and European brands. As shoe factories go, it's a nice one.

4 Bringing home the buffalo. Farmers in the northwestern village of Mai Chau walk their livestock through the rice fields.

5 The staple industry of the 'conical hat village' southeast of Hanoi. Small-scale production keeps families afloat and away from the big cities.

6 An illegal 'frog' market in Hanoi. So called because of the way the traders jump up and run when they see the police coming. Women like these generally commute into Hanoi each day bringing produce with them or buying it in wholesale markets.

7 Residents of Nguyen Quy Duc Street in southeastern Hanoi protest against the imminent destruction of their shops and homes, December 2006.

8 Nguyen Quy Duc Street in May 2009. The old shops have gone to be replaced by an unpaved parking space. The poor have been moved out to make space for those with cars.

9 A badminton court in Lenin Park. A typically Vietnamese solution to providing sports facilities in an overcrowded city.

10 A newly-married couple offer tea and cigarettes to the guests at their wedding party, southeastern Hanoi.

11 The new face of Vietnamese youth. Rapper Kim performs at a hip-hop gig in southern Hanoi.

12 A DJ performs at the same hip-hop gig in southern Hanoi. There are small but vibrant hip-hop scenes in both Hanoi and Ho Chi Minh City. The rhythm offends the older generation.

13 The impossible achieved. In November 2007 almost no-one in this picture would have been wearing a helmet. Within a month, almost everyone was. A victory for propaganda, persuasion and punishment.

14 The internet has spread far and wide. Here kids in the Mekong Delta develop hunched shoulders and repetitive strain injury playing online games, February 2007.

15 The citadel excavations in June 2009. Evidence of Hanoi's thousand year history has been saved from destruction by the lobbying of archaeologists and historians.

16 Local kids hanging out in Lenin Park on the only modern public play area in Hanoi. They are about to attract the attentions of the police.

17 The Mausoleum of Ho Chi Minh in Ba
Dinh Square, central Hanoi. Against his express
wishes, President Ho's body has been turned into
a visitor attraction and political rallying point,
February 2007.

18 Nong Duc Manh, the General Secretary of
the Communist Party of Vietnam and the most
important politician in the country, May 2006.

19 Nguyen Tan Dung, the Prime Minister
and second most important politician in the
country, May 2006.

20 A Buddhist monk and a military officer
participating in the National Assembly, May
2006. Vietnam's electoral arrangements give
guaranteed representation to the military and
Party-controlled 'civil society' organisations,
May 2006.

21 'Greet the Party, Greet Spring' reads the official slogan on a local neighbourhood notice board in southwestern Hanoi ahead of the Tet Lunar New Year Festival 2007.

22 Human rights lawyer Nguyen Van Dai. Dai was jailed in May 2007 for 'spreading anti-state propaganda'.

23 A plain-clothes security officer guards the home of 'cyber-dissident' Pham Hong Son in October 2006. During the Asia-Pacific Summit, dissidents were barricaded inside their homes to prevent them meeting journalists or disrupting the event.

24 Junks in Ha Long Bay; the jewel of Vietnam's tourist industry. Over-exploitation of the Bay is destroying its unique environment, June 2006.

25 The memorial on Kham Thien Street to the people killed when the street was razed by the US Christmas bombing of 1972. There's little sign of destruction now but memories linger, June 2006.

26 A motorbike in the village of Dong Ho is laden down with sacks containing votive goods made of paper which will be burnt as offerings to ancestors.

27 The wreckage of a US bomber lies in a lake in central Hanoi, February 2007.

28 The consumer society, Hanoi. A vast display of tinned baby milk and other foodstuffs.

29 Part of the vast new Ministry of Defence complex in central Hanoi, January 2007.

30 Remembering the war. A women's delegation at the Military Museum, central Hanoi, July 2006.

31 Celebrating American Independence Day, 2006 in the grounds of the American Club, Hanoi.

32 A delivery bike sets out with freshly-made bust of Ho Chi Minh, passing a copy of the Statue of Liberty waiting for a buyer at a sculptor's shop in northern Hanoi.

33 A bucolic backdrop to conspicuous consumption. Soon-to-be-weds have their album pictures taken in the ground of the Ethnology Museum, Hanoi.

34 The terraced hills of the northwestern highlands, near the town of Sa Pa. The villages are home to ethnic minority peoples, who make a living from the passing tourist trade.

35 *(above)* Girls from the Hmong minority stitch handicrafts for tourists in Ta Van village, near Sa Pa in the northwestern highlands. The Hmong find themselves close to the bottom of Vietnam's unwritten ethnic hierarchy.

36 *(right)* The renewal of religion 1. Pagoda at the foot of Nui Sam mountain in the Mekong Delta, one of the holiest sites in southern Vietnam.

37 The renewal of religion 2. With ostentatious displays of piety, women like these have found meaning and status through pagoda rituals. Quan Su Pagoda, central Hanoi. Buddha's birthday, 2006.

38 The renewal of religion 3. Women making offerings for the lunar New Year at Ba Da Pagoda. Tet 2007.

39 A quiet day in Hanoi's Old Quarter, June 2006.

their agenda. Only a very few are prepared to call for an end to the Party's monopoly on power and usually only when they are safely out of power. The reformist former Prime Minister Vo Van Kiet and the conservative former Party General Secretary Le Kha Phieu both openly discussed the issue, but their interventions probably owed as much to their sense of frustration because of their inability to get their own way while in office as to their interest in political pluralism.

There is no doubt that politics in Vietnam is changing. Things that would have landed people in prison a few years ago, such as openly discussing the fact that politics is changing, are now commonplace. But these innovations are intended to shore up Party rule, not undermine it. Party leaders still see themselves as the guarantors of the country's stability and development, and doggedly maintain their position at the centre of national life. Each year at Tet, the lunar new year, a slogan appears on billboards, banners and even planted in flowerbeds, 'Mung Dang, Mung Xuan' – 'Greet the Party, Greet Spring' – as if the Party's presence is as much a part of life as the seasons. The phrase itself is the echo of an idea dating back to feudal times, later promoted by Ho Chi Minh, that the ruler lives in harmony with nature. The Party, which rose to power by opposing the old imperial system, with its mandarins and royal rituals, has evolved into a new mandarinate. In dynastic times the king relied on just a thousand mandarins to rule the country; most of the actual 'governing' was subcontracted to local officials. They had the authority to rule in the king's name and great autonomy in the way they did it. The king only had to step in when his authority was usurped or abused. The mandarins, selected by merit, money and connections, were the state's guiding hand. The king's policy was never wrong – only the officials' implementation of it. And this is the position the Communist Party is now adopting. It guides the state but stands above criticism, blaming any failures on the state's implementation, not its policies. But in reality the Party can't let go of the levers of power. It has vastly more than a thousand mandarins each and each, from the lowest levels of the state to the highest, is intimately involved in the implementation of policy.

It's common for foreigners to assume that the reformers' victory is inevitable; that the great march of History will take Vietnam into the promised land of free markets and, later, to political pluralism. In Vietnam that appears to be no more than the mirror-image of Karl Marx's belief in the inevitable victory of the proletariat. There is nothing inevitable about what is happening in Vietnam; the outcome will be the result of day-to-day choices made by the Party and the people. Calls for democracy might be genuine or they might be simply a tactic to allow one particular point of view or set of patronage connections to prevail over another. It's clear that there is widespread frustration with the glacial pace of politics, and with the endless rounds of coalition-building and consultation required to agree policy and get it turned into practice, but they could just as easily become calls for a strong single leader as for a multi-party democracy. The Party is experimenting with openness to try to make the current system more effective, but any transition to a new system – a truly open and democratic system – is still a long way off. In the meantime, the effect of the millions of dollars, euros and pounds of foreign aid spent on good governance has not been to bring about multi-party democracy but to make one-party rule more efficient.

★

6

The rise and fall of Bloc 8406

On 11 May 2007 the Chief Judge of the Hanoi People's Court, Nguyen Huu Chinh, brought his chamber to order, called his two defendants forward and squashed the brief flowering of Vietnam's democracy movement. It was a show trial; special arrangements had been made to relay the four hours of proceedings to a side room full of diplomats and the international media. By lunchtime it was all over. When it was done, two of the most outspoken critics of the Communist Party had been silenced. The two, both human rights lawyers, were convicted of 'spreading anti-state propaganda'. Judge Chinh sentenced veteran campaigner Nguyen Van Dai to five years in jail and Le Thi Cong Nhan, who'd been a member of the dissident movement for less than a year, to four.

The trial of Dai and Cong Nhan was one of four, which, over the course of six weeks, decapitated the democracy movement. The trials ended a year of unprecedented activity in which dissidents announced a political manifesto, declared four new political parties and two independent trade unions, published underground newspapers and formed a broad alliance of almost all the country's critical voices. It also demonstrated the Communist Party's determination to retain its monopoly on political power and its paranoia about the threat it faces from 'hostile forces'. What did the dissidents achieve? On the surface, very little. The Party's vast security apparatus made sure its rule was never seriously challenged. But the events of 2006 and 2007 created new underground networks of activists and new ways of organising them, and strengthened the links between dissidents inside the country and their supporters outside. Their legacy might yet unsettle the country's rulers.

There have been dissidents in communist Vietnam ever since the state was founded. In the mid-1950s a group of writers and artists used the pages of two publications, *Nhan Van* and *Giai Pham*, to demand greater cultural freedom. In the late 1960s, one faction of the Party, accused of being 'pro-USSR', was purged by another, ostensibly 'pro-China'.[1] In the late 1980s several former senior leaders of the communist guerrilla movement in the south formed the Club of Former Resistance Fighters to demand better treatment for the south and to protest against corruption in the Party. All these movements were different but all those involved had one thing in common: they were Communist Party members who disagreed with the leadership. They were not, at least initially, anti-Party.

The Party managed them in different ways. The *Nhan Van–Giai Pham* group and the 'pro-USSR' people spent long periods in 're-education' camps. The Former Resistance Fighters were too influential to be tackled head-on. Instead, the leadership was co-opted into the official veterans' movement and the organisation disbanded. But many of the dissidents continued to nurture their grievances and became progressively more alienated from the Party. Although they were spied upon and their movements controlled they were never eliminated. The Party doesn't shoot its enemies any more. Throughout the 1990s they continued to meet privately and occasionally smuggled out letters and articles to be published overseas. Their demands were officially ignored by the Party leadership at the time, but over the past decade the Party has actually addressed almost all of them. The National Assembly has been given greater powers, the press has greater independence, it's now easier for individuals to complain about injustices, campaigns are mounted against corruption, there's more artistic freedom and southern politicians are no longer marginalised. The Party leadership would never admit it, but the dissident movement did, to some extent, set the reform agenda.

What is there left for dissidents to complain about? Ultimately it boils down to a single clause in the Constitution: Article 4, which states that the Communist Party of Vietnam, 'is the force leading the state and society'. From this Article, or rather the political principle behind it, flow all the grievances of the contemporary dissident movement in Vietnam. Corruption, economic backwardness, the loss of border territory to China, the limits on media freedom, the constraints on individual and artistic expression, their own marginalisation – all these things are blamed, by the dissidents, on the Party's monopoly of power. It follows then, in their view, that the answer to all these problems is the abolition of the Party's leading role. But while the Party has been prepared to concede ground in many areas of life (as the rest of this book describes), it seems absolutely determined to maintain its political monopoly.

* * *

The story of the 2006 dissident movement begins in the central city of Hue, the imperial capital, during the nineteenth and early twentieth centuries, now eclipsed by Hanoi and Ho Chi Minh City. Hue was special mainly because of the activities of one man – a Catholic priest, Father Nguyen Van Ly. A veteran dissident, Ly had been jailed three times since 1975 for agitating against the communist system, spending a total of 15 years in jail and the rest under forms of house arrest. But his political evangelism had found fertile ground in the city – particularly among some of his fellow priests. Towards the end of 2005 they saw an opportunity to evangelise political pluralism. Ahead of its Tenth Congress, as part of a conscious strategy to be seen to be listening to the people, the Party was actively seeking comment and criticism. The official discussion was channelled through Party-controlled structures and therefore contained within strict limits. Although newspapers printed articles critical of corruption (this was the time of the PMU18 scandal: see Chapter 7) at no point was the Party's right to rule publicly questioned. But here was a chance for the dissidents to say the unsayable.

In January 2006 Ly, along with two other Hue priests, Phan Van Loi and Nguyen Huu Giai, and a fourth based in Saigon, Chan Tin, drew up an appeal for freedom of speech, entitled *We are No Longer Afraid. We Ought to Know the Truth*. Making reference to the International Covenant on Civil and Political Rights, the Constitution of Vietnam and also the Second Vatican Council, it invoked 'the blessing from the Almighty through the intercession of our ancestors' and condemned the Communist Party for 'Poisoning and suppressing the conscience of the people, turning them into masses of obedient servants'. It demanded an end to the Party's monopoly on power and called on Party members and the armed forces to desert, and for non-communist parties in Vietnam to assert themselves. When it was finished, the priests circulated the text among the dissidents, accumulating signatories.

At the same time, Ly began work on another document: *Manifesto for Freedom and Democracy*. He had two co-drafters: one from Saigon – Do Nam Hai (who described himself as an engineer but who'd worked as a bank official until he was fired for political activity) and Tran Anh Kim, a former army colonel from the northern province of Thai Binh. By early April, two weeks before the Party Congress was due to open, they were ready. The Appeal was formally published on 6 April and two days later (with the withdrawal of one signatory and the addition of three more), out came the *Manifesto*. The date was 8 April 2006, so the 118 signatories became known as Bloc 8406.

The first article of the *Manifesto* baldly declared: 'In the August 1945 Revolution, the entire Vietnamese nation made a choice for national independence and not socialism.' It's hard to imagine anything more calculated to enrage the Communist leadership. But brave as it was, it was also rather long-winded. Its first page reviewed the history of Vietnamese politics since independence was declared in 1945 and the second sought to blame the country's problems on the Party's monopoly of power. Only on its third, and penultimate page, did the *Manifesto* get around to listing its demands: 'a pluralistic and multiparty system', 'a clear separation of powers among . . . the branches of government' and for freedom of opinion, assembly, election and religion, the right to freely organise trade unions and to strike. In short, the minimum demands of a Western-inspired democratic movement. On its final page the *Manifesto* outlined the non-violent methods of its 'freedom fighters'. It argued that 'Once having a clear and correct knowledge, the people will act appropriately and effectively.' And that was about it. There was little about how the people should be educated or what should happen afterwards. It was long on idealism but short on specifics.

The signatories were a Who's Who of Vietnamese dissidents stretching back, in some cases, 40 years. Many of them had been lonely voices for decades; others were new faces – a younger generation of activists pushing for more radical change. More than a third came from Hue – far more than from either Saigon or Hanoi – and 14 of them were Catholic priests. There were just nine signatories from Hanoi – although all were significant figures, including the former dean of the Party-controlled Marxist-Leninist Institute of Philosophy, Hoang Minh Chinh, and a lawyer: Nguyen Van Dai. These two represented the old and the new faces of the movement. The different routes along which Chinh and Dai became dissidents reveal how much the political situation in Vietnam has changed over the past two decades.

Hoang Minh Chinh was a Party loyalist and hero of the independence war against France who fell foul of the 'pro-Chinese' faction of the Party in the late 1960s and was imprisoned. He became a dissident and was jailed again in 1981 and 1995.[2] His war record accorded him some respect, though, allowing what became known as 'the democracy group' to gather around him – mainly people like Chinh, victims of Party purges who wanted to see the Party reform and allow greater freedom of expression. In 2005 Chinh had been allowed to travel to the United States to be treated for prostate cancer. While there he had given testimony to the House of Representatives' Committee on International Relations and ferociously criticised the Party's treatment of religious and political dissidents. Despite this he received little more than lukewarm support from the exiled Vietnamese-American anti-communist community because of his continuing loyalty to the ideas of Ho Chi Minh. Nonetheless, on his return home, he felt the Party's wrath.

> The crowd, increasingly violent, began to attack us with tomatoes, including efforts to hold my shirt and break water bottles on my head, cursing and threatening my relatives who were protecting me. . . . The emergency police unit responded, after several calls from my family, by sending over three officers. They looked at the scene and, before leaving, said: 'This is the consequence of what Mr. Chinh has done in America. We don't see any violence and there's nothing for us to intervene.' . . . Some members of the mob successfully broke the window panes, jumped in and tried to force the door down while others used sticks to hit other windows and threw bottles of stinking shrimp paste inside my house. It was a scary horrible moment. Suddenly, they quietly told one another to 'retreat' as many of them shouted, 'now we don't need to talk to that Hoang Minh Chinh, even if he invited us.' They had apparently been ordered to leave, since they all disappeared within five minutes.[3]

Chinh wasn't deterred by this attack, nor by any of the criticism aimed at him in the national press, and carried on holding discussions in the 'democracy group'. On 1 June 2006, Chinh would declare it the country's first opposition political party – the 'Twenty-First Century Democracy Party':

DP (XXI) The name was a conscious reference to the original Democracy Party, founded in 1944, which had been allowed to operate alongside the Communist Party in the Democratic Republic of Vietnam from independence until it was suppressed in 1985. Chinh had been its General Secretary between 1951 and 1956. This heritage was important to Chinh, who wanted to reclaim the original spirit of Ho Chi Minh's national revolution while jettisoning much of its later baggage. But although the DP(XXI) had an impressive lineage, it didn't have much in the way of contemporary support. Its continuing allegiance to the legacy of Ho Chi Minh – even though Chinh interpreted it as a non-communist legacy – wasn't attractive to the new generation of disaffected citizens who wanted a clear break with the past. Another Bloc supporter interviewed in early 2007 suggested it had barely ten members, mainly in Hanoi and Saigon.

Nguyen Van Dai's disillusion with the Communist Party rulers began much later than Chinh's and was from the perspective of an outsider, not a loyalist. He was an electrician, one of the tens of thousands of Vietnamese guest workers labouring across the eastern bloc in the late 1980s. Such opportunities were coveted by Vietnamese, for whom even the spartan living conditions of the Comecon were a vast improvement on their domestic situation. Dai owed his ticket abroad to his father's membership of the Communist Party. But when European communism collapsed in 1989 things changed radically for Dai. For the first time he was able to read newspapers produced by Vietnamese exile groups and saw parallels with the situation back home. When his East German employer went bankrupt the following year he returned to Vietnam to study at Hanoi Law University with the intention of 'doing something for my country'.[4]

After graduating in 1995 he began by working as a legal adviser to the Hanoi Law Company, but in 1997, when a change in the law made it possible, he and a friend became two of the first ever independent candidates to stand for election to the National Assembly. They weren't successful. At the end of 1999 Dai was asked by the Vietnamese Assemblies of God (unregistered and therefore illegal Evangelical Christian gatherings) to represent a woman from Vinh Phuc province, Nguyen Thi Thuy, who had been imprisoned for holding unauthorised religious services in her house. Her appeal failed, but shortly afterwards, Dai says, 'I felt God calling' and he joined the legally registered Hanoi Evangelical Church. He'd had some contacts with Vietnamese evangelicals in Germany but it took ten years for Christianity to become the bedrock of his life – and his political dissidence. His choice of evangelical Protestantism was bound to arouse the ire of the secret police, for whom ideas imported from the United States are automatically suspect. In April 2004 he was one of 12 lawyers who tried to set up what Dai describes as 'a lawyers' group for justice'. But the Hanoi Bar Association ordered them to disband the organisation or have their licences revoked. The 11 other lawyers dropped out, leaving only Dai. 'I think it was my Christian belief,' he says. He further irritated the authorities at the end of that year by defending six members of the then illegal Mennonite Church accused of 'resisting persons doing official duty'. And then, in April 2005 he began to defend political dissidents too.

Until this time, being a dissident in Vietnam had been a lonely – and largely fruitless – activity. Most were either elderly, disillusioned former Communist Party members like Chinh or religious refuseniks like Father Ly. They were few in number and divided by ideology and personality. And there wasn't much they could do. The security services had effectively, indeed ruthlessly, squashed any attempts at insurrection over the previous few decades. The system might tolerate occasional protests over local issues like land disputes, but any explicitly political demonstration would be extinguished within minutes. However, things began to change – as Chairman Mao had predicted decades before when he had warned his own Party that 'When you open the windows, the flies also come in'. The upturn in the fortunes of Vietnam's dissidents after 2005 proved him right. It was a direct consequence of the Party's desire to integrate the country into the global economy.

* * *

2006 was a unique opportunity for Vietnamese dissidents. The country was in the final stages of joining the World Trade Organisation. Negotiations with individual WTO members were followed by drawn-out multilateral talks and then an equally drawn-out process in the US Congress to award Vietnam Permanent Normal Trading Relations (PNTR) status, an adjunct to WTO membership. In addition, Vietnam held the rotating chair of APEC, the Asia-Pacific Economic Co-operation group, during 2006, and was due to host its annual summit in November. Twenty-one leaders had been invited, including the presidents of the USA, Russia and China and the prime ministers of Australia and Japan. Vietnam was also seeking a non-permanent seat on the United Nations Security Council. All of this meant the Communist Party was vulnerable to criticism from abroad and therefore less able to crack down on dissent with its usual efficiency.

There was another factor too. By 2006, broadband had fully penetrated Vietnam; internet shops were available on most city streets. Through the net, dissidents managed to surmount the physical barriers the state had erected around them and bridge the gaps of physical distance, of ideology and – at least as important – of ego, which, until then, had kept them divided. Services originally intended to allow teenagers to flirt with each other provided invigorating links with Vietnamese exiles in the United States and elsewhere. Websites such as PalTalk host chat rooms in which hundreds of people can type messages to each other and simultaneously listen to an audiostream or watch video. In effect, each chat room is an interactive radio 'narrowcast'. Narrowcasters can give out information, make speeches, discuss developments and take questions and comment from the other participants. Suddenly dissidents in Vietnam had access to a new world of ideas and to a reservoir of supporters. Until then many people had been reluctant to trust each other, never knowing who was an informer; but a few overseas activists acted as 'brokers' – in effect vetting the dissidents who contacted them and putting them in touch with one another. They also began to provide cash.

With the cost of living so cheap in Vietnam, relatively small amounts of money raised abroad could go a long way. Supporters groups sprang up in Australia (Bloc 1–7–06), the US (Bloc 1–9–06) and the UK (Bloc 10–12–06) and sent in money for dissidents' living expenses and equipment. With hundreds of thousands of overseas Vietnamese remitting money to relatives each month it was easy to disguise the transfers. They weren't particularly clandestine; most went via Western Union. Once inside Vietnam, the money was moved by couriers to where it was needed. When police stopped the car of one dissident, Nguyen Phuong Anh, on 15 December 2006, they confiscated 4.5 million Vietnamese dong, the equivalent of about $300, about six months' wages for the average worker. He told them he had planned to buy clothes for needy paper boys.[5] The money was crucial. It paid for computers, dozens of mobile phones, and hundreds of SIM cards to enable the dissidents to stay in touch even as the security services tried to disconnect them.

But useful as the internet was to the dissidents as an organising and discussion tool, it was much less effective as a proselytising force. The national firewall prevents the casual web-surfer accessing dissident websites and intercepts unwelcome emails. That didn't stop one middle-aged Ho Chi Minh City-based activist, though. At night, after his family had gone to bed, he would trawl Vietnamese discussion sites and blogs harvesting the email addresses of anyone making critical comments. Then, with his harvest complete, he would send out two or three hundred emails with details of dissidents' activities. He would tell them about strikes and how to form trade unions and about lobbying activities in the United States. But he couldn't send all the messages from one email address because he feared the security services would soon track him down. So instead, he laboriously maintained dozens of different accounts and sent just a few messages from each one. It worked, and he managed to stay below the police's radar. But even this very direct mailing had limited success; the phantom spammer estimated his response rate was less than 1 per cent. So even with all these technological innovations the number of active dissidents remained small.

There was still very little for the dissidents to actually do. Veterans like Hoang Minh Chinh had once been a source of information about what was going on inside the Party, but the supply of disillusioned idealists willing to spill the beans has dried up. Where once people joined the Party to build socialism and were outraged when they found corruption, by 2006 they were joining it to build their own careers and found corruption quite useful. All that was left was the online realm – a virtual world where plotters could imagine and wish for a different Vietnam, but one that had little impact on the actually existing one. By 23 May 2006, when it launched a campaign to boycott the following year's National Assembly election, the Bloc claimed 560 supporters – a significant number for the dissident movement but negligible compared to the total population. In August the Bloc published its *Process to Democratise Vietnam in 4 Stages and 8 Steps*. The plan was simplistic in the extreme:

1. Realise freedom of speech and the press.
2. Reactivate, establish and develop non-communist and democratic political parties.
3. Compile a temporary Constitution and hold a referendum.
4. Accomplish democratisation in Vietnam.

It shared with the original Manifesto the Bloc's apparent belief that it could bring down the Communist Party simply by propagating its own message to the people. Nowhere was there any mention of practical methods of political organisation, community outreach or other activities to win the support of the masses.

* * *

A42, the political department of the Ministry of Public Security, was in difficulty. At any other time it would simply have rounded up the troublemakers. But with WTO approval still in the balance and the APEC summit drawing close, a large-scale crackdown wasn't politically possible. Instead it maintained a campaign of low-level harassment, stopping short of anything that might seriously provoke the international community. So homes were raided, computers confiscated, computer disks and memory drives seized and activists taken off to police stations for 'working sessions' with A42. But it was all such low-level activity that it received virtually no coverage outside the dissident community.

Nguyen Van Dai became the main source of information about what was happening. His Thien An law firm, tucked away in a small courtyard in the shadow of Vincom Towers, the only shopping mall in Hanoi worthy of the name, became a virtual news agency for dissident activity. He employed four staff and, although the office was far from lavish, it was well equipped with computers, telephones and internet devices. When it was eventually closed down, the police took away five PCs. They probably weren't bought from the proceeds of defending the victims of human rights abuses. Many people wondered why Dai was able to get away with his activities for so long, why he wasn't detained like so many of the people he was defending. Some in the diplomatic community suggested that he might be an informer or even an agent for A42. Others thought that the authorities found it useful to have a public figure like Dai as a 'control channel' to help them keep an eye on the dissident movement and that the information he distributed played a useful role for A42 because it warned potential dissidents what would happen to them if they became politically active.

However, not everyone was put off. One person attracted by the message of Bloc 8406 was another lawyer, 27-year-old Le Thi Cong Nhan. Ten years younger than Dai, she had become a dissident at a much earlier age – seven.

'I was keeping my parents' position in a queue to receive food from a state shop in 1986,' she says, 'and I just thought, "Why do I have to do this?" ' She looked like so many young women of her generation: round face, bobbed hair and glasses, moderately but not excessively fashionable. She was a good lawyer and spoke reasonable English and had been hired, via the British Embassy, to defend a British-Vietnamese woman facing a possible death penalty for drug smuggling.

Cong Nhan, ironically, has a very communist name. It means 'worker': her grandfather changed it when she was one month old, hoping to curry favour with the authorities. It didn't do much good. Her parents were teachers, and she says their low pay meant there was rarely enough food in the house. She was already a lawyer when, in August 2006, 'After a long period of careful thought', she became a supporter of Bloc 8406. Two weeks later she became one of the founding members of the second political party to declare itself during 2006, the 'Viet Nam Progression Party' (VNPP). Like the Bloc, the Progression Party's membership also centred on Hue: the other three founders (Nguyen Phong, Nguyen Binh Thanh and Hoang Thi Anh Dao) all lived in the city.[6] And again, the inspiration was Father Nguyen Van Ly. Ly was not a member of the Party – he'd been banned by his archbishop from joining – but he admitted to being an adviser.

The Progression Party took quite a different perspective from Hoang Minh Chinh's Democracy Party: it rejected the legacy of Ho Chi Minh totally. It was not a position likely to attract mass support in Vietnam, where children are taught to love Uncle Ho from their first days at school. Nor was it one which many of the older dissidents would support. Still, the two groups agreed on the basic principles expressed in the 8406 *Manifesto*, particularly the call for multi-party democracy. The Progression Party launched itself with an Interim Political Platform containing huge amounts of detail on its organisation: outlining, for example, ten internal committees (including a Finance Committee, Accounting Committee *and* an Auditing Committee) and regulations for members wishing to leave the party. 'The withdrawal of the member will be documented with information such as: name, date of birth, occupation, date of joining, membership number, reason for withdrawal or possibly no withdrawal reason given. One copy of this document will be given to the withdrawn member, two copies will be filed in the party offices.' But in contrast to these highly detailed bureaucratic arrangements, the VNPP's plans for taking power were vague in the extreme. Its plan was to assemble a group of pro-democracy parties and 'force the Communist Party of Vietnam to agree to participate in a pluralistic political arena'. Quite how this would happen was left unsaid.

If it did have a secret plan for taking power, the Progression Party seemed to borrow it from the Solidarity movement in communist Poland. This may have been inspired, in part, by the VNPP's overseas Vietnamese supporters, many of whom were based in Poland. It hoped to politicise the scattered islands of localised discontent in the country and turn them into a social movement. A priority, therefore, was to set up its own, independent trade union. It seemed an opportunistic choice: the VNPP's interim platform had little to say on workers' rights. Indeed the only thing it had to say on economic matters was that it would 'Re-establish and exercise the full and legitimate right of the Vietnamese People to private ownership,' which suggests that it might have been more favourable to the interests of the owners of capital than to those of the proletariat.

Almost immediately after she joined the Progression Party, Cong Nhan was visited at home by officers from A42. She was taken to the police station, told that she was guilty of plotting to bring down the state and questioned for three days, in the course of which she says she was told that 'many bad things could happen to me'. When she refused to attend any more questioning sessions the police bombarded her with calls and text messages threatening her with arrest. One officer reminder her that the police were listening to all her phone calls. But then, suddenly, the tactics changed. 'They sent me flowers, invitations to dinner and the cinema, even a new mobile phone.' The emails now called her brave and kind and asked her to explain her motivations and dreams for the country. At the same time, though, A42 were leaning on her family and friends to press her to stop her activities.

A42 uses Vietnam's traditionally tight family structures as an extension of its own networks. In September 2006 Nguyen Van Dai was called by his father and told that if he continued to act as a lawyer for dissidents, the two of them wouldn't be allowed to meet. One of the staff in Dai's office, a young woman, described how the police had met her friends and told them that she was working for a bad person and that they should try to make her stop. 'But I know what Dai is doing and I support it, so I didn't listen,' she said later. Because of pressure like this, being a dissident in Vietnam is lonely and difficult. Few people, even if they have complaints about life in Vietnam, are willing to take the considerable risks involved in supporting dissident activity. The movement has been thoroughly demonised by the Party and the official media, to the extent that its members are commonly regarded as treasonous criminals.

Vast resources – official, unofficial, familial – can be mobilised against an individual who chooses to speak out. Long questioning sessions, public denunciations, personal attacks in the national media and, occasionally, physical attacks are all tactics used by A42. Dai was subjected to one public denunciation session which harked back to the catastrophic land reforms of the 1950s, according to an account circulated by the organisation which Dai helped to set up, the Committee for Human Rights in Vietnam.

> On the evening of 8 February 2007, the communist government mobilized about 200 people, between the ages of 60 to 80 at the Peoples' Committee of Bach Khoa Ward. They called it The Conference of the People and proceeded with reading aloud Mr. Dai's biography, afterwards falsely accused attorney Dai as a member of The XXI Democracy Party, calumnying him as a traitor who has sold out his country. During the whole two and a half hours of this ordeal, they did not allow attorney Dai to utter a single word. Finally, they concluded that attorney Nguyen van Dai is guilty on two counts, violating Article 88 and 258 of the Criminal Code. They demanded to disbar and revoke his law license, to close down the Thien-An Law Office, and to pursue criminal actions against him. Using the security force and the extremist's threat they pressured him into signing the affidavit, but lawyer Nguyen van Dai declared: 'You all can kill me, but I will never sign it'. In the end they conceded.[7]

To stand up against this kind of pressure requires a particularly determined constitution. So it's perhaps not surprising that, as in Eastern Europe in the 1970s and 1980s, it's those who care least about what society thinks of them who stick it out; uncompromising, often quite difficult people. A significant number of them are Christian – Catholics such as Father Ly and Father Phan Van Loi were central to the Bloc's foundation and both Dai and Cong Nhan were members of evangelical churches. One very small party, the 'Vietnam Populist Party', run by a Texas-based exile, was represented inside Vietnam by a Baptist minister, the Reverend Hong Trung. There's also a significant strand of dissident Buddhist thought, represented by the banned Unified Buddhist Church of Vietnam (See Chapter 10 for more on the UBCV). But again its dissident leanings and pariah status in mainstream society minimise the chances of its messages gaining traction with the rest of the population. As with the Christian and secularist dissidents, its members' faith in their cause may give them the strength to continue but it also cuts them off from wider society.

In September 2006 Le Thi Cong Nhan had no idea of the trouble that she was about to get into. But things rapidly got nasty. Having had no success with interrogation, flattery or peer pressure it appears that A42 opted for intimidation. In October she was due to fly to Warsaw to take part in a conference organised by overseas supporters of the Progression Party to launch its trade union. She got as far as the foot of the steps to the plane before she was stopped and told she couldn't travel. The next day, as she rode on her motorbike to change her ticket, she was pushed and jostled and nearly fell off. She believed her attacker was from A42. This wasn't an isolated incident; over the next few weeks the dissidents Pham Hong Son and Do Nam Hai were also pushed while riding their motorbikes. Nonetheless, communist Vietnam's first independent trade union, the Independent Labour Union of Vietnam, was launched on 20 October. But in a sign that the dissidents hadn't managed to bridge all their differences, Vietnam's second independent trade union, the United Workers' and Farmers' Association (UWFA) was launched ten days later. Of the two rival unions, the UWFA had the greater vitality. Its founders, Nguyen Tan Hoanh and Tran Thi Le Hang, were already activists, having previously organised strikes before going into hiding.

For about a year before they went public the founders of the UWFA had been in contact with one particular group of Vietnamese exiles in the USA. The group later evolved into the Dang Vi Dan, the Vietnam Populist Party (VPP, also known as the For the People Party), and for a while the two groups co-operated. But then they fell out over strategy. The founder of the VPP, the Houston-based Nguyen Cong Bang, advised the UWFA activists to keep a low profile and build up an underground network. He argued that going public would provoke the authorities into arresting them and scare off other potential recruits. But the UWFA wanted to go a different – more overt – way and switched their allegiance to another American-based organisation, the People's Democratic Party, which supported their more confrontational stance. They had enough of a network to remain hidden from the security forces for some time. But Nguyen Cong Bang's prediction proved correct. Within six weeks of the UWFA going public, its ten leading activists were in detention. Others continued its work, but by early 2007 it was an underground operation, small and isolated.

Bloc 8406's supporters also tried to spread their message by starting an underground newspaper. *Tu Do Ngon Luan* (Freedom of Speech) was launched a week after the original *Manifesto* on 15 April. Once again, the instigators were the rebel Catholic fathers: Nguyen Van Ly, Phan Van Loi and Chan Tin. It wasn't the first time that dissidents had issued some kind of publication in the country, but it was the first to maintain any kind of regular production schedule. Somehow it managed to come out fortnightly throughout the troubles which followed. *Tu Do Ngon Luan* was circulated online so it could be downloaded, photocopied and distributed relatively easily. For some reason its production was never interrupted by the security services, and even though Ly was later imprisoned, his fellow clerical journalists remained free to edit and publish the paper.

In early August, five activists in Hanoi, including Nguyen Van Dai, announced they were to produce another paper which they called *Tu Do Dan Chu* (Freedom and Democracy). Shortly afterwards they were ordered to report to the police every day for lengthy questioning sessions.[8] Their homes were searched and much of their electronic equipment and paperwork confiscated. They were also banned from meeting and from leaving Hanoi. Despite this, the paper's first issue appeared on 2 September and it managed to produce five more until it was suppressed in early 2007.

The dissidents and the security forces were on a collision course. As the Asia-Pacific summit approached the leading figures in Bloc 8406 became gradually bolder. They forged links with the dissident Buddhists of the UBCV and on 16 October 2006, just a month before the summit, the two groups launched the biggest dissident movement seen in Vietnam since 1975. Its name, the Alliance for Democracy and Human Rights of Viet Nam, was a deliberate echo of Aung San Suu Kyi's National League for Democracy in Burma. For the first time almost all the dissident voices inside Vietnam had managed to bridge their differences and forge a common front against the Communist Party. The challenge to the Party's monopoly of political power was clear. At other moments it would not have been tolerated but with American and Australian leaders about to arrive in Hanoi, a round-up of the usual suspects was not politically possible.

It was not a position the Party enjoyed being in. There seemed to be disarray within the leadership about what to do. In early October the government spokesman Le Dung acknowledged the existence of the Bloc for the first time when he told the French news agency AFP that, 'Recently, people have misused the label of democracy, with false arguments, misrepresented and fabricated the situation in Vietnam and gone against the legitimate aspirations of the Vietnamese people.' But then, a week later, at his official press conference, the Party line had changed and he began his statement by saying, 'We don't recognise this Bloc 8406', before repeating the line about the misuse of democracy. It looked as if his superiors had thought better of admitting the existence of an organised opposition body inside the country.

There did seem to be a significant strand of opinion within the Party leadership that thought the dissidents could be left to chat among themselves in the privacy of their own internet chat rooms, so long as they didn't try to proselytise or draw attention to themselves on the streets. Vo Van Kiet, the former Prime Minister, would later tell the BBC Vietnamese Service that the authorities must not avoid 'talking to those who have a different view' on Vietnamese politics, adding that 'the dialogue should be honest'.[9] But there were also those within the Party for whom this was anathema and who were urging tough action. The compromise they reached was not to arrest the dissidents but to make sure that they couldn't in any way disrupt the upcoming summit. The security forces literally barricaded almost all the Hanoi-based dissidents inside their homes for the whole week. Le Thi Cong Nhan wasn't even allowed out to defend her client, the British woman accused of drug smuggling, despite the Embassy's copious protests.

Large police guards were placed on the dissidents' apartments, signs were put up banning foreigners and photography from their neighbourhoods and their telephones were cut off. Anyone calling received a pre-recorded message informing them the number had been suspended, 'at the subscriber's request'. A few months before the summit there had been talk among the dissidents of organising a demonstration for the delegates to see. The lock-down made sure that it never happened. A few foreign reporters in town for the summit made attempts to meet the dissidents. None of them even got close.

Members of the United Workers' and Farmers' Association were also detained and, in one of the most egregious examples of the crackdown, a lawyer linked with the Democracy Party (XXI), Bui Thi Kim Thanh, was forcibly committed to a mental institution – with the approval of her husband, who disliked her campaigning in support of dispossessed farmers. After interrogation in Ho Chi Minh City, police took her to a local psychiatric hospital but doctors there couldn't find any evidence of mental illness. So she was taken to the Bien Hoa Central Psychiatric Hospital, which provided a more compliant diagnosis.

The diplomatic community's attitude to all this dissident activity was complex, hedged with considerations for the wider political context and hampered by the difficulties of operating in an authoritarian state. Some diplomats were suspicious of certain key activists, having had their fingers burnt after previous encounters when supposedly secret meetings were publicised – provoking protests from the government and a reduction in access to senior officials. So when, for example, the Progression Party sent a letter to every embassy announcing its establishment, they received only one reply (from the Spanish Embassy). The others didn't want to risk getting another telling-off.

But the wider question diplomats had was whether the dissidents were helping or harming what they hoped would be Vietnam's gradual path towards stable democracy. Among that part of the diplomatic community which was at all concerned about human rights – most of the richer countries – there was greater concern for stability. Virtually all the European embassies fund co-operation programmes with some aspect of the existing system: the National Assembly, government ministries, the Audit Office, official trade unions and so on. All of them do so in the hope that this will help effect a gradual and ordered transition to a more open system. There was a strong belief that taking a vocal stance on the dissidents would harm their 'reforming' work inside the system. There was an equally strong view that the dissidents' activities made the authorities more nervous and therefore more reluctant to relax their hold on political power. When foreign journalists asked the then American Ambassador, Michael Marine, his view on this he told them it was 'A difficult question. . . . To what extent the [Communist Party] Central Committee believes that expanding the space for discussion will strengthen the country remains to be seen.'[10] He then went on to describe Bloc 8406 as 'true patriots' – a remark which incensed the government and prompted furious condemnation from its spokesman.

Instead, several embassies – particularly the Swiss and the Swedes who enjoy excellent relations with the Vietnamese government because they were the first Western countries to establish diplomatic relations with it – took a keen interest in individual human rights cases. They drew a sharp distinction between defending human rights and supporting the political aims of the dissidents. Although the official line was that there shouldn't be any political prisoners at all, there was a realism in their approach. They would focus on a few key cases, hoping to win two or three releases at each of the twice-yearly presidential amnesties.

* * *

The authorities' paranoia is not entirely misplaced. Various US-based zealots have periodically hatched hare-brained plans to instigate uprisings in Vietnam. Their plans have underestimated both the security forces' degree of control and the allegiance the vast majority of Vietnamese have to their country. Most people are, in fact, relatively pleased with their improving lot and quite happy to be loyal citizens of the Socialist Republic. But from their faraway vantage point, the exiles convince themselves that this must be the result of propaganda and that if only they could break its stranglehold on the media, the Communist Party would be overthrown. During 2006 it emerged that one California-based group, the Government of Free Vietnam, had attempted to do exactly that through an intricate plot to hijack the frequencies of radio stations in southern Vietnam.

The Government of Free Vietnam (GFV) was founded in 1995 in Garden Grove, the most famous 'little Saigon' in the United States, by a former boat person, Nguyen Huu Chanh. Its leadership includes former senior officials of the government of the pre-1975 Republic of Vietnam. It originally advocated the military overthrow of the communist government and Chanh himself is accused by the Vietnamese government of organising bomb attacks on its embassies in London, Cambodia, the Philippines and Thailand during 2000 and 2002. The group officially renounced violence after the 9–11 attacks in 2001.

The GFV went to great lengths – setting up an adoption charity in Cambodia, using it to smuggle in components for radio transmitters and recruiting at least four local supporters. The plot seems to have involved three Vietnamese-born US citizens, in particular a Florida-based Republican Party activist, Nguyen Thuong Cuc (also known by her married name, Cuc Foshee). It all ended in failure: police rounded up all the plotters. Luckily for them, they were brought to trial in late 2006 while the US Congress was considering whether to approve the status of Permanent Normal Trade Relations (PNTR) with Vietnam. With the Republican Senator for Florida, Mel Martinez, threatening to block the PNTR vote, the judge knew what had to be done. The Americans were given unusually lenient sentences – equivalent to the time they'd already served in custody – and then immediately released and deported. Senator Martinez lifted his veto and PNTR was passed. The Vietnamese accomplices remained in jail.

But even more patient, realistic plans can end in disaster. Cong Thanh Do was another California-based former boat-person who, under the alias of Tran Nam, spent five years building up a network of activists inside Vietnam using chat rooms like PalTalk and internet telephony services like Skype. In 2004 he secretly formed the Peoples' Democratic Party (PDP), which attracted several dissidents, including the leadership of the UWFA. He worked almost entirely alone, not even telling his family what he was up to. Other exiles he communicated with online didn't know his real name. But he came to international attention when, on 14 August 2006 he was arrested in the southern beach resort of Phan Thiet and accused of plotting to blow up the US consulate in Ho Chi Minh City. His family thought he was at a wedding, but in fact he'd been trying to meet his personal underground network.

Within days he and his six recruits had been picked up – the fruit of five years' work undone. The terrorist charges were intended to discredit him in the eyes of the American government, but when the security services couldn't produce any evidence to support them, they were switched to disseminating anti-government information. After a month in jail he was expelled from the country. Eight months later, at the People's Court in Ho Chi Minh City, the leadership of Do's PDP inside Vietnam – the Party Chairman medical doctor Le Nguyen Sang, journalist Huynh Nguyen Dao and lawyer Nguyen Bac Truyen – were convicted of spreading propaganda against the communist state and sentenced to five, four and three years respectively. The PDP was extinguished inside Vietnam.

* * *

In early 2007, once President Bush had gone home and Vietnam's WTO membership had been safely approved, the authorities ignored all diplomatic protests and conducted what Human Rights Watch later described as 'one of the worst crackdowns on peaceful dissidents in 20 years'. If there were voices in the Party advocating a cautious engagement with the dissidents they had been overruled. The dissidents also overreached themselves. Perhaps they had begun to believe their own propaganda; begun to believe they really were creating a greater political space for dissent. They became more united – the Progression Party and the Populist Party formed an alliance, the Lac Hong Group. But, more dangerously, they left the safe confines of cyberspace and began to try to take their message out to the people.

The trigger in the cases of Dai and Cong Nhan was their effort to organise human rights training for university students in Hanoi. Dai had ignored the warnings from his neighbourhood warden, the 'peoples' tribunal' and the admonishment of A42, and continued his activism. He'd become reckless, even circulating material from the US-based Montagnard Foundation – a fanatically anti-communist organisation which accuses the Vietnamese government of perpetrating genocide against ethnic minorities in the Central Highlands. It was one thing to form an alliance with the dissident Buddhists; quite another to become friendly with the Foundation. Perhaps it was his evangelical Christianity, but Dai appeared to be deliberately taunting the authorities.

Police broke up the second human rights training event in February 2007 and arrested the two lawyers. The students taking part were persuaded to denounce their teachers as traitors. Dai and Cong Nhan were questioned and released. A month later they were charged with spreading anti-state propaganda and committed for trial. Over the next three months the leaderships of Bloc 8406, the Progression Party, the Peoples' Democratic Party and the United Workers' and Farmers' Association were imprisoned, and their organisations systematically dismantled. The Democracy Party reverted to its role as a discussion group and the Alliance for Democracy and Human Rights became little more than a shell. Significantly though, not everyone was arrested. A42 seems to have picked its targets carefully. The people it went after were the stars, those who had achieved some kind of profile, rather than the foot soldiers. They were also the ones with international contacts, working with activists abroad and receiving the funding. The media talked of 'destroying the snake by cutting off its head'. And by targeting certain individuals in this way A42 seemed to do exactly that

The trial of Father Ly and the founders of the Progression Party in Hue on 30 March 2007 made international headlines when Ly attempted to shout out an anti-communist poem of his own composition: 'Communist trial of Vietnam, A lewd comedy for years, Jurors a bunch of baboons, Servants of dictators, who are you to judge?' and was promptly muzzled by the burly hands of a plainclothes security officer in full view of the world's TV cameras. Thus in little under a year the story of Vietnam's dissidents turned full circle. Having emerged from Hue, the movement was crushed, 11 months later, in the city's courtroom. The hands across Father Ly's mouth provided an apt metaphor for the fate of Bloc 8406. The colloquial Vietnamese word for censorship is *bit mieng* – literally, to cover the mouth.

* * *

And that, more or less, was the end of Bloc 8406. In retrospect, the flowering of dissent during 2006 seems the result of a unique opportunity – the deliberate 'hands off' policy by authorities fearful of potential international reaction. In spite of their best efforts, the dissidents remained a tiny and isolated group. At most, Bloc 8406 acquired around 2,000 open supporters within the country – about one in 40,000 of the Vietnamese population. Their idealistic comparisons with Poland and Solidarity were misplaced. In the 1980s, Poland's economy was stagnant, Vietnam's is growing; Solidarity had the backing of the Catholic Church but there is no equivalent mass support in Vietnam and the activists were not the same either – not so much shipyard trade unionists as capital-city lawyers. They didn't have the same community roots. The parallels are less with Poland than with Czechoslovakia. The Czech dissident movement, the group known as Charter 77, comprised outspoken intellectuals who remained isolated and unknown by the mass of the population until the Party leadership finally cracked in 1989.

But the 2007 crackdown didn't mark an end to online activism or to protest. There are still large numbers of dissident-minded individuals inside the country, many of whom are veterans of previous crackdowns. Some of them are organised and some still maintain links to groups overseas. Perhaps they have laid down an infrastructure which may yet weaken the current system. Internet use continues to spread and even as the security services' surveillance of it becomes more effective, so do techniques of evading it. Bonds have been formed between activists in different places and from different backgrounds, and mechanisms are in place for transferring information and money.

The dissidents' other significant achievement has been to bring about a shift among exiled anti-communist activists. A new generation seems to be taking over; people who are less interested in hopeless revolutionary plotting and more willing to patiently engineer peaceful change. Groups like the Government of Free Vietnam have been outflanked by the well-funded and well-organised Viet Tan. Like the Government of Free Vietnam, Viet Tan was founded by former members of the Saigon regime and, also like the GFVN, in its earlier incarnations it tried – and failed – to wage an armed struggle in Vietnam. However, in September 2004 Viet Tan committed itself to peaceful campaigning and went public. It has excited the interest of many Vietnamese exiles, and also the paranoia of the Vietnamese security services and official media, which have labelled it a terrorist organisation. Nonetheless, it's continuing to send its activists into the country to build up support and to generate finance for a sustainable, home-grown democracy movement.

The events of 2006–7 seem to have generated a new *modus vivendi* between the dissidents and the security forces. The dissidents who were arrested and jailed were not those who simply held dissident thoughts or even wrote about them online. They transgressed the Party's limits of tolerance in much more significant ways – in particular by breaking its monopoly of political organisation with independent parties and trade unions. They were also involved at a much deeper level with activists based outside Vietnam, they took money from anti-communists overseas and they tried to take their message to people in the offline world – in the universities, factories and streets of Vietnam. Dissidents who did not do these things – the majority of signatories of the original *Manifesto* – may have been harassed or questioned by the police but they were not jailed.

Calls for reform were once heard almost exclusively from disillusioned but still senior Party members. Now, the franchise has widened, with such calls emanating from a tiny fraction of the urban professional classes. However, there seems little sign of them winning support from the wider public. By plotting with foreigners and accepting financial support from overseas Vietnamese they have damaged their credibility at home. But who knows what may happen in the future? So long as Vietnam's economy booms, they're likely to be safe. But if it falters and disenchantment grows then there may come a time when the dissidents' message speaks to such a significantly large segment of the population that, one day, the Party may be forced to reach some kind of accommodation with it.

7

A sharp knife, but not too sharp

The gang of men lounging in the Hanoi Botanic Gardens were enjoying themselves. They were on a break from a training course, it was mid-December, the weather was cool and the Gardens provided some respite from the roar of city traffic. Traffic was the men's livelihood – they were paid a salary for controlling it and most made a tidy income from the side perks. Hanoi's traffic police are notorious. Any minor infraction is an excuse for an informal transaction, no receipt offered or asked for. But some of these cops were into something much bigger than roadside bribery. They were about to go centre stage in the biggest corruption scandal in Vietnam's recent history. Officers from Police Department C14 had been investigating one of them, Bui Quang Hung, since receiving an anonymous letter in late August accusing him of organising betting on football matches – a serious criminal offence. They swooped on Hung and his mates under the big trees in the Gardens on 13 December 2005 and the arrests got a brief mention in the press, but it took another month before the wider ramifications started to emerge.

The scandal arose just as the Communist Party was making final preparations for its Tenth Congress. The Party was making a high-profile effort to be seen consulting the people, and the people's biggest concern was corruption. Not just the traffic police kind of corruption, annoying as it is – more the sense that rich and connected people were getting even richer through bribery and kickbacks. So when the newspaper *Lao Dong* (Labour), owned by the Vietnam Federation of Trade Unions, reported on 16 January that the arrest of Officer Hung had led police to the Director-General of a corporation who had bet at least $1.8 million on European football matches, outrage was sure to follow. In the following days others printed more revelations. The Hanoi police force's own newspaper *An Ninh Thu Do* (Capital Security) made the most of its inside sources. Evidence from Hung's computer suggested vast sums were being bet: $320,000 on a game between Manchester United and Arsenal in the English Premier League, and $268,000 on Barcelona-Real Betis in Spain. And the alleged punter? It was Bui Tien Dung, the boss of Project Management Unit 18 (PMU18 for short) the best-funded development agency in the country.

PMU18 had been set up in 1993 to handle road-building projects for the Ministry of Transport. Over the following 13 years it had handled around $2 billion of contracts – partly funded by the Vietnamese government, but also by the World Bank, Japan and European countries. It had built some very important roads and bridges, but, among those in the know, its senior management had a reputation for taking massive kickbacks in exchange for contracts, for using aid money to buy cars as bribes and for fast and loose living. Until the Botanic Gardens arrests, they seemed to be able to get away with anything. But now the lid on their hidden world had been lifted. In the following four months the media, and the country at large, would be consumed with the scandal. They revelled in the allegations and the prurient details of personal lives. Two newspapers in particular – *Tuoi Tre* and *Thanh Nien* – seized the opportunity to splash stories across the front page and their circulation soared. It would be the most liberating period in the history of socialist Vietnam's journalism.

It was obvious to these papers' readers that PMU18 enjoyed some very powerful connections. The question was, how far up did the corruption go? One answer appeared to come on 21 March when PMU18's former boss, Nguyen Viet Tien, who'd risen to become Deputy Transport Minister, was summoned for questioning. The papers had been tipped off in advance and covered developments in glorious detail. At the end of April, *Tuoi Tre* (Youth), published by the Ho Chi Minh City branch of the Youth Union, printed readers' letters and also an op-ed by Duong Trung Quoc, a reformist member of the National Assembly (see Chapter 5) calling on Tien's boss, the Transport Minister Dao Dinh Binh, to resign. Nothing like this had ever been seen before. Other papers, particularly *Thanh Nien* (Young People), published by the Vietnam Youth Federation (an umbrella body for all youth organisations, including the Youth Union), joined in the chorus.

On 4 April, exactly two weeks before the Party Congress was due to begin, Binh did resign. The following day Tien was arrested and accused of using state funds to build a four-mile road to his relatives' farm, of misusing state vehicles and deliberately causing a $2 million cost overrun on a bridge project. Having forced two politicians from office, the papers aimed their investigations at even bigger fish. On 13 April, *Tien Phong* (Pioneer, published by the Central Committee of the Youth Union) alleged corruption in the Government Office – the Prime Minister's secretariat. They printed details of a lunch at the Melia Hotel, one of Hanoi's smartest, organised by a business associate of Dung, the PMU18 boss, five days before he was arrested. The lunch had been attended by the head of the then Prime Minister's Office, Doan Manh Giao; Giao's deputy, Nguyen Van Lam and Major-General Cao Ngoc Oanh, chief investigator at the Ministry of Public Security. Lam was already in trouble. The papers reminded their readers that three years previously he'd accidentally left a bag at Hanoi airport holding ten envelopes, each containing around $10,000. Both his brothers-in-law, the papers alleged, had been business partners of the PMU18 boss. In spite of all this, Lam had been, for a time, head of the government's Anti-Corruption Office. All this information had been coming directly from the police investigation. Loyalty among the elite had clearly broken down, dirt was being dished on an ever widening number of people.[1] After the revelations, Major-General Oanh denied any wrongdoing but nonetheless resigned his seat at the Party Congress. It was a disaster for his career – he had been tipped to become Deputy Minister of Public Security.

On 16 April though, the papers finally overstepped the mark. *Thanh Nien* published an article which would spell disaster for several more careers – but this time within the newspaper itself. In a story titled 'Bui Tien Dung reveals 40 others took bribes to cover up', the paper for the first time suggested that among those bribed were 'dozens' of 'important people'. Although the paper was careful not to name names, the implication was obvious: that corruption had reached the highest levels. Even suggesting this was politically explosive. The papers had gone too far and that was, more or less, the end of the revelations. The papers' main source, the officer in charge of Department C14, another police major-general, Pham Xuan Quac, denied the story and *Thanh Nien* was forced to defend its own journalists in print. The flow of material from police to press dried up.

Why the sensitivity? The explanation seems to lie in one important fact about PMU18 which was never published in the Vietnamese press but which was common knowledge among those at the top. One of the managers of PMU18 was a man called Dang Hoang Hai. Hai is the son-in-law of the most powerful man in the country, Party General Secretary Nong Duc Manh. Hai was never accused of wrongdoing but was reputed to be a close ally of the arrested Deputy Minister, Tien. By even suggesting that people of this status had been bribed, *Thanh Nien* had exceeded the limits of media freedom in Vietnam by a considerable margin. The shutters came down. The Party Congress was held and elected a new leadership. The officials who'd been implicated in the scandal missed out on promotion. After the Congress few new details about PMU18 were published and media reports tilted towards glowing coverage of anti-corruption measures being taken by the new Prime Minister, Nguyen Tan Dung. Behind closed doors though, things were turning against those who'd exposed the scandal. In December 2006, the anti-corruption Prime Minister issued a directive calling on government agencies to step up their inspections of newspapers, magazines, television stations and internet sites and crack down on those that violated the law. An official at the Ministry of Culture and Information suggested the speech was a response to 'inaccurate reporting' which had linked 'innocent people' to the PMU18 scandal. The same month Major-General Quac, the chief police investigator and the main source of the newspaper stories, was quietly retired.

On 19 January 2007, almost exactly a year after the first revelations appeared in the press, the police formally wound up their investigation. One immediate result was that Major-General Oanh – and by extension all the other senior officials who attended the lunch at the Melia Hotel – was cleared of wrongdoing. The official verdict was that bribery was not on the lunch menu. That changed the whole course of events. On 22 March, the police started investigating the journalists who'd investigated the scandal. The journalists had obviously got some things correct, because on 7 August 2007 Bui Tien Dung, the boss of PMU18, was convicted along with seven others and imprisoned for 13 years – six for gambling and seven for bribery. Bui Quang Hung, the traffic cop in the Botanic Gardens, received six years. However, the political wind had changed. The first public evidence was the dismissal of *Tuoi Tre*'s two widely respected deputy editors, Huynh Son Phuoc and Quang Vinh, at the end of August. Then, in October, ex-Deputy Transport Minister Tien was given bail. The following March the investigation into him was suspended, and then on 7 May 2008 his Party membership was restored. 'Tien the corrupt official' had been completely rehabilitated.

Five days later the Ministry of Public Security arrested the two journalists who'd done most to reveal the scandal: 56-year-old Nguyen Viet Chien and 33-year-old Nguyen Van Hai – the home affairs editors of *Thanh Nien* and *Tuoi Tre* respectively. The police also arrested retired Major-General Quac and his former deputy, Senior Lieutenant-Colonel Dinh Van Huynh – by now identified as the sources of most of the stories about PMU18. The papers exploded. Front-page headlines like 'The journalist is the victim' and 'A parody of justice' attacked the arrests and inside pages were filled with critical comment and testimonials on behalf of the detained men. One commentator suggested that 'there must be other dubious things involved'.[2] But after three days the storm subsided. The papers suddenly went meek and mention of the case was almost dropped. Punishment wasn't long in coming. On 1 August the Ministry of Information and Communications announced that the deputy editors-in-chief of both papers were being fired, along with a senior manager from each paper. The press rebellion was over. Newly appointed editors made sure journalists toed the official line and across the country, the contents of once-fiery newspapers turned from meek to bland.

On the morning of 14 October 2008 dozens of journalists stood outside the Hanoi People's Court waiting for the trial of their colleagues Chien and Hai and the two policemen Quac and Huynh. The two journalists espoused very different positions. Hai, the younger man, expressed remorse and at one point broke down in tears. Chien, the older, was defiant, insisting he had done his job as a journalist and had nothing to apologise for. The judge specifically asked him, 'Was the information about 40 individuals offered money by Bui Tien Dung to fix the case accurate?' To which Chien replied, 'I think it is accurate because I got it from not only one but four sources of information. I have already submitted the tapes to the investigation authority about this.'[3] The following day the judge delivered the verdict. The journalists were convicted of 'abusing free and democratic rights to breach the interest of the state and legal rights of organisations and citizens'. The remorseful Hai received two years of non-custodial re-education. The defiant Chien got a year in jail. The policemen were convicted of 'deliberately revealing state secrets'. Retired Major-General Quac received a warning but his former deputy was sentenced to a year in jail.

We may never know exactly what happened in the PMU18 case. The story of the scandal still has many pages missing. Why was PMU18 selected for investigation? Was it an accidental effect of the initial betting circle arrests or was the unit deliberately targeted by someone? Was the media coverage orchestrated by people with scores to settle? Did Major-General Quac want to bring down Major-General Oanh? Did other people want to bring down the Deputy Transport Minister Nguyen Viet Tien and was that a way of trying to bring down the Party General Secretary, by linking his son-in-law to the scandal? Rumours abound, facts are hard to come by. All we know is that if those were the intentions, then they rebounded badly. Quac was retired, Oanh and Tien were rehabilitated and Nong Duc Manh remains General Secretary. The journalists paid the price for their efforts to tell their readers the truth. On 16 January 2009 the government announced that Chien was being freed early as part of the annual Tet amnesty for well-behaved prisoners. Exactly three years after the first story about the PMU18 scandal, the episode came to an end. In a final irony, the announcement was made by one of the Deputy Ministers of Public Security – the man who took the job Major-General Oanh was being lined up for before the scandal broke.

* * *

Every Tuesday a group of mainly grey-haired men gathers outside an imposing colonial building on Nguyen Du, one of the avenues bequeathed to central Hanoi by the French. Old friends are greeted, new members of the gang are introduced and, as far as they can over the traffic noise, the old hands make small talk. But this is no retirement club. This is the weekly gathering of Vietnam's media elite: around 100 of the country's editors-in-chief. It's not a press conference, what goes on inside the Ministry of Information and Communications (MIC) is never reported and no one outside the select group of regular invitees has ever been allowed in – although a few insiders have spoken quietly about what goes on. This is where the Communist Party manages the media. The Tuesday gathering used to be held directly under the auspices of the Communist Party and hosted by the Party's internal Ideology Commission. But in 2006 it was felt this no longer fitted with the new image Vietnam was trying to present to the world – that it was a normal state governed by the rule of law – so responsibility for the meeting was transferred from the Party to the government. But it was exactly the same meeting, with more or less the same attendance and the same purpose.

Once all the editors are seated, a senior official, usually Deputy Minister of Communications Do Quy Doan, opens proceedings. It's rarely a discussion, more often a critique. The man from the Ministry reads out a list of items in Vietnam's newspapers, magazines, radio programmes, television bulletins and websites which the Ministry thought were 'negative': such-and-such a publication, the page number, the title of the article and the reasons why it has offended the Ministry's sensitivities. It's the first warning, a simple ticking-off. As *Thanh Nien* and *Tuoi Tre* know well, repeated failures bring tougher penalties – editors-in-chief can be ordered to replace their editors and publications can be fined, suspended or even banned altogether. The instructions continue with a look ahead to the coming week: which issues will be good to highlight, which ones won't and why. In early 2007, when there were outbreaks of cholera in some parts of the country, the Ministry warned the Tuesday meeting that coverage of the disease might hurt the tourism industry. While it's quite permissible to write stories that highlight social problems, one veteran of the briefings says everyone there knows that, in general, the media 'shouldn't write too many negative stories'.

Some editors are spared the burden of attendance. The publishers of *Nha Dep* (Beautiful Home) magazine don't have to spend their Tuesday mornings closeted with their colleagues. But that doesn't mean they aren't subject to its edicts. However unlikely it might seem, the risk that *Nha Dep* might run an article on political reform and interior design is regarded as sufficiently great for the Party to need to keep a watchful eye over its content. *Nha Dep* can only be printed because it is formally published by the Vietnam Association of Architects: a professional body which is registered with the Union of Vietnam Literature and Art Associations, which is in turn a member of the Vietnam Fatherland Front – the Party-controlled umbrella organisation to which most 'civic' organisations ultimately belong. There are no legal, independent media in Vietnam. Every single publication belongs to part of the state or the Communist Party. A series of formal links stretches from the Party Politburo at the top, through Party or government 'supervisory organisations' (*co quan chu quan* in Vietnamese) to the editor-in-chief of the publication, and then on to the editor and the journalists. Through these links every journalist can be held directly accountable to the Party leadership for what they do and don't write. This isn't to say that the Politburo itself is scrutinising *Nha Dep* for ideological promiscuity (though its members are probably reading it for tips on decorating their holiday homes) but it is, in theory able to direct the magazine's content – and that of any other publication in Vietnam – should it step out of line.

In this sense there is no press freedom in Vietnam. The country is regularly placed in the bottom 10 (out of 170 or so) in the Reporters Sans Frontières annual 'Press Freedom Index' – slightly above North Korea and Burma. But the lack of 'media freedom' hasn't prevented a huge media boom. Proof can be found at every street kiosk in Vietnam where a selection of the 800 or newspapers and magazines produced in the country will be on sale. In the days before *doi moi* there was often just one, *Nhan Dan* (The People), the official organ of the Communist Party's Central Committee. Two decades later and the home-grown magazine industry includes not just *Nha Dep* but even 'Vietnam Golf', replete with advertisements for Lexus cars and Rolex watches. ('Vietnam Golf' is published by the Hanoi Golf Club, which is under the Sports Department of Hanoi City People's Committee, which, of course, is ultimately under the control of the Politburo. The same rules apply, even to golf.) And as the range of titles has proliferated, so has the range of subjects which the Party has allowed the media to discuss. The agenda of today's newspapers and magazines would have been utterly unacceptable just a decade ago. Corruption, scandal and gossip are all part of the modern media mix.

This wasn't how it was meant to be. Right from the beginning of *doi moi*, Party leaders wanted the media to act as an agent of reform. The Politburo knew that hundreds of thousands of people had grievances about corruption and mismanagement by local officials and that it didn't have the capacity to address them all. So, in effect, it delegated some of the power of inspection and exposure to the media.[4] A new Press Law, formally approved in 1990, specifically gave journalists the right to gather their own information and made it an offence to obstruct their work. Simultaneously the end of Soviet aid meant the end of subsidies. Newspapers and magazines had to actively sell their product – and therefore offer something readers actually wanted to buy. Just as in every country with a freer press, editors discovered that the best thing for selling papers was crime. And who better to publish crime stories than a newspaper owned by the police themselves? Readers of

Cong An Thanh Pho Ho Chi Minh (Ho Chi Minh City Police) are treated to a diet of sex and murder – with reportage straight from the horse's mouth. The editorial line of the paper both terrifies the audience and reassures it that the police are on hand to catch the bad guys and keep the streets safe. It's a successful mix, making it easily one of the country's biggest selling papers.

The once near-monopolistic *Nhan Dan*, on the other hand, is kept afloat by the obligation placed upon every Party and government office to buy a copy. If it were left to survive on its street sales it would have gone bust long ago – it's almost impossible to find in newspaper kiosks. The people don't want to buy 'The People'. *Nhan Dan* is not alone. *Quan Doi Nhan Dan* (the army newspaper) and *Hanoi Moi* – published by the Hanoi City Communist Party branch – are also kept going by compulsory purchase arrangements. Instead consumers have turned to papers which have built a reputation for uncovering corruption, exposing malpractice and widening the boundaries of what it's acceptable to print. The three leaders are the ones which pursued the PMU18 story most vigorously: *Tuoi Tre, Thanh Nien* and *Lao Dong*.

As these papers have stretched the journalistic envelope they have discovered the limits beyond which the Party's media managers feel they shouldn't trespass. The Party is paying careful attention to the development of the media from its 'brain', the complex of mainly yellow-painted buildings adjacent to the National Assembly in Hanoi, the epicentre of Vietnam's political life. While archaeologists scratch away at the remains of the thousand-year-old Citadel on one side of the road, on the other, in a drably modern office block, the Party's Propaganda and Education Commission (the renamed Ideology Commission) debates how far and fast the media should change. The interior of the block is decorated in the style of a western suburban business park. Grey wallpaper, carpets and woodwork, a blank metal lift, over-filled ashtrays – there's no sign of luxury. The offices are scattered with newspapers and there are few secretaries; the ideologues have to rinse their own teacups. But lack of opulence shouldn't be confused with lack of power.

The Propaganda Commission has lost one of its key roles – hosting the Tuesday meeting – and its staff are at pains to point out that the media is now managed 'according to the law' by the MIC. The Commission, they insist, is just a think-tank developing the Party's media policy. Except that it's a think-tank to which government departments must genuflect if they wish their policy to be approved. The functionaries' desks are laden with requests for direction and guidance from ministries and provincial authorities. The staff regularly write pseudonymous articles for national papers setting out the Party's line on various issues. The Party's structures reach into every newsroom – which frequently causes tension between editors' sense of responsibility to their journalists and readers and their duties as Party members. It hardly needs to be said that all editors-in-chief (the people with official supervisory responsibilities who attend the Tuesday meetings) have to be Party members. The same is true of most managerial positions; something which persuaded one excellent journalist on *Tuoi Tre* not to try to rise up the paper's hierarchy. 'If I wanted to be a manager I would have to become a Party member, but I don't want to. Joining the Party requires at least one, perhaps two years of study and it's so boring. You have to learn the history of the Party by heart.' According to this journalist, the most influential figure in the paper is the newsroom secretary, who is always a Party member. 'They decide what goes on the front page and in the other parts of the paper.'

Under Article 6 of Vietnam's Press Law, the media have two mutually contradictory obligations: 'To provide honest information about the domestic and international situations'; and, 'To carry out propaganda, disseminate information about and contribute to the building and protection of directions, orientations and policies of the Party and the law of the State'. Ever since 1986 and the first instructions to the media to expose 'negativism', there's been a battle between conservatives in the Party and the liberal press over these contradictory obligations. Journalists can fully obey the law only if the truth coincides with the policies of the Party. If it doesn't, they have a choice about which clause to obey. Since the consequences of violating clause 2 are worse, it's usually the obligation 'to provide honest information' which suffers.

There are plenty of people within the Party who would like to see greater freedom in the media but also others who are far more suspicious – and policy has to please both groups. At times the Party experiments with openness to see what happens. Then, when things get out of hand, it tightens things up again. In the run-up to the Tenth Party Congress in 2006 there was clearly a loosening, and in the aftermath, clearly a tightening. In the PMU18 case, the loosening appeared connected to the way different interests in the Party were using the media against their rivals. But there are also wider issues involved: the Party needs new ways to manage public opinion in a rapidly changing society, and is debating whether tighter or looser controls work better. Over the long term there has evidently been some kind of 'ratchet' effect – journalists have pulled things in their direction and then the Party has pulled back, but not as far back as before. The net result has been that more subject areas and new ways of writing about them have gradually been permitted.

* * *

The Party is always playing catch-up. Like most things in the new Vietnam, the media hasn't evolved through a considered process of policy-making but through *pha rao* – 'fence-breaking' by entrepreneurial, some might say piratical, business bosses. They may be Party members but they also have their own interests – and these often come first. Vietnam's media industry is already behaving, in some respects, like their western capitalist counterparts: the search for profit is prompting circulation wars, dirty tricks and ever-more risqué content. This is most noticeable in television. For years after the end of the war there was only one TV channel to watch – assuming the viewer had the means to watch it. Vietnam Television was just as stimulating as any state-owned monopoly provider of socialist propaganda could be expected to be. In 1990 the number of channels doubled to two, but the visual diet didn't improve. Then, a decade later, VTV got competition. The story is a superb illustration of the informal way things are done in Vietnam, where the law is less important than the people implementing it.

VTV's own subsidiary, the Vietnam Multimedia Corporation (confusingly known as VTC) was initially created to build a new national TV infrastructure. When it was transferred to the control of the Ministry of Post and Telematics in July 2003 senior people there saw an opportunity to make some big money – and not by building transmission towers. Instead, they used their new asset to set up an entirely new, and rival, media network with six channels. Since then, the competition between it and VTV has become intense, particularly over the rights to money-spinning spectacles such as the Olympics, the football World Cup, and Miss World.

In 2006 VTV, in what was a relatively new development, bought the rights to legitimately broadcast the Miss World pageant. Sadly for the channel the event took place just as one of the biggest storms in years, Typhoon Xangsane, hit the country, killing 70 people. As a mark of respect VTV decided to delay its broadcast. No such scruples concerned VTC. It stole the pictures from the transmission put out by the Hong-Kong-based Star Channel and re-broadcast them. But, in an equally novel turn of events, VTV sent in the lawyers – first of all to demand that VTC stop broadcasting and, when they didn't stop, to demand compensation. VTC was forced to admit wrongdoing and settle with VTV. It was the second time it had done so in just a few months. Earlier it had had to compensate FPT, another rival, a reported $450,000 for broadcasting World Cup football matches without permission.

Such disputes show how deeply embedded commercial motives have become in Vietnam's media industry, even though all the companies involved belong to the state. Competition can be fierce, even within the same company. VTC's difficulties over Miss World were enthusiastically detailed by the website VietNamNet, even though both were owned by the Ministry of Telecommunications. The managers of the companies saw each other as serious rivals, competing both for attention and, more seriously, for advertising revenue and profit. Indeed when VietNamNet set up an internet TV operation it co-operated far more with VTV than it did with its supposed sister company VTC.

VietNamNet's TV operation was equally piratical. It started broadcasting news programmes on the web and then, in November 2004, on the Hanoi cable TV system, even though it had no government licence to do so. To keep inside the law, it simply titled its news bulletin 'comprehensive information'. So long as VNN's overall boss could keep his bosses and any other potential objectors happy, everything could keep running. But there were problems with living in legal limbo, as one reporter for VNN-TV found out when she went to interview the Minister of Telecommunications. She thought it would be simple to question the man who was, on paper, her ultimate boss. But the Minister inexplicably declined to be filmed – although he was willing to offer a statement. Only later did the reporter realise that the Minister was covering his back. If he'd been seen on camera giving a news interview he could no longer pretend that VNN-TV wasn't a news programme; he would have confirmed, in effect, that it was operating without a licence. Better to turn the interview down than be exposed, even though anyone who mattered already knew informally exactly what was going on. VNN-TV lasted less than three years. Officially it closed because it wasn't making money. But the reason it wasn't making enough money was because it couldn't reach a big enough audience without a broadcasting licence and, in contrast to its equally piratical rivals, the reason it couldn't get the licence was because ultimately its patrons didn't have enough influence with the right people.

The search for profit usually tops almost all other considerations – including, from time to time, ideological instructions. It's sometimes a major battle for the Party to keep control. The local TV networks in Hanoi, and particularly in Ho Chi Minh City, now make so much money from advertising that they don't need state subsidies – and if they don't need the money why should they take the state's instructions? The answer so far is that Party discipline has been stronger than the lure of cash but such divided loyalties are becoming more and more difficult to manage. So much so that the Prime Minister was forced to issue his December 2006 directive ordering tighter control over the press, in which he said Vietnam would never allow privately owned media.[5]

But one media outlet is already almost entirely privately owned. The hugely popular online site, vnexpress.net, started life as a project of FPT, the Corporation for Financing and Promoting Technology, wholly owned by the Ministry of Science and Technology. Under its highly entrepreneurial management (led by Dr Truong Gia Binh, former son-in-law of General Giap: see Chapter 1) FPT has grown from its original 13 employees into an employer of several thousand, with a series of IT outsourcing contracts for companies in Japan and Europe. It is also one of Vietnam's largest internet service providers and telecoms companies. In 2001 it set up its own online news site – and just like VietNamNet-TV it did so without a government licence. Initially vnexpress.net was classified as an 'internet content provider', meaning that it could only publish material that had already been published elsewhere. By selecting the stories which the site's editors thought would most interest readers and by focusing on information rather than ideological comment it rapidly reached a huge audience. Its business plan required it to reach 200,000 users within a year and a half. It achieved this within four months. But by the end of its first year in business it had already made profits from advertising of $70,000. It was the only unsubsidised website in the country. After more than a year of lobbying, vnexpress.net eventually received its licence from the Ministry of Culture. It was surprisingly easy.

At the time it seemed to the leadership of vnexpress.net that the Ministry didn't really see the point of an online newspaper or understand its potential significance.

As it has evolved, the parent company of vnexpress.net, FPT, has grown far away from its roots. Just 8 per cent of its stock is still owned by the state, around 80 per cent by its employees and foreign investors (including the venture capital arm of the US chip-maker Intel), with the remainder held by investment houses based in Vietnam. Thus one of the most important Vietnamese news outlets is almost wholly owned by private interests in contradiction of government policy. Its survival rests less on the law than on the balance of relationships between the company's patrons and potentially hostile forces in other parts of the Party and government. FPT has become one of Vietnam's biggest companies and its connections run deep into the Party leadership and into the boardrooms of some of the biggest global corporations. It has no shortage of allies to call upon if it's ever put in a difficult position. For the time being vnexpress.net, its most controversial subsidiary, exists in a curious legal limbo.

* * *

The Party may be sanguine about fence-breaking by home-grown entrepreneurs but it is distinctly paranoid about foreign media organisations. Foreign correspondents based in the country and international news outlets are governed by a completely different set of rules to local ones. The government still tries to block out unwelcome messages transmitted from abroad. Satellite dishes were banned in 1997, except for certain government offices, local authorities, smarter hotels and radio and television stations. If viewers want to see international channels they have to subscribe to cable. But anyone watching BBC World News or CNN International on Vietnamese cable networks learns not to set their watch by them. Broadcasts are recorded and then transmitted with a 30-minute delay to give the censor sufficient time to stop the signal if there are 'provocative' news items such as any mention of Vietnam – in case it might be offensive – or of political change in China or Cuba. The only time the delay was removed was during the Asia-Pacific summit in November 2006, presumably because the authorities didn't want all the influential foreigners in town to realise what usually happens and because they could be reasonably confident that almost all the coverage would be positive. Curiously the censorship only covers news channels. While BBC World News signal is frequently disrupted, it's quite possible to watch any number of offensively gung-ho documentaries on the Discovery Channel about the effectiveness of US military hardware during the Vietnam War.

Overseas papers too are subject to censorship, but the regime has failed to keep up with the electronic revolution. From time to time, foreigners in Vietnam find foreign publications vandalised. Editions of the *Financial Times* or the *International Herald Tribune* will have silver paint sprayed over an article which MIC has decided is too negative.[6] When, in April 2008, the *Economist* magazine published a supplement on Vietnam, most readers inside the country found it lacked something: the final page. The last article in the supplement was about the future prospects of the Communist Party and a team of MIC minions had carefully razored out each one. Given that the article and others the minions block out remain easily accessible on the web, the idea that this bowdlerisation will prevent the information from circulating within Vietnam is absurd, yet the practice continues. It's the sight of the article on display which offends the censors. The ritual of censorship seems to be more important than the effect.

Because the government knows it can't stop foreign media organisations publishing or broadcasting whatever they want about Vietnam, it puts controls on the other end of the news process – the gathering of information. Under the Press Law, foreign journalists are supposed to send a request to the Foreign Ministry's Press Department five days before they carry out any journalistic activities. Every trip, every interview, every phone call has to be cleared by the government five days in advance, by law. In theory then, if a journalist wanted to call a doctor in southern Vietnam and ask about the severity of an outbreak of bird flu, they would need to wait at least five days to get an answer, by which time, of course, bird flu could have spread to the entire country. Suffice to say then that all of Vietnam's small band of foreign journalists break the law, almost every day. The fact that most of them manage to keep their working visas might suggest the government doesn't really care about the law. Except that it does. Like many laws in Vietnam, it hovers over the heads of those it affects, ignored and unused, until the authorities have a reason to use it.

I had personal experience of this several times. As the BBC reporter in Hanoi almost everything I produced was illegal in the sense that I only ever went through the grinding channels of official bureaucracy when I really had to. And that didn't cause any problems at all, so long as my reports concentrated on Vietnam's negotiations to join the WTO or official visits by foreign leaders. But the moment they strayed into more 'difficult' territory, the Foreign Ministry's Press Department got serious about the law. The day after I made a telephone appointment to meet a political dissident I was called to the department to be reminded of the need to clear all activities through its staff. When I arrived at the dissident's house I was met by a large reception party of security officials along with a helpful student with fluent English who was 'just passing' and could translate the police's objections to my presence. On another occasion a report about allegations that the authorities were removing street children from Hanoi ahead of the Asia-Pacific summit prompted the head of the Press Department to warn me loudly in the corridors of the summit that my visa was in jeopardy. Subsequent reporting on the dissident movement, once the summit had finished and Vietnam had joined the WTO, caused further official warnings, then a decision not to renew my visa and two weeks' notice to leave the country.

Foreign news organisations with Vietnamese-language output are not allowed to have permanent correspondents based in Vietnam. Recently, however, the authorities have relaxed their attitude towards them. The BBC's Vietnamese Service is now allowed to send reporters to Vietnam for short periods. They are always visited by police agents when they arrive and their work is monitored, but in between they seem to have relative freedom to operate, so long as they steer clear of the most sensitive topics. The BBC Vietnamese Service website has now become one of the most important news providers in the country. It was unblocked by the national firewall in 2005 and now any internet user in the country can view it. When the local media was cowed in the wake of the PMU18 dismissals and court cases, traffic to the BBC Vietnamese site grew and grew. As a result it is receiving more and more tip-offs about stories within the country from sources frustrated by the inability of local journalists to tackle controversial topics in the way they once did.

There are certain issues for which sites like BBC Vietnamese are the only choice. One of the most startling was the death of the former Prime Minister Vo Van Kiet. He died in hospital in Singapore on 11 June 2008 and the news spread quickly around the world. But in Vietnam, nothing was reported at all for a day and a half.[7] When the Thai army launched its military coup in Bangkok in September 2006 the delay was even longer. It was several days before Vietnam could be told that Prime Minister Thaksin had been over-thrown. In situations like these it's simply too risky for any Vietnamese publication to take an editorial position, in case it should clash with the view subsequently adopted by the Party leadership. That would prompt severe criticism at the Tuesday meeting. Certain events almost never get covered – the riots in Tibet in March 2008 and the protests in Burma in September 2007 just didn't happen as far as the domestic media were concerned. At times like these, Vietnamese audiences turn to foreign websites. The Party doesn't seem sufficiently concerned to try to prevent the information getting through the national firewall (see Chapter 4 for more on the fire-wall) but neither does it allow its publication at home. Again, the ritual of censorship seems to be more important than the effect.

Trying to outwit the censorship, however, can cause serious trouble. Intellasia is an independent website specialising in reporting business news from Vietnam. Founded in 2001, it had been run by two Australians – one based in Vietnam, with 14 local staff, and the other in Australia – without trouble for six years. The first inkling Peter Leech, the Hanoi-based partner, had that trouble was coming was a fax at the end of June 2007 from the then Ministry of Culture and Information (MoCI – before it became the MIC) warning him that some of the news articles on its website said 'bad things about Vietnam'. For a while the site had been including items about polit-ical dissidents in its mix of stories. These were items which had already been published by the main international newswire services and were there-fore in the public domain. Leech argues that these amounted to no more than 'a few dozen over a couple of years' – a tiny fraction of the 50,000 it produced in that time. Four days after the fax, the site's Hanoi offices were raided by officers from A25, the police unit which deals with 'cultural crime', along with officials from MoCI who accused the office of 'running an illegal website'.

The problem for Intellasia was that it had positioned itself between two sets of laws. The site itself was registered as intellasia.com and its internet server was physically based in the US. Intellasia should, therefore, have been registered as a foreign news organisation, the Hanoi office as its Vietnam bureau and Leech as the local foreign correspondent. However, the company was operating as if it were a local website, and should therefore have been using a '.vn' domain name such as intellasia.com.vn. It's a crucial distinction because in order to register a Vietnamese domain, the site would have to be hosted on computers inside Vietnam and therefore subjected to Vietnamese controls. It's illegal for Vietnamese organisations to host their sites on straight .com domains – though many large organisations routinely do so. As in so many areas of life in Vietnam, regulations weren't a problem until some other line was crossed – and then they became very problematic indeed.

Within a matter of weeks Leech, his wife and the office staff had been repeatedly summoned for questioning, the company had been attacked in several newspapers, particularly *An Ninh Tu Do* (Capital Security owned by the Hanoi police) and Leech fined $1,200 for publishing a defence of his actions on the company site. He finally left the country (and, temporarily, his wife and child) in late August 2007 having been warned that, unless he did, more severe action would be taken against him. In subsequent days his American-based website was swamped with computer-based 'denial of service' and 'brute force' attacks and blocked by Vietnamese internet access providers. At the time of writing, the site is still running but the editorial outlook has changed. Articles about the prospects for foreign investment in Vietnam have been joined by ones headed, 'Vietnam: enter at your own risk' and others equally critical.

This is an extreme example, but it shows the difficulties the authorities are facing in trying to regulate online media. It may well be that the motivation for this persecution was mainly *pour encourager les autres* in the absence of a specific legal framework for websites whose very nature crosses borders and regulatory regimes. For some time now the Party has been wrestling with the question of how to manage blogs – personal websites published on sites based overseas (such as Yahoo 360 and Facebook). For the most part the staple fodder of Vietnamese blogs is the same as on others from Singapore to Sweden: pop music, film stars and gossip. While most of it is harmless chatter, the Party is worried about the possible implications of a popular medium that isn't under its control.

Their concern turned into anxiety in late 2007 after what could have been a trial run for their worst nightmare. When China announced that it intended to annex the disputed Paracel and Spratly Islands in the South China Sea (see Chapter 9 for more), the Vietnamese blogosphere experienced a spontaneous outpouring of rage, uniting Vietnamese inside and outside the country. Angry bloggers spread word of unauthorised demonstrations in front of China's embassy in Hanoi and its consulate in Ho Chi Minh City. Even more unsettling for the Party, later protests were timed to coincide with protests at other Chinese missions around the world. The authorities were in a difficult position: although unwilling to allow independent demonstrations they were both sympathetic to the cause and unwilling to be seen suppressing it. In the end, several hundred people turned out at demonstrations in Vietnam, mobilised entirely through the internet and without official support.

The more daring newspapers and most of the online news sites reported the protests. The official *Nhan Dan* did not, concentrating instead on the Foreign Ministry's diplomatic protest to Beijing. But then came the Tuesday meeting and a predictable instruction from the Information Ministry to end the coverage of the protests. However, the bloggers hadn't been to the Tuesday meeting and in cyberspace the coverage continued. Debate raged back and forth over the adequacy of the Vietnamese government's response to the Chinese move, and the government was powerless to stop it. Eventually the discussion died away but it was clearly a wake-up call for the authorities. Two weeks after the first demonstration, the Information Ministry held a conference to review the work of the media, at which the majority of officials attending 'said they would support draft regulations on controlling weblogs'.[8] Nguyen The Ky, head of the Press Department of the Party's Central Propaganda and Education Commission (the organisation in the bland office block which monitors media development) told the conference: 'It's all right some bloggers have recently showed their patriotism, posting opinions about the Paracels and Spratly archipelagos on their weblogs. But some have sparked protest, causing public disorder and affecting the country's foreign affairs.'

The conference approved draft regulations intended to prevent bloggers from posting subversive or sexually explicit content online. Do Quy Doan, the Deputy Information Minister, told the meeting: 'Bloggers will have to be responsible for not only their uploaded information but also information they access. Once we have obvious regulations, I think no one will be able to supervise weblogs better than the bloggers themselves.'[9] In the meantime the police resorted to old-fashioned methods of control. When 55-year-old Nguyen Hoang Hai – who blogged under the nickname Dieu Cay – called for more Spratly protests while the Olympic Flame was travelling through

Vietnam in April 2008, he was quickly detained. He'd apparently been under surveillance since taking part in the earlier street protests. In September he was jailed for 30 months on the rather unlikely grounds of tax evasion, having rented out his property to an eyewear company. The charges were widely regarded as trumped up.

For several months officials argued over whether and how to control blogs. In December 2008 the Ministry introduced its new regulations under which only 'personal' information can be published on blogs. Anything which violates an earlier Government Decree (No. 97) is banned. This includes anything that 'Opposes the state . . . undermines national security, social order and safety, causes conflict or discloses national security, military or economic secrets'[10] – sufficiently broad wording to include almost anything the authorities don't like. Given the development of the internet it is hard to believe that the new regulations are anything more than a comfort blanket for the authorities. They know there are well over a million Vietnamese blogs on the web, and systematic monitoring is impossible. Enforcement is likely to follow the pattern already established for the rest of the media: the authorities will tolerate the rules being ignored until some particular mark is overstepped – and then they will step in and make public examples of a few violators and keep the rest in line.

To some extent control has been made easier by the way the market has developed. The first generation of bloggers took to Yahoo's 360 site and then Facebook – both based in the United States, beyond the reach of the censors. But more recently bloggers have switched to the first such site developed in Vietnam, with a Vietnamese-language interface. Zing.vn is owned by VinaGame, which produced the staggeringly successful online video game Vo Lam (Swordsman). From a standing start in mid-2007, Zing.vn took less than six months to become one of the top five most popular websites accessed from Vietnam.[11] With sections devoted to games, music, film and beauty it clearly knows who it's targeting and many bloggers have switched to it from Yahoo. This is a happy coincidence for the authorities. Controlling blog postings on a Vietnamese-located website will be much easier than on foreign sites. While they won't be able to censor every posting before publication, pressure can be brought to bear on the site's managers to remove certain kinds of content and dissuade others from posting similar material.

But already some journalists are using blogs as uncensored online newspapers, a way to get stories into the public domain without scrutiny from editors. One of the most famous is a blog called 'Osin'. Osin is the creation of a veteran journalist best known by his *nom de plume*, Huy Duc. Duc was once a reporter for *Tuoi Tre*, but got into trouble and moved to *Thanh Nien*, got into trouble again and left to set up a newspaper under the umbrella of the Saigon Business Association, *Sai Gon Tiep Thi*. But he wanted more freedom to publish his thoughts so in August 2007 he created Osin. He named the blog after a character in a Japanese television soap opera which became incredibly popular in Vietnam. Osin was the servant who slaved away to earn the money to live her dream. Duc sees himself as a 'word slave' – writing to survive but his blog has built him an international reputation. 'On average there are about 15,000 page views each day', he said in early 2009. 'In the past year there have been about 2.5 million.' Duc/Osin writes about the kind of issues which even the liberal papers won't touch: corruption in high places, intra-Party intrigue and international relations. From time to time he has received warnings about some of his postings but never, he said, demands to remove anything. 'Many people, including some members of the Politburo, have read the blog but only a few complain and that is when there is an entry criticising and naming them directly. However Osin is one of the blogs that some officials have used as an example in their demands to the government to have regulations about bloggers.'

But in August 2009 Duc wrote an article on the Osin site which overstepped the mark. In it he criticised the former Communist rulers of Eastern Europe and described the Berlin Wall as a 'wall of shame'. A few days later he was fired from his newspaper, yet again. The paper's editor-in-chief, Tran Cong Khanh, told the AP news agency it was because, 'The attitude of his entry did not reflect that of our newspaper.'[12] Others thought that this was just an excuse to punish a journalist who'd tried to push the boundaries of the Vietnamese media too far in too many directions. He became the most high-profile victim of the crackdown on blogs. Duc remained philosophical, blogging that he'd lost many jobs in his career and was thinking of writing a book.

* * *

The crucial question is where all this will lead the country's journalists now that they've had a sniff of freedom. Out in the bleak western suburbs of Hanoi, all four-lane boulevards and concrete institutions, stands the Party's own training school, the Ho Chi Minh Political Academy. This is where cadres come for the instruction necessary to advance in the structures of power. An annexe houses the Academy's Press and Communication Institute which was, until recently, the only place for Vietnamese journalists to train. The barrack-like buildings within its dusty grounds are designed to induct workers on revolutionary press organs rather than unleash talent in a creative industry. But there's been such an explosion in the media industry – in January 2007 the Party calculated there were '13,000 well-trained journalists together with tens of thousands of contributors and supporters who provide direct or indirect services to journalism'[13] – that the Academy has had to give up its monopoly and outsource training beyond its walls. Courses are now being offered at the National University in Hanoi and at Ho Chi Minh City University in the south. The curriculum, however, has hardly changed: it's long on Marxist-Leninist studies and the history and theory of the media but short on practical skills, hands-on experience or guidance on modern journalistic standards.

There's plenty of evidence of low standards. Many editors are more concerned about selling papers than checking their facts. Interviews are regularly 'adapted' to fit the needs of the story and, from time to time, entirely invented. It's customary for journalists to receive a tip for turning up to press conferences. Ostensibly it's to cover expenses but it's become more like a fee, a virtual requirement if a company or government office is to receive good coverage. Even 100,000 dong (around $6) is more than a day's wages for an average person in Vietnam – about a quarter of the wage of a journalist in Hanoi. PR agencies are known to keep a list of those who write bad things about their clients. They get special named envelopes that contain a fraction of the standard tip. It is simple bribery but hard for a jobbing journalist to turn down.

One man who's trying to improve the situation is Le Quoc Minh, editor-in-chief of vietnamplus.vn – the overseas-oriented website of the official Vietnam News Agency. Based in the VNA's Stalinist edifice on Tran Hung Dao Street, amid the graduates of the Ho Chi Minh Academy, Minh knows the difficulty of changing the way anything is done. But more importantly he knows how to overcome those difficulties. A big factor in his favour is that his late father, Le Phuc, was once Vice-President of the National Union of Arts and Cultural Associations, a senior figure in the Party's cultural apparatus. In the Vietnamese system, important fathers tend to protect their sons – even in the afterlife. Minh has set up his own website, dedicated to improving standards among his colleagues. Vietnamjournalism.com concentrates on practical advice: how to cover and write stories, how to do research and how to behave ethically. It's not a campaigning site; it doesn't lobby for changes to government laws or regulations. Instead it's a one-person reform programme, the effects of which will only be seen in the long term.

Minh has received some financial support from foreign donors concerned to improve standards of journalism as a step towards reforming the 'governance' of Vietnam. But he's sceptical of the value of such initiatives. The rush of well-intentioned cash from abroad to transform the local media has so far had little obvious effect on its output. The journalists who are selected to attend foreign-funded courses – whether for a few days inside the country or for longer abroad – tend to be the most easily spared from the daily rota and thus younger and more junior. They attend their Western-taxpayer-funded courses, learning how to be independent tribunes of the public interest. But then they return to their old newsrooms, where nothing has changed, and are bludgeoned into submission by the weight of seniority above them. Many of the bright young journalists expensively trained by foreign aid money end up so frustrated and bored that they rapidly find alternative employment in the press offices of foreign embassies, international organisations and multinational corporations.

But it's worth reflecting on what will be lost if ever Vietnam's media are 'reformed' along western lines because, at present, their official operating instructions stand in deliberate opposition to the mores of their westernised cousins. There are few countries where an Information Minister will berate the media for 'catering to majority tastes' as Nguyen Quy Doan did in 2003, adding that some parts of it considered themselves 'to be a normal commodity'. By standing against the obsessive pursuit of novelty and topicality, Vietnam's old-fashioned media should be praised for at least trying to present a more egalitarian agenda and for defending the rights and dignity of those who usually get left out or left behind by western media: the poor, the elderly, the disabled, inhabitants of rural areas and ethnic minorities, to name but a few. Old people, particularly war veterans, are honoured rather than ignored in the search for the latest trends. The poor are made to feel valued rather than pathetic. The old-fashioned media don't regard it as their job to peddle false aspirations to them.

The Vietnamese media is changing rapidly. What seems radical one day rapidly becomes commonplace. The authorities are no longer completely in charge – they are fighting to remain in control of the forces they have unleashed. It's a bumpy ride, but the Party hasn't remained in power for so long without learning a lot about managing public opinion. However the gulf between them and today's public is expanding. The bedlam of blogs, game shows and glossy magazines is both generating and transmitting the aspirations of an intensely aspirant people. It has both transformed and been transformed by an ever more sophisticated urban culture. The professors in the Ho Chi Minh Academy and the ideologues in the Party Propaganda Commission are keeping a close eye on developments and tinkering with the rules – all the time trying to understand how to use the modernising media to ensure its place at the apex of political and social life.

But discussion is kept within safe limits. Criticising the implementation of policy is acceptable; criticising the Party directly is not. At root, the Party still wants the media to be a tool for managing society – keeping corruption within acceptable limits, raising awareness of social problems and applauding efforts to tackle them. Looking too hard at why corruption continues to flourish or social problems go unsolved is not encouraged. In the words of one editor: 'You can't fight the top officials because they are the Party. Scapegoats will be found. . . . They want the knife to be sharp but not too sharp.'[14] So far the Party's media managers have proved reasonably adept at the task. But a new generation is coming up through the ranks of media professionals – one which is literate in international culture and has a different set of goals to their current bosses. The struggle in the next few years will be over how far this generation is co-opted into the existing media management system and how far that system can be stretched before it fights back with a sudden retrenchment in media freedom.

★

8

See it before it's gone

The morning mêlée on the boat steps was in full swing. Bus-loads of brightly coloured tourists sought shade under the souvenir shops' awnings. Guides grabbed permits from the booking office and ushered their sweltering charges past the barriers. Tour parties headed left and right: snakes of Koreans, Chinese, Americans and Europeans teetering along the tide-wet concrete, searching out the wooden junk to begin their tour of Vietnam's greatest visitor attraction, the World Heritage Site of Ha Long Bay. Balancing bags and cameras while dodging box-loads of food and laundry overhead and the ropes and moorings underfoot, they eventually reached their designated gangplank, the relief of gaining floating sanctuary heightening the expectation of seeing one of the wonders of the natural world. As their junk was pushed back from the landing stage, 300 others pressed in, waiting their turn to collect their tour group.

Ha Long Bay is truly spectacular. More than 2,000 limestone towers erupt from the sea. From afar they look like the back of the descending dragon which gives the Bay its name. Each one is its own little nature reserve, the steep cliffs and flat summits providing home for clinging greenery and intrepid wildlife. Some hide magnificent caves and intricate natural sculptures. In among them, protected from storms by dozens of natural harbours, fishing communities in floating villages make a decent living selling seafood, and increasingly soft drinks and sweets, to the passing trade. And what a trade. In 2008 more than 1.5 million people traversed the landing stages and sailed among the peaks of Ha Long Bay. Forty per cent of all foreign visitors to Vietnam went there. Ha Long Bay has become the icon of the national tourist industry. When Régis Wargnier filmed the opening scenes of *Indochine* in Ha Long Bay in 1991, the whole area had fewer than 100,000 visitors a year. Now it has more than 20 times that.

A short drive from the northern border, the Bay is getting busier every year as more and more Chinese develop the money and the taste for foreign travel. Vietnam is the nearest place to go and Ha Long Bay the nearest sight to see. For many of them the backdrop seems immaterial. Being abroad is more important than seeing abroad. Groups spend their time afloat sleeping, chatting or playing cards rather than looking at the view. A few hours in a foreign country is followed by a bus trip back across the border to the safety and comforts of home. What they take home is status. What they leave behind is Vietnam's problem. Ha Long Bay is not just an icon of the tourist industry, it's a symbol of the country's environmental crisis: the dash for growth, the yearning for a decent living, the lure of cash, the conflicts between business interests and regulations, the confusion between different layers of authority and, above all, the unsustainable rush for reward *now*, without regard to the future. Ha Long's beauty endures but beneath the surface it's dying. Its fate could well be the fate of large parts of the rest of the country too.

When Wargnier came to Ha Long the shore was lined with mangrove forests. Now they've been stripped, the land reclaimed and a wide road pushed along the coast. The newly named Ha Long City has grown out of the fishing towns of Bai Chay and Hon Gai. The sea view is undiminished, but the land has become a jumble of gaudy high-rise hotels and entertainment spots: casinos, karaoke bars and at least one cock-fighting venue. But aesthetics are the least of the Bay's problems. For more than a century the area of Cam Pha, just north-east of Ha Long has been the centre of the Vietnamese coal industry. Blighted desolation covers tens of square kilometres and heavy rains fill its rivers and streams with coal dust. So much dust has flowed into the sea that it's now economically viable to mine it. Coffer dams are built, the water is pumped out and the sludge collected, dried and turned into the charcoal burners seen on every side street in the country. Some of the solid coal is transported by uncovered trucks, blackening the towns and fields along their routes with soot. Most is carried by sea. As the tour boats return from Ha Long Bay they're given a close-up tour of the dozens of lighters queuing outside Hon Gai harbour. Vietnamese coal is a big export earner. In 2008 they were worth around $1.5 billion. Two-thirds goes to China and most of the rest to Japan.[1] Other lighters take the coal along the coast to Vietnam's own power plants. Coal dust, oil, bilge water, heavy metals and the other detritus of the shipping industry contaminate the water. All of this within half an hour's boat ride of the limestone peaks. To make matters worse an international shipping route has been dredged through the middle of the Bay. No matter that there's a well-established deep-water port in the city of Hai Phong just up the coast, the authorities in Quang Ninh, the province which includes Ha Long Bay, decided that they needed one of their own. Ships of up to 70,000 tonnes can now dock in Hon Gai. A few are cruise ships but most are container vessels and bulk carriers with much lower environmental standards. And all of them stir up dust and sediment in the Bay's shallow waters, coating the sea bed in a life-drenching blanket.

And these aren't the only sources of pollution. Ripped-up mangrove forests used to be the vital barrier which preserved Ha Long's coral and fish life – slowing down the rivers and streams flowing into the Bay and filtering out the soil they carried. That kept the sea clean and allowed the delicate corals to flourish. When the mangroves went, the silt flowed free, covered the corals, preventing them photosynthesising, and killed them. Then the fish which fed on the coral died, and so on, up the food chain. Thirty years ago the waters in and around Ha Long Bay teemed with life and were harvested by fishermen who had worked the sea for generations. Most of them were ethnic Chinese, descendants of people who'd moved back and forth between China and Indochina for centuries. But in 1979, after relations between Vietnam and China collapsed (see Chapter 10 for more on this) the fishermen, and most of the rest of the Chinese community, were expelled. Around 30,000 are thought to have left, creating a huge gap in the market for anyone who thought they could fish. Most of those who tried were poor, without proper equipment and lacking knowledge of the sea. In place of nets, lines and generations of skill they used explosives, electric shocks and poison. Breeding populations were decimated. Those who want to make a living from fish now do so with intensive farms in the floating villages. But the oils in the feeds leak into the water along with all the other waste, making the problem even worse.

Marine biologists test the clarity of water by lowering a circular board known as a Secchi disk into the depths. It's common in tropical waters to be able to see the disk as far as 30 metres below the surface. Less than two metres is regarded as bad. In parts of Ha Long Bay international environ-mentalists lost sight of the disk just 15 centimetres below the surface. The problem goes all the way to the bottom. The water is green and turbid, filled with dust – and worse. All the tourist boats in Ha Long Bay are supposed to be fitted with septic tanks to catch and process their passengers' toilet waste. It's a regulation of which the Ha Long Bay Management Board, a part of the provincial administration, is proud. Unfortunately the board has failed to provide sufficient facilities on shore for the boats to unload all the waste. Only a very few boats, the luxury end of the market, have the necessary four tanks on board to process the by-products of their trade properly. All the other boat owners can do is sail around until the motion of the boat has broken up the contents of their (single) tank into an unidentifiable soup and then quietly empty it into the water. The shit of a million and a half boat passengers a year is being dumped directly into Ha Long Bay.

Some of the people in charge of managing the Bay know they have a problem and some parts of the central government are trying to force them to clean up. But the Ha Long Bay Management Board has no powers over coalmining or commercial shipping – it can only make recommendations to its boss, the Provincial People's Committee, which also has to listen to the demands of business. The coal mines are run by Vinacomin, a state-owned enterprise. It makes huge profits and provides thousands of jobs. The tourist industry seems to be doing fine too. Tickets and permits generate $3 million per year for the Management Board. 'Where's the problem?' they ask. But visitor numbers are no longer growing so fast and few international visitors return to Ha Long Bay; growth is at the cheap end of the market. International advisers say the board has done minimal serious research into tourists' impressions of the place; certainly nothing that focuses on the quality of the experience or how that has changed over time. Most of the policy devel-opment for one of the world's most important natural environments is being led by special interests and guesswork. UNESCO, the United Nations body which listed Ha Long Bay as a World Heritage Site in 1994, is trying to help; making recommendations to improve the place. In 2007 it successfully got jet-skis banned from the Bay. But it completely failed to prevent the construction of a new cement plant near the Cam Pha coal mines. Where environmental protection only affects the little guys it is implemented. Where it conflicts with big business it is ignored. As a visitor attraction Ha Long Bay survives, but as a natural environment, it is dying.

Central government appears impotent, unable or unwilling to force the provincial authorities to improve the situation. The problem is exemplified by the Ministry of Natural Resources and Environment, MoNRE. The conflict of interests begins with the name: the environment comes a poor second. The Deputy Minister in 2007, Dang Hung Vo, an outspoken reformer, understood the problem but could offer little evidence that the government was going to take determined action. 'I'm strongly aware that many industrial economic zones lie in sensitive geographical areas and that this has led to environmental disasters. In Ha Long Bay we understand the need to preserve the balance between economic development and the environment. We have quite good solutions for this.' But he was not forthcoming about what those solutions might be. There is minimal pressure on the authorities from outside government as well. Although more stories about pollution are now being printed in newspapers, editors are regularly warned not to publish material which might scare away tourists. Instead, the vast majority of local media stories about the Bay are positive – increasing visitor numbers, new regulations to protect the environment (regardless of whether they are implemented) and admiring reviews by visitors. During 2008 the Management Board devoted a quite ridiculous amount of attention to trying to ensure that the Bay won a place in a global internet vote, organised by a private Swiss foundation, to find the 'New7Wonders of Nature'. UNESCO refused to have anything to do with it. The results had little merit other than reflecting the number of online votes each country could mobilise, and yet the board thought this worth more of its time and resources than providing sewerage facilities for the floating toilets. The Vietnamese media fell into line behind the campaign rather than questioning the board's priorities.

* * *

This focus on Vietnam's international image rather than on domestic realities seems to affect the country's entire approach to the environment. Vietnam has signed up to all the right pieces of paper – it's one of the few Southeast Asian countries to have ratified the four big conventions on conservation – but it's also an environmental disaster in slow motion. The problem, as in so many areas of Vietnamese life, is implementation. There are people who understand the problems: Vietnam had its first national park in 1962, its first National Conservation Strategy in 1985 and a Plan for Sustainable Development in 1990. On the surface it looks impressive. But laws have great loopholes in them, pieces of legislation contradict each other and when it actually matters regulations can be bent, dodged or ignored.

The disaster is more acute because of the rich diversity of Vietnam's forests just a few years ago. It seems strange to call Vietnam's landscape 'untouched' when it was, for a decade, deliberately targeted by a US policy of what some have called 'ecocide': deforestation, the draining of wetlands, the use of carpet-bombing and even the seeding of rain clouds to stimulate mass flooding. Vast areas of natural habitat were destroyed.[2] One reason why Vietnam is currently one of the few countries whose forests are growing is because so much was destroyed during the 1960s. (The problem is that what is now being grown is plantation acacia and eucalyptus for the furniture industry.) But the war and the lack of development afterwards also preserved large parts of the country from industrialisation, and from the 1980s onwards international conservation groups and a few home-grown experts have put a lot of effort into trying to keep them that way.

About 6 per cent of the country has been turned into national parks or nature reserves. Some of these places are among the most spectacular landscapes in the world: huge karst limestone pillars, dense mountain forests, mangrove swamps and pristine islands. They're home to some of the rarest creatures on the planet, including elephants, rhinos and tigers. Every few months zoologists discover species they thought had become extinct: the hairy-nosed otter, the world's rarest animal; an oryx-like member of the cow family called the *sao la*; the white-lipped keelback snake and dozens of orchids and other plants. But at the same time habitats are being destroyed, the animals hunted for eating or traditional medicine, the snakes bottled in jars of rice wine and the orchids stripped for collectors. There is one set of rules for the rich and powerful and another for the poor. Vinacomin's continuing pollution of Ha Long Bay is one example. Another is the wildlife trade.

At the western end of Ha Long Bay is its biggest island, Cat Ba. Designated a Global Biosphere Reserve by UNESCO, it should be a jewel in the Bay's crown, but it's turning into a dump. Almost all the island is included in the Reserve and about half has been declared a national park but neither designation has prevented the development, since 2001, of a boom town resort on its southern coast. A strip of tall, thin, five-storey budget

hotels lines the seafront, like a slice of Hanoi rising out of the sea. Bigger
hotels lie on the edge of town. This thin strip of land receives more than
350,000 visitors a year. And, just as in Ha Long City, the main attractions are
the bars and restaurants along the seafront. Some openly feature wildlife on
the menus, others are more discreet. Organised gangs can supply almost
anything within a couple of days. Deer, turtles, snakes, lizards – tastes are
broad and the National Park can provide them all. The local authorities on
the island make minimal efforts to prevent the trade. In fact the People's
Committee of Cat Hai district (which governs the island) has repeatedly
tried to get the National Park abolished or drastically reduced in size in
order to expand the area available to hotel development and the number of
customers for wildlife meat. Their motivations are purely based on short-
term gain with little thought for the future.

Cat Ba is far from unique. In almost every town in Vietnam there are restaurants advertising *dac san* – 'speciality' food. Some offer genuine local specialities, but the name doesn't usually imply *haute cuisine*. Customers go there to
demonstrate their status and virility to their friends and clients. The menus
may appear innocent, but behind the scenes a parade of pangolins, porcupines
and palm civet cats can be killed to order. The greatest kudos goes to those who
can buy the most expensive, most endangered, most sought-after meat available. The trade is vast. A survey by researchers at Hanoi Agricultural University
published in 2008[3] calculated that a million animals – some dead, some kept
alive for extra freshness – are being illegally bought and sold in Vietnam every
year. Figures from the Agriculture Ministry, responsible for controlling the
trade, suggest its inspectors intercept just 1–2 per cent of it. The cumulative
effect of so many wild animals being removed from their natural environment
every year is devastating. In the early 1990s Vietnam's forests became a giant
larder for Vietnamese and Chinese consumers, but after two decades feeding
their insatiable appetites the cupboard is looking bare. The story of one
national park shows how bad things have got. Pu Mat, on the border with Laos,
was a hub of the wildlife trade in the 1990s with dozens of illegal traders operating. Ten years later their catch is down 80 per cent and only a few traders are
left.[4] Increasingly the remaining traders have to buy animals from Laos itself,
Cambodia and even as far away as Malaysia and the Philippines.

There is a small, but dedicated, community of people in Vietnam trying
to stop the wildlife trade. Vu Thi Quyen is one of its leaders. In 1999 Quyen
was working with an international NGO in Cuc Phuong, Vietnam's

first national park, to educate local people about conservation. She and a colleague decided that such important work shouldn't be left to foreigners and set up the country's first indigenous environmental organisation: Education for Nature, Vietnam (ENV). It wasn't easy. As a 25-year-old woman she wasn't taken seriously, but after two years of lobbying ENV was eventually allowed to register. Most of its work is in schools – encouraging new generations to live more environmentally friendly lifestyles than their parents. But, uniquely for a Vietnamese organisation, ENV has a strident campaigning agenda and access to top politicians. It sees this 'pincer movement' – tackling the entrenched bureaucracy simultaneously from above and below – as the only way to protect the country's dwindling wildlife. One of its most successful initiatives has been a wildlife crime hotline.

National radio and TV run ENV's advertisements encouraging people to call in with tip-offs. ENV then takes up many of the cases itself, reminding restaurants they are breaking the law and calling in the authorities where violators refuse to mend their ways. It maintains case files on around 1,500 restaurants and uses more than a thousand volunteers around the country to check up on them at regular intervals. It also runs a big publicity campaign to try to stigmatise bear bile. Hundreds of Asian brown bears, known as 'moon bears' because of the crescent-shaped patch on their chests, are taken from the wild each year to feed the bile trade. As a result the species is classified as 'threatened' by the International Conservation Union. ENV has recruited pop stars and football players to portray drinking bile as a backward, antisocial habit. To some extent it appears to have worked. The price of bile fell from highs of $15 per millilitre in 2004 to just $1.50 in 2007. But it hasn't wiped out the industry.

In 2005, after sustained lobbying from ENV and international organisations, the Agriculture Ministry introduced new rules to end the hunting of wild bears. Bear trading was made illegal along with the extraction, advertising and selling of bile. It was a smart plan. Rather than ban the keeping of bears – which could have led to their wholesale slaughter or abandonment – they were tagged with a microchip, making any unregistered bears easily identifiable by inspectors. By preventing new animals entering the trade they hoped to gradually phase out the trade. Registration went well, and 4,000 animals were 'chipped', but it rapidly became clear that bear farms were not going out of business. In July 2008 national Forest Protection Department inspectors were tipped off about 80 unregistered bear cubs being kept at a farm in Ha Tay province on the outskirts of Hanoi, but were prevented from actually getting into the farm by provincial officials. When they returned with police, intending to confiscate the cubs, they discovered they had been moved to another farm in Ha Long City. ENV and the local authorities set up a surveillance operation outside that farm and three others nearby. Over four days they counted 33 tourist buses going in. They then managed to get inside and saw the groups, mainly Koreans, being given a live demonstration of the bile extraction process, drinking bile and then being offered it for sale. The entire operation was illegal and yet it was advertised with billboards on the highway. It was clear that the owners of the farm enjoyed some protection from authorities in Quang Ninh province.

The bear bile crackdown has been effective against 'mom and pop' operations making small amounts of money from one or two caged bears and unable to afford the bribes necessary to secure official protection. Large-scale bear-farming operations seem in most cases to have successfully evaded the regulations. Even worse, in April 2008 after the discovery of the 80 cubs in Ha Long City, the Agriculture Ministry decided it wouldn't confiscate them and sent out a new circular, Correspondence 970, which undermined all the previous legislation banning the keeping of endangered animals. It instructed provincial governments that merely 'keeping' protected animals was not a criminal offence and only merited administrative fines. At a stroke all the effort of the previous three years appeared to have been undermined. Nonetheless Quyen and her staff at ENV remain optimistic that things are gradually improving. They've been consulted by members of the National Assembly over the new draft Law on Biodiversity and believe that new regulations will slowly advance the cause of wildlife protection. The problem they face is that this law, like many other pieces of Vietnamese legislation, is being written to allow many interpretations. It is expected to outlaw wildlife trading but also to legalise the breeding of endangered species for profit. This messy compromise has been strongly criticised by international conservationists but it's partly the result of a noisy controversy in early 2007 which pitted international concerns about animal protection against raw political power.

At that time ENV, perhaps against its better judgement, joined a group of international conservation organisations in taking on one of Vietnam's richest men in what seemed to be a clear-cut case of illegality. In 2006 Wildlife At Risk (WAR), an international NGO based in Ho Chi Minh City, discovered that Ngo Duy Tan, the owner of the Pacific Beer Company, was keeping and breeding tigers of unknown origin in his private zoo. Tan was far from ashamed of what he was doing. He proudly declared to the authorities and the media that he had saved six baby tigers from death when they were offered to him by 'a peddler' in 2000. In the intervening years, the six had bred to become 24. This was entirely illegal. The law specifically bans breeding tigers of unclear origin. (From a conservation point of view, if species are to be preserved then their origins need to be known, otherwise captive breeding generates cross-breeds which are useless for conservation and can never be returned to the wild.) WAR called in the big guns. Six organisations, including the World Wildlife Fund (WWF) and the International Conservation Union called for tough action against Tan to demonstrate that Vietnam was serious about cracking down on the wildlife trade. But then Tan demonstrated where real power lies in Vietnam.

Former Prime Minister Vo Van Kiet, usually hailed as a political liberal and economic reformer, wrote an article for the press in which he stated, 'There is no reason to consider the case of Mr Tan to be illegal.' After that intervention, the law and the opinions of international conservation groups counted for nothing. In March 2007 the current Prime Minister ordered the Agriculture Minister to investigate the case. A meeting of all the relevant enforcement agencies was called for 23 March, but the day before, the Agriculture Minister, Cao Duc Phat, also usually hailed as a reformist and a technocrat, flew down to Tan's zoo to discuss what to do about the tigers. The following day the agencies' meeting made two entirely contradictory decisions. Firstly they agreed that the tigers should be confiscated but then they ruled that the owner could 'temporarily continue breeding them'. It was a nonsense: the law was upheld in name and then completely ignored in reality. It was a big setback for efforts to end illegal wildlife trafficking. The clear message was that the rich and connected can flout the law with ease. Worse, the law has now been changed to legitimise what had previously been illegal. Few are convinced that the Agriculture Ministry is serious about its conservation duties. As the Ministry of both Agriculture and Rural Development (MARD) its priority has long been economic growth in rural areas. Conservationists describe its attitude to the environment as 'jurassic'. With such official vacillation and continuing demand for wildlife products, the potential rewards for traffickers vastly outweigh the risks.

But even if MARD did take its conservation duties seriously, the problem would not go away. The 2008 Hanoi Agriculture University survey[5] estimated that a third of the wildlife being traded is exported to China, mainly through two major crossings on the northern border. The chances of this trade being stopped seem remote. A survey reported in the Communist Party's own newspaper *Nhan Dan* in July 2002 said three-quarters of the staff who worked there were regularly accepting bribes.[6] It's not hard to see why. Wildlife traders are thought to make over $20 million profit each year – 30 times the total budget of the Forestry Protection Department's monitoring and enforcement arm. A forest ranger makes a pathetic $50 a month. The average wildlife restaurant makes that much profit every couple of days. Even dedicated officers face an impossible battle because no part of the state bureaucracy is free of corruption. There have been cases of illegally caught live animals being transported in police cars, hearses and even prison vans. In one incident a live bear was dressed as a patient and put in an ambulance surrounded by several 'concerned relatives'. The Forest Protection Department is woefully under-staffed. The average ranger is responsible for around 1,400 hectares of forest, a vast area, and the people the rangers are up against are very determined. Most of the hunters are dirt poor and frequently members of ethnic minorities, for whom hunting makes the difference between survival and starvation. Most of the traders are from the *Kinh* majority population who make vast amounts of money and they are often protected by people with power and influence. In particular, the military seem to be almost immune from prosecution. That's true of both the wildlife trade and of the illegal timber trade too.

Vietnam's forests suffered almost as much from post-war logging as wartime destruction. Between 1976 and 1990 Vietnamese loggers destroyed nearly as much of the country's forest cover as the United States did with Agent Orange in the 1960s: 2.5 million hectares.[7] Most of the northern mountains were completely deforested. The combination of war and logging has left a quarter of the country classified as 'bare' or 'denuded'. As a result of these twin environmental disasters the government, in 1992, banned the export of logs and sawn wood and cut felling quotas by almost 90 per cent. Logging was then banned in five million hectares of remaining 'natural forest' and the government set about replanting five million hectares to use as plantation wood for industry. The plan is to close all natural forests to logging by 2010. Like the bear bile plan, it looks good on paper but it has affected only the small guys in the trade. The big operators continue to take wood from natural forests in defiance of the law. But it's getting ever harder to find good supplies of timber in Vietnam, so the trade has gone over the border into

Laos and Cambodia. The mountainous regions along the borders are strategically sensitive areas controlled by the military. Either the military are incompetent, or they are deeply involved in forest destruction.

* * *

The prevailing attitude to land, trees and animals in Vietnam is that they are resources to be exploited as profitably as possible. Perhaps this shouldn't be surprising in a country which has only recently escaped dire poverty. The national priority is to secure livelihoods for a large and growing population. But there's an added factor in Vietnam: the dogmatic Marxist-derived belief that the environment is just another resource to be used up in the service of humanity. The pattern has repeated itself across every sector in which the Communist Party has directed investment. The legacy of state planning and output targets set in faraway Hanoi combined with the huge number of impoverished people desperate to improve their standard of living has caused boom and then bust in sector after sector: coffee, cashew nuts, rattan and shrimp-farming are just a few examples.

This is just as true offshore. The waters around Nha Trang on the central southern coast should be teeming with life. Clear blue waters, vast coral reefs and plentiful sunlight. But they aren't. The reason so many aquamarine-painted boats are lined up in the harbour for tourists to photograph is that there are no longer any fish to catch. Nha Trang is being marketed for the global tourism industry; a new high-rise Sheraton has just opened on the seafront. The beach is lovely, but the ecology has gone. Studies by WWF, the Vietnamese government and the UN have shown that, all along Vietnam's coastline, inshore fishing is in a state of serial depletion – meaning that even if fishing were banned today it is unlikely that stocks would recover. It's the result of economic reform, political decentralisation and collateral damage from foreign aid.

Ninety per cent of Vietnam's fishing industry is privately owned and much of it is seasonal. Fishermen work in the fields or on building sites part of the year and go to sea when fish are available and they need extra income. As the economy started to grow, more people had the resources to buy a boat. Between 1986 and 2000 numbers tripled. In the late 1990s, in an attempt to increase food supplies, many inshore fishermen were given international development funding to buy bigger boats so they could fish further out to sea. But although they had new equipment, they didn't have the skills to find fish offshore. Instead they retreated to the waters they knew best. With their bigger boats and bigger nets they reaped a bountiful harvest, made good money and filled local markets with fish. But after a few good years, the seasonal fishermen, with their small boats and basic equipment, started to notice that their catches were falling and conservationists began to sound the alarm. The situation became so bad in the central provinces of Quang Tri and Quang Binh that fishing communities began to suffer malnutrition.

The government drew up a new Fisheries Master Plan for 2006–10, a Strategy to 2020 and then a Fisheries Law of 2007, all of which were applauded by international experts for recognising the problem and focusing on conservation. The Plan called for half the country's inshore fishing fleet, 40,000 boats, to be scrapped by 2010. One leading idea was to sink them to create new coral reefs. The obvious problem was what to do with the fishermen. The Agriculture Ministry wanted them to move into aquaculture – cultivating fish in ponds and farms – or work in industrial zones. But new jobs aren't being created quickly enough to match the decline of the fish stocks. During 2008, as the cost of engine fuel rose, fishermen pressured the provincial authorities. Their response was to delay plans to reduce their local fleets and turn a blind eye to destructive fishing – using dynamite, electricity and fine nets to increase the fish catch. Instead they lobbied the government for more subsidies. In May 2008 the Agriculture Ministry announced it was offering a grant of $3,500 per year to fishermen buying boats with engines over 90 horsepower – big enough to get to offshore fishing grounds. Once again the result is likely to be even greater over-exploitation of inshore waters. The political reality is that the provincial leaders have greater influence than the conservation-minded experts back in Hanoi.

To try to preserve what was left of Nha Trang's marine life, the World Bank funded the creation of the Hon Mun Marine Protected Area (MPA) around a group of islands a short distance offshore. At its inception, the MPA could boast 40 per cent of all the known species of hard coral. In places there is still plenty to see but even its manager believes that it's only got five years of viable life left. The owner of a diving company in Nha Trang is even more pessimistic. 'Diving here is dead. It's finished,' he says morosely. The MPA charges visitors a few dollars if they want to swim, dive or snorkel in its waters but provides little in return. The money seems to go elsewhere. Boats fish openly and illegally in the area; some still use explosives. The MPA's rangers do nothing – they have been intimidated into silence by threats to them and their families. Tour boats drop anchor on the coral and dump litter over the side. The only part of the MPA which seems to be working, indeed one of the very, very few environmental projects in Vietnam which appears to be in any way sustainable, is the multimillion-dollar bird's nest enterprise on the northern side of Hon Mun island.

Here the Khanh Hoa Salanganese Nest Company guards its territory very carefully. The cliffs and caves on Hon Mun island are where the German's Swiftlet breeds, using nests made from their own saliva. While other species also make their own nests this way, the German's Swiftlet is the only one that doesn't use twigs or other materials for support, making Khanh Hoa bird's nest soup a highly prized delicacy in the restaurants of East Asia. By studying the life cycle of the birds and working out the least destructive times to harvest the nests, the company developed what appears to be a sustainable business plan. The company, known as SaNest, pays the MPA authority millions of dollars for the right to collect nests twice a year from the cliffs and caves where they live. SaNest employs its own well-motivated guards, armed with assault rifles, who protect the cliffs from poachers and chase away divers – even those who've paid the park admission fee – with speedboats. But the company's enlightened approach has not transferred to the Marine Protected Area, the local fishing industry or the tourist trade.

The Communist Party may have embraced the market but it still thinks in terms of output quotas and production targets. The priorities are economic growth and poverty reduction. But fisheries are not like ingots of steel or bales of paper, they can't just be 'produced' by increasing the amount of resources available. Nonetheless, the Vietnamese fishing industry is still planned on the basis of arbitrary targets set by people far away from the realities of falling catches and dynamite fishing. The publication of independent research and critical analysis is very unwelcome to provincial Party elites whose promotion prospects depend on meeting quotas and fulfilling targets. Instead they resort to inflating figures to give the impression that they are successfully managing the situation. Newspapers continue to report good news from the fishing industry, despite the obvious problems that so many communities are suffering. One clear symptom is the increase in the price of what were formerly regarded as 'trash fish', which would once have been thrown away or turned into fertiliser. Now they are sold in the market and eaten.

* * *

Many of Vietnam's environmental problems are still being swept under the carpet, but some are now so glaring that they can't be ignored. City pollution has finally become a hot topic. Vietnam has socialist traffic. In most developing countries rich people own cars while poor people walk, but in egalitarian Vietnam almost everyone can own or share a motorbike. They make up 98 per cent of all the vehicles on the road. In Hanoi there's one motorbike for every two people and every day, according to the city's planners, another 700 appear on the streets. In Ho Chi Minh City in the morning and evening rush hours, the roads are simply places where tens of thousands of motorbikes stand almost stationary, their riders jostling for tiny pieces of advantage, roaring noise and filth into the air. And it's not just the city air which is suffering.

Most urban water supplies are not only undrinkable, but lethal. They've been so for years, but the situation became so bad in Ho Chi Minh City that finally, in January 2008, the city authorities began to talk openly about the problem. They had little choice: the city's inhabitants could smell the pollution and see the dead white fish floating in the grey-black canals. But, as is often the case when the public gets concerned about something in Vietnam, the first official response was to blame the foreigner – which is why a Taiwanese monosodium glutamate (MSG) manufacturer on the banks of the Dong Nai River became the first to feel the new pinch.

The Dong Nai River rises, clear and fresh, in the Central Highlands, makes its way through rapids and waterfalls down to the plain, breaking into several streams, before eventually flowing into the South China Sea. It sounds idyllic, but along its course the Dong Nai passes 77 urban zones and runs through three of the five most polluted provinces in Vietnam – as defined by a 2008 World Bank survey. These three (Dong Nai, Binh Duong and Ho Chi Minh City itself) have attracted huge amounts of foreign investment, particularly in low-cost manufacturing – textiles, garments, metal-working and food processing. Companies have come in search of cheap labour and minimal environmental regulation. Two-thirds of the industrial parks in Vietnam have no central waste-water treatment plants and many of those in the south are built in environmentally sensitive wetlands. For years farmers along one of the branches of the Dong Nai, known as the Thi Vai, had been complaining about their fish and crops being killed by toxic waste, but nothing was done. In early 2008, however, a Japanese shipping company claimed pollution in the Thi Vai had eaten away three millimetres of the steel hull of one of its vessels docked at the river's mouth and refused to allow any more of its ships to operate there. This was a direct threat to the region's economy: the authorities were forced to act.

The MSG-maker, Vedan, became Vietnam's first pollution fall guy. That Vedan should have been caught polluting came as no surprise to Professor Doan Canh, from the Institute for Tropical Biology in Ho Chi Minh City. His research team first discovered the company was pumping untreated waste into the Thi Vai in 1997. At the time, he says, Vedan was the only significant polluter on the river. He called for stricter controls but was ignored. 'We submitted the report to the Ministry of Science, Technology, and Environment,' he said after the company was eventually charged with pollution. 'But what a pity that the report received scant attention.' By late August 2008, a 15-kilometre stretch of the river was biologically dead. Fish farms along it had lost all their stocks and Vedan was still dumping over 100 million litres of untreated waste into the river each month. The company had laid three illegal underground pipes to dispose of waste it didn't want to pay to treat. The temptation to do so was obvious. When, at last, Vedan was called to account, the total fine which could be imposed was just $16,700. The authorities, desperate to make an example of the company, then demanded a more significant $7 million in what they called 'unpaid environmental fees', but the company delayed and argued over the payment. Some officials wanted the company shut down but it became clear that Vietnam's environmental laws weren't strong enough to make this happen. Instead Vedan was forced to dig up the illegal pipelines and reduce production to the level that its waste treatment plant could actually cope with.

But even as Vedan was being prosecuted, the other companies which had set up factories along the Thi Vai carried on pumping out waste as normal. The Vietnam Environment Protection Agency estimated that another 200 companies near the river were continuing to discharge 34 million litres of waste into the river each day. With fines so low and the cost of waste treatment so high, it was the economically rational thing to do. But the issue of pollution had finally made it on to the newspaper front pages and gradually the people of Vietnam learnt just how badly polluted their rivers were. They learnt, for example, that only 14 per cent of city wastewater is treated; that all the waste from Hanoi and Ho Chi Minh City's hospitals is dumped, untreated, into rivers and landfill; that dumps were illegally accepting toxic waste and that they were leaking run-off into the local water supplies. A few other foreign companies were made examples of: Hyundai's shipbuilding joint venture was said to have tried to dump 60 tonnes of toxic waste and another Korean company Miwon, also an MSG-maker, was fined $2,000, also for polluting river water. Officials began to point the finger at Taiwanese and Korean companies in general, accusing them of trying to dodge regulations and of systemic illegal practices.

But while it was easy to blame the foreigners, minimal attention was paid to companies that pollute at least as badly – but do so under state ownership. The most polluted urban district in Vietnam, again according to the 2008 World Bank survey, is not a modern industrial zone in Dong Nai but the Cam Gia ward of Thai Nguyen city, about 75 kilometres north of Hanoi. It had the misfortune to be an early beneficiary of Russian and Chinese development aid. From the 1950s the city became home to companies which might have been chosen from the devil's own list of noxious processes: the Thai Nguyen Iron and Steel Company; the Thai Nguyen Asbestos-cement Slate Factory; the Thai Nguyen Coke Coal Manufacturing Company; the Thai Nguyen Coking And Chemical Factory; and the Hoang Van Thu-Thai Nguyen Paper Mill Company. As you bump over the railway lines entering the steel complex its vast size becomes apparent. It's the kind of place that would once have been painted in bright colours and celebrated in socialist-realist propaganda posters – ruddy-cheeked heroes, blast furnaces and electricity pylons. In reality it's like a slice of the Urals in the tropics: grimy-faced workers, smokestacks and slagheaps. The 11,000 employees and their families living nearby endure the worst water pollution, the second-worst land pollution and the third-worst air pollution of any district in Vietnam.

Problems aren't confined to big cities. When industrial production was decentralised in the 1960s, partly to avoid American bombs, great concrete aliens landed in the middle of paddy fields across northern Vietnam. One of these vast edifices lies in Phu Tho province to the west of Thai Nguyen: the Lam Thao fertiliser plant. Below its prefabricated ramparts live communities in homemade huts, digging out the clay soil to make bricks. The chimneys up the side of the plant pour out sulphur dioxide and other noxious gases. On rainy days, the villagers are doused in sulphuric and hydrochloric acids. When the American researcher Dara O'Rourke went there in 1997 a local woman joked, 'Well, at least we don't have to add any spices to our soup.'[8] Before it was built, in 1962, local farmers grew fruit; now the trees are dead and the district is known as 'the cancer village'. The local doctor

Le Van Ton says 15 people died from cancer in 2007 (out of a population of 7,000) and the number is increasing every year.[9] The wastewater used to run into the fields but after years of pressure from villagers the company built a small channel and a treatment plant. But the channel leaks and the plant frequently fails. The waste gets into the ground, the streams and eventually into the Red River, and then on to Hanoi itself.

There are, at last, signs that things might be beginning to change, mainly because of pressure from communities like those around Lam Thao. The ugly facts of pollution are now impossible to hide and anger is rising. International experts who've worked with the Vietnamese authorities say they have taken notice of the protests that have erupted in China over environmental issues and are moving pre-emptively to try to head off similar unrest at home. It's been a long time coming: farmers have been complaining about pollution for years. Now, however, it's the urban middle classes getting upset and the politicians have started listening. The National Assembly has held widely publicised hearings into pollution scandals, the Prime Minister and officials from MoNRE have admitted there are big problems, and, in a sign that the authorities really are serious, the Ministry of Public Security has set up a new Environmental Police Department. The World Bank report has also helped the government understand that pollution will eventually damage economic growth (if people become sick or if investors and tourists stay away) and also that international aid is available to help with cleaning up the mess.

* * *

Pollution is a huge issue for Vietnam but another environmental problem has the potential to become such a disaster that, if the worst predictions come true, the rest of the contents of this book will become irrelevant. It will force mass migration and possibly economic collapse and political chaos. The question is whether anything can be done in time to prevent or mitigate its effects. A report for the World Bank in 2007 concluded that Vietnam will be one of the five countries worst affected by sea level rise and that any rise over a metre would be 'potentially catastrophic'.[10] No one, of course, knows if things will get that bad. The International Panel on Climate Change (IPCC) has forecast a likely rise of just 59 centimetres by the end of the century but others have argued that once certain temperature thresholds are reached, further rapid rises could become much more dramatic. Even if this

does not happen, if the more conservative forecasts are correct, the consequences in southern Vietnam – if nothing is done – are likely to be severe.

A one-metre rise would flood 5 per cent of Vietnam, including some of the
most populated and economically useful parts of the country. Six million
people would be directly affected. The highest point in the province of Ben
Tre, for example, is just 1.5 metres above current sea level; the province is an
island, surrounded by rivers and sea, so even a small rise will have drastic
consequences. Without some kind of preventive action almost half of Ho Chi
Minh City could flood. The city is already very vulnerable: the Saigon River
only has to rise 1.35 metres above its median level to overtop the dykes.
Some parts get inundated every month. In November 2008 the city experienced the highest recorded tides for 49 years, breaking embankments and
putting several districts under water. The Delta is so flat that the Mekong is
tidal as far inland as the city of Can Tho, 80 kilometres from the sea. At very
high tides in the last months of the year, the drains back up and sewage fills
the streets. Children swim amid the waste. If the sea level rises then tides and
storm surges will become even higher and the potential destruction starts to
reach disastrous proportions. So many industrial parks are located in the
Delta that half the country's manufacturing base would be under threat.

If, as is expected, weather becomes more extreme and typhoons shift
their track, storm surges are likely to become more frequent. Central
Vietnam is repeatedly lashed by typhoons – which are forecast both to
increase in number and to become stronger. This part of the country is
already one of the poorest and such a calamitous climate will drive away
investment. There's also evidence that typhoons are moving further south,
hitting parts of the country less prepared for natural disasters. The effects on
people and property are also likely to become more extreme, with severe
consequences for the country as a whole: falls in the rice crop, increases in
poverty, enforced migration and the loss of transport and other infrastructure. People forced to leave low-lying areas will put pressure on resources in
other areas, particularly if they head towards areas already under strain –
such as the cities and the highlands. The loss of prime agricultural land and
the reduction in the number of rice crops cultivated each year would cause
a dramatic fall in food supplies and a rise in prices. Regular sea-flooding will
further increase the salinity of soils in the Mekong Delta, further reduce
crop yields and destroy local fish and shrimp farms.[11] The question facing
Vietnam and the international community now is what to do about it.

Ever since the IPCC and the World Bank highlighted the risks to Vietnam, there's been increasing interest from foreign governments wanting to demonstrate their environmental credentials. The outside world is, in effect, offering to fund a huge-scale programme of public works: dyke building, flood prevention schemes and new infrastructure, with opportunities for kickbacks at every level. For Vietnam it means the possibility of continued large-scale aid – just as its economy reaches the status of a 'middle-income country' when many donors would be scaling back their support. Technical experts in the Ministry of Agriculture and Rural Development privately acknowledge that the reason their political masters are pushing for large-scale dyke building is mainly economic. They're actually fairly sanguine about the likely effects of sea-level rise. There seems to be a feeling within MARD along the lines of: 'We're Vietnamese, our people are hardy and ingenious, we won the war and we'll beat this too.'

There is a considerable risk that if the international community piles into Vietnam with large amounts of money and grandiose plans the money will be spent on the wrong things. There are major downsides to building bigger dykes. In some circumstances they prevent water draining away after storms, exacerbating flooding. Dykes also affect rivers' flow and the amount of sediment that they drop – causing channels to silt up or erode. These things can be managed with adequate planning but the haste with which foreign donors want to be seen spending their money, combined with the chronic short-term thinking and systemic corruption of Vietnamese local authorities, could end up creating problems almost as big as the ones they are meant to solve – at a cost of many billions of dollars. Environmentalists attending climate-change planning meetings have described an almost panicked mood in foreign delegations desperate to get projects started, even though proper assessments haven't taken place. 'Sea level rise is a medium-term problem, we don't want short-term actions and long-term disasters,' says one.

Billion-dollar building plans would probably fail to help the people who need it most: the very poor who are already being affected by the changing environment. In the south-central coastal city of Quy Nhon, areas next to the sea are occupied by slum housing. Strong currents have eroded the seafront and hundreds of homes have already been washed away. At high tides and in bad weather the remainder flood with sea water. The same thing is happening in Danang, where only a few years ago Save the Children Fund (UK) helped build concrete housing for people whose homes had been destroyed in typhoons. Inland, mountain communities are being cut off as extreme storms wash away roads and destroy bridges. In all these places the heaviest burden will fall on those least able – in terms of finance, education or access to power – to cope with it. And yet these people are being left out of government planning. Their residency is unregistered and their lifestyles are marginal. They don't show up on official statistics so little account is being taken of their needs. A new dyke that has been built to protect the city of Danang cost $600,000 for each kilometre of its length. If it was a typical state construction project anything between 10 and 30 per cent of the cost would have been lost in kickbacks to officials and intermediaries. Those whose houses were washed away on the beach got nothing.

* * *

The irony is cruel. Vietnam is one of the least significant contributors to climate change yet will suffer its effects more than most. As the world's 13th most populous country, however, it won't be long before it starts moving into the pollution big league. The population is growing and increasingly able to afford the consumer goods people in richer countries take for granted: motor-bikes, televisions, refrigerators, air conditioners and the other accoutrements of modern living. The government is building electricity networks and power stations, manufacturers are building industrial plants, and the result is a rapid increase in the emissions of greenhouse gases and other pollutants.

Environmental authorities face many hurdles. There is no regular moni-toring of pollution, central ministries have little capacity to enforce regula-tions and it's easy for polluters, animal traffickers and other rule-breakers to buy off local officials and avoid penalties. Vietnam's priorities will remain economic growth and job creation for some time to come. Already foreign companies with plans for 'dirty' factories are 'shopping around' different provinces, choosing those more willing to bend rules if it means jobs and cash for them and their constituents. If the government is unable to keep the country's supposed environmental jewels like Ha Long Bay and Nha Trang in good condition, it's highly unlikely that it's going to be able to motivate and properly direct its 64 provinces to think about things that might happen in a decade or two.

Every province wants growth; few are willing to tell those responsible for pollution, over-exploitation of resources or environmental destruction to stop. The rules made in Hanoi will get stronger but it will be a long time before the people in the provinces properly implement them. It's too late to save some things. It's unlikely that Ha Long Bay's marine life will ever recover, denuded forests will remain bare and many rare species will probably become extinct. The spectre of sea-level rise overshadows all these problems. No one knows exactly what will happen but the experts' consensus view is that Vietnam will suffer severely and in ways which can't yet be fully predicted. Vietnam still has some beautiful places and some amazing wildlife. See them before they're gone.

9

Enemies into friends

It wasn't, perhaps, the best choice of date. Whoever arranged the port visit for Pacific Command couldn't have had a strong sense of history, otherwise why send two US warships up the Saigon River exactly 30 years after the day which set the seal on the United States' defeat in Indochina? The minesweeper USS *Patriot* and the rescue vessel USS *Salvor* steamed into harbour on 2 July 2006, the 30th anniversary of the date when the two Vietnams were formally unified, 15 months after the fall of Saigon, the day in 1976 when Saigon and its surroundings were formally renamed Ho Chi Minh City. It wasn't a day celebrated with great fanfare, but for those with long enough memories it summed up the futility of American military involvement in Vietnam – from the US decision in 1950 to fund and supply the French colonial occupation to its evacuation of Saigon a quarter of a century later.

The commander of the USS *Patriot* in July 2006, Richard Brawley, was pioneering a new kind of US military involvement. Washington is playing a patient game – not asking too much but gradually making friends with a military whose mantra has been paranoia and suspicion ever since the fight against the French. It's a process of forgetting old wounds and forging new ties, based, not on the horror of history, but on the hoped-for horizons of the future. To facilitate the *rapprochement* a new version of history, acceptable to the hegemon, is being imposed, not just by the stronger party but by the weaker one too, in the hope of future strength. It's the Hollywood version: the man-to-man struggle in the jungle, the conflict between American boys and an unseen enemy, between cumbersome Goliaths and wily Davids. No room in this version for mass slaughter by B-52s and napalm, the death squads of the pacification programme or the airborne intoxication of Agent Orange. In the Hollywood version Vietnam's horror is displaced by America's.

Unknowingly the sailors on board the *Patriot* and the *Salvor* were a part of the process. 'They've never had a chance to experience what modern Vietnam is about,' Captain Brawley told the media. 'They only get the impression from Hollywood movies and history books.' The ships were in town for five days, long enough for the 180 sailors on board to celebrate American Independence Day. And what better way to mark the occasion than with a trip to the Cu Chi tunnels, the battleground where, between 1966 and 1970, Viet Cong guerrillas had inflicted grievous casualties on the US 25th Infantry Division, where the wily Davids had run rings around the cumbersome Goliaths? A diver on board the *Salvor*, Jon Sommers from the Alaskan city of Anchorage, told reporters he 'was thinking of doing a tour there, maybe taking some pictures'.[1] Vietnam would remain a war movie to him and his shipmates.

It was the fourth visit by the US Navy to Vietnam since the two countries began developing a military side to their relationship in late 2003. The last visit before that had been the airlift from what was then still Saigon at the end of April 1975. But no one was mentioning that – certainly not the Vietnamese side. The official welcoming party was led by Colonel Dang Phuc Hoa, and his official welcoming comment was that 'The visit will continue to consolidate the bilateral relations that will facilitate the fight against terrorism as well as ensure security in the region and in Vietnam.' Vietnam doesn't really have a problem with terrorism, nor is it much of an issue in the South China Sea, but it is something that both sides can agree to fight against without much controversy. Regional security, on the other hand, is slightly more delicate.

The ships' visit was sandwiched between a pair of more conventional diplomatic delegations. The then US Defense Secretary Donald Rumsfeld had been the month before and the head of US Pacific Command would arrive two weeks later. Rumsfeld's visit was no whistle-stop. Even in mid-2006, with the Iraq and Afghanistan conflicts raging, he found time to spend two nights in Hanoi. There was clearly some sensitivity about the whole event, though. Ta Minh Tuan, an analyst with the Foreign Ministry's think-tank, put it this way: 'Vietnam is very careful to manage its relationship with the United States and China. Vietnam doesn't want to arouse any anxieties from the Chinese so they try to keep it low profile.' But that wasn't the only reason. Even 30 years after the end of the war the presence of a US Defense Secretary was still a sensitive issue for many Vietnamese, both in the leadership and outside.

On the surface, Hanoians appeared quite sanguine about Rumsfeld's presence. Even on Kham Thien Street, which was devastated in the Christmas bombing of December 1972, no one was prepared to openly criticise someone who was part of the Nixon Administration at the time. The street is now a typical Hanoi thoroughfare, lined with a haphazard collection of four- and five-storey buildings, a riot of neon signs and a vast cobweb of electrical cables. The 20,000 tonnes of bombs dropped in the 11 days of the Christmas bombing killed about 1,300 civilians in Hanoi, but the only physical evidence of the night which brought mayhem to this part of the city is an austere memorial on the south side of the road, set back behind locked metal gates. People who reached the shelters on Kham Thien Street that evening still remember the terror and then the bewilderment of emerging several hours later into a flattened neighbourhood they could no longer recognise. Eighty-two-year-old Dung Ha was one of them. But though he describes those who ordered the bombing as 'bad people' he looks to the future, not the past. 'If I had a chance to talk to Mr Rumsfeld I would say please come to Vietnam and open business more than with other countries. In terms of politics we have various kinds of points of view that are similar to the US, and other things in which we are not different from the US are the fields of love, economy and society.'

Even though he and others on the street spoke without the obvious presence of a government minder, the sentiments they uttered felt like a script. They were the lines repeated all over the country whenever a foreigner, particularly a journalist, asks about the past. Those who don't want to repeat them don't say anything at all. In an alley behind the memorial sat an old lady who was in the shelter when the bombs hit. She wouldn't give her name. 'That night I was so scared that I forgot everything, I lost my memory. My family only returned to this place after the signing of the peace agreement because I was so scared. Everybody was terrified. The whole place was flattened and we could hardly find the way to come back.' Her response to terror was amnesia. When asked what she might say if ever she met Donald Rumsfeld, her response was silence. 'I am too old and I don't know what I would say to him.' And her opinions about the United States? 'I am very simple, I don't think much. Much bombing and many people killed.' Her silence was more eloquent than her neighbours' clichés.

It's true that younger generations are more optimistic and outward-looking. A woman in her twenties, Chan Thu Wah, selling counterfeit American jeans on Kham Thien Street, was typical. 'We look forward to closing the past and opening the future. Vietnam's young generation is dynamic and smart and if they have the chance to study in the United States I hope the US government will recognise their ability. The US is the most powerful economy in the world and it also has the highest level of human development.' The vast majority of Vietnam's population have no direct memory of the war. Most have little indirect memory either. Few parents talk to their children about what they really experienced. Some just prefer to forget the trauma but there's also a deliberate strategy of 'official forgetting'. Even as TV dramas trot out the tired old tropes of virtuous communist fighters battling perfidious oppressors, novels that portray the genuine horrors of the conflict, such as Bao Ninh's *Sorrow of War*, are ignored, and any attempt to find a wrinkle in the sanitised story of ever-better relations with the United States is squashed flat. Expressions of individual memories of the war have been suppressed in the officially approved history.

In August 2006 the *Los Angeles Times* published details of an early 1970s Pentagon investigation which found evidence that every US army division to serve in Vietnam between 1965 and 1973 had committed war crimes. The accusations were extensive: in addition to the 1968 massacre at My Lai, army investigators confirmed 320 incidents in which almost 200 civilians were killed and many more injured, tortured or sexually assaulted. The investigation had also received allegations from soldiers in the 9th Infantry Division in the Mekong Delta, that their units had killed more than 10,000 civilians in less than a year during Operation Speedy Express. Taken together it amounted to as clear an indictment of the American military's behaviour during the war as could ever be expected to come from official US sources. It wouldn't have been hard for the Vietnamese government to condemn atrocities against civilians or to call for a thorough investigation and prosecution of those responsible. But this was the official response from its spokesman. 'In the past thirty years the country has been rebuilt. However we still have much to do to overcome difficulties. The people of Vietnam shall never forget but in our policy of living in peace we look to the future. The important thing is that we should try to prevent the recurrence of such a tragedy.'[2]

But the official 'policy of living in peace' *has* required forgetting. When Senator John McCain was running for the US presidency in 2008, the Foreign Ministry's Press Centre facilitated trips by several overseas journalists to meet the people who claimed to have rescued him when he was shot down over Hanoi in 1967 and who guarded him while he was in prison. Unsurprisingly, the official history they presented was bland and benign. Reporters from Associated Press, Agence France-Presse, CNN, the BBC, Al-Jazeera, the *Washington Post*, and the *International Herald Tribune* were taken to meet Colonel Tran Trong Duyet, who was in charge of the 'Hanoi Hilton' – the Hoa Lo Prison where McCain and the other POWs were kept until their release in 1973. The story he wove them was classic 'official forgetting': the prisoners were well treated, had enjoyed friendly relations with the guards and now everyone was looking to the future. But a Hanoi-based journalist, Matt Steinglass, went further and patiently tried to track down some of McCain's other captors.[3] One, whom Matt had previously interviewed, just disappeared, and his employer, the Veterans' Association, claimed to have no knowledge of him. Then, a few weeks later, Matt met the man, still in his official capacity with the Veterans' Association, at a US Embassy function. A third man declined to comment other than to call McCain ungrateful. A couple of days later Matt discovered he'd been taken to hospital with dangerously high blood pressure. The stress of recalling unwanted memories had perhaps been too much for him.

Many Vietnamese who fought the war find themselves trapped in voiceless rage. They know why they fought, they know what they and their fellows suffered, they know how unjust it felt – but they're banned from expressing any of it in public because the Party has decided that the country needs the support and resources of the United States. To tell the truth would damage the relationship. Trapped in the middle, they must remain silent or disappear. The sheer monstrosity of the war: the industrial-scale killing, the deployment of technologies which inflicted such long-term harm for so little short-term gain, the grotesque distortions wrought upon bodies and environment and the unimaginable psychological torment of its participants – the monstrosity which makes it so hard for Americans to reconcile themselves to their past involvement with Vietnam demands, in consequence, that Vietnamese must forget it as the price of 'normalisation'. If the atrocities had been the actions of a few rogue soldiers, apologies might be easier to make. But the awfulness of the most grievous aspects of US involvement in Vietnam is that they were *state policy* and that is far more difficult to apologise for.

What is Vietnam getting to make all this forgetting worthwhile?[4] In short, its basic needs: development and security. Without normalisation with the US the country would still be languishing under an economic embargo, starved of World Bank and most other multilateral aid, outside the WTO and missing out on billions of dollars' worth of foreign investment. It might also have become a vassal of China. Vietnam has traded the memories of its recent past for the promise of a prosperous and secure future. Vietnam's teenagers and university students have few qualms about the deal. They openly idolise the United States and its icons. When the head of Microsoft, Bill Gates, visited Hanoi in April 2006, so many university students climbed into the trees to watch him arrive on the campus of the Economics University that branches collapsed. A few months later, when then US Treasury Secretary Henry Paulson came to speak at the same hall, the place was packed out with hundreds of eager-eyed students desperate to learn how to become a successful investment banker. Paulson blew them away. He took off his jacket, rolled up his sleeves, spoke without notes and walked among the students taking their questions. Under a banner proclaiming that 'The Communist Party of Vietnam will be glorious for ever' (found in almost every public building), he extolled the virtues of study, enterprise and a good work–life balance. The contrast with the usual dry fodder the students usually receive in their lectures was sufficient to win another thousand converts to the American cause. But relations between Vietnam and the United States are not 'normal', and so long as the official forgetting continues, they never will be. These issues appear quiet now but, just as the 'comfort women' came back to haunt Japanese–Korean relations 50 years after the end of the Second World War, perhaps subsequent generations of Vietnamese will one day make them noisy again. Once their basic needs are met, the students applauding Hank Paulson may one day come to take a different view of his country.

* * *

Forgetting and remembering are integral to Vietnam's other key strategic relationship, the one with China. But if good ties with the US depend on suppressing memories, Vietnam's turbulent relationship with China stems from their reinvention. The similarities between Chinese and Vietnamese cultures are easily apparent, particularly when compared to the differences between Vietnamese cultures and those in the rest of 'Indochina'. Yet in what Charles Dickens once called 'the narcissism of minor difference' the country more or less defines itself in opposition to China. Most of the main streets in Vietnamese cities are named after heroes and heroines, real or mythical, who fought the Chinese: Hai Ba Trung, the two Trung sisters who led a rebellion in AD 40; Ngo Quyen, whom Vietnamese regard as the first ruler to separate the country from 'China' in 938; Ly Thuong Kiet who fought the Sung in 1076; Tran Hung Dao who defeated the Mongols in 1284; Le Loi/Le Thai To who defeated the Ming in 1428; and Nguyen Hue/Quang Trung who defeated the Qing in 1789. Most of this is anachronistic myth. At no point until 1979 did two countries corresponding to the present borders of 'Vietnam' and 'China' go to war against each other. Conflicts in previous millennia were mostly battles pitching rebels, regional lords and self-proclaimed kings against various empires and raiders from the north. All, however, have been subsumed into the twentieth-century nationalist myth of a transcendent Vietnam forged in the crucible of resistance against China.

Even the name of the country was generated in opposition to China. In 1802 Gia Long, the first Emperor of the Nguyen Dynasty, had wanted to call his new country 'Nam Viet'. But the Chinese Emperor objected. To him, *Nam Viet* – southern Viet – implied a territorial claim on 'northern Viet', the provinces of south-western China incorporated into the Han Empire long before. The Chinese Emperor insisted the new country be called *Viet Nam* – meaning 'to the south of Viet'. The Nguyen reluctantly agreed but then unilaterally chose to use a different name, *Dai Nam* – the Great South – in their own documents in preference to the one imposed upon them by China.[5] The name 'Viet Nam' was revived by nationalists in the early twentieth century, mainly in opposition to the French division of the country into three: the two protectorates Tonkin and Annam, and their colony, Cochin China.

These nationalists took a very different view of China than their ancestors. Throughout most of the twentieth century Vietnamese nationalists and communists repeatedly took sanctuary and inspiration from China. Without Chinese support from the 1940s up until the end of the 'American War', the Vietnamese communists would not have prevailed. But at the grass roots, even their best efforts to promote harmony between the peoples failed. In the early 1970s schoolchildren were taught a song with lyrics of comradeship: 'Vietnam and China are connected by rivers and mountains . . . they are like lips and teeth . . . when the lips are parted the teeth feel the cold'. But by the end of the decade, with the two countries at war, the lyrics had been unofficially changed. 'Vietnam and China are like connecting courtyards . . . they share a toilet and quarrel over the deposits. The Chinese always want a larger share.' Underlying concerns about China's geopolitical manoeuvrings is simple prejudice. The Chinese community in Vietnam calls themselves *Viet Hoa*. Most Vietnamese from the Kinh ethnic majority refer to Chinese as *tau* – a derogatory word which could be translated into English as 'chink'. The term applies equally to the country's own Chinese minority *ba tau* and to Chinese over the border, *bon tau*. These are not hidden terms; they are part of everyday conversations. The prejudice comes from fear. Vietnamese see themselves as more creative and cultured than the Chinese, but unable to compete with the impenetrable network of Chinese business interests. They regard this seemingly closed community with its alleged tentacles stretching all around East Asia as destined to take over the whole region.

Like the Red River, which brings both nourishment and disaster from China into Vietnam, the conflicted relationship between the countries' two communist parties has brought both succour and catastrophe to Vietnam. Communist China has at times treated communist Vietnam in a manner both their imperial predecessors would recognise. In the 1950s, Beijing pushed Hanoi to follow its land reform policies, with disastrous results. In the late 1960s, China tried to export its 'Cultural Revolution' to Vietnam via the thousands of advisers it had sent there, but this time Hanoi resisted.[6] During the early stages of the 'American War' the Chinese leadership wanted Vietnam to fight a prolonged 'people's war' to keep the US bogged down, rather than negotiate an end to the fighting. But after Beijing opened relations with the US in 1972, and it became obvious that Hanoi would win the war, the Chinese position changed: they opposed Vietnamese unification.[7] But the Vietnamese, while still trying to keep China's vital support for its war effort, refused to give in to these changing demands; they didn't want to be China's buffer state.

Instead, Hanoi courted greater support from the Soviet Union and tried to distance itself from China. But almost as soon as the war was won in 1975, the Vietnamese leadership became over-confident. With the USSR bankrolling it,

Vietnam could pay less and less attention to the demands of Beijing. China, locked in its own conflict with the USSR since the late 1950s, began to fear it was being encircled. In 1978 Vietnam joined a 'pro-Soviet' arc of countries on China's borders stretching from Russian Vladivostok, through Central Asia and on to Afghanistan, India and Southeast Asia. Vietnam, on the other hand, feared that it too was being encircled as China developed relations with the Khmer Rouge in Cambodia. Backed by the Soviet Union, Hanoi acted with ever greater arrogance towards Beijing: ignoring its protests against its military alliance with the USSR, against the ill-treatment of Chinese citizens resident in Vietnam, against the increasing number of armed clashes on their shared border and then, as things became worse, against Hanoi's assertions of sovereignty over the Paracel and Spratly Islands in the South China Sea.[8]

China, of course, was not an innocent in this process. In particular, its support for the Khmer Rouge rulers of Cambodia had facilitated genocide there and a series of increasingly bloody attacks on Vietnam. In Christmas 1978, in response to the deaths of hundreds, perhaps thousands of civilians in cross-border raids, the Vietnam People's Army invaded Cambodia and overthrew the Khmer Rouge. In an attempt both to relieve the pressure on its Khmer Rouge allies and to punish Vietnam for its insubordination (and having received a green light from Washington),[9] China then invaded northern Vietnam in February 1979, famously 'to teach them a lesson'. But it was the Chinese who learnt things the hard way. The battle-hardened Vietnamese halted the Chinese advance and forced them to retreat. The relatively recent building projects in Lao Cai and many other northern Vietnamese towns are evidence of the destruction wrought by the Chinese as they left. The Chinese then continued the war by other means: backing the Khmer Rouge guerrilla war in Cambodia and increasing tension in the South China Sea until, in 1988, the two sides fought a brief naval battle there.

But by the late 1980s Vietnam was in crisis. The occupation of Cambodia and the need to guard the northern border had caused the regular army to grow to 1.25 million soldiers. One US estimate put military spending at almost a fifth of GDP in 1985.[10] War was bleeding the country dry. Something had to be done. With Mikhail Gorbachev introducing perestroika it became obvious that the Soviet Union wasn't prepared to bankroll Vietnam indefinitely. A change of policy was required.

The then Foreign Minister, Nguyen Co Thach, and his allies argued that the main threat facing the country was economic backwardness and that overcoming it would require co-operation with the sources of international finance and technology – the West. His approach was endorsed by the Politburo in May 1988. Its still-secret Resolution 13 approved a 'multi-directional orientation' for the country in place of its single reliance on the USSR.[11] It was a dramatic change and could have been a moment for Vietnam to join the capitalist camp, but this initial opening was overtaken by events. In September 1989, two months after the crushing of the Tiananmen Square protests in Beijing and amid the collapse of communist regimes in Eastern Europe, the Party hierarchy was gripped by the fear that Vietnam would be next. General Secretary Nguyen Van Linh told the Central Committee that its priority was to defend socialism and that those who believed in the good intent of the United States were 'naïve'.

By the summer of 1990, different parts of the leadership were heading in different directions. Foreign Minister Thach camped out in New York for several weeks hoping to meet US government officials. It wasn't until the end of September that he finally got to meet Secretary of State James Baker. By then it was too late. He'd already been outflanked by the old guard. On 2 September General Secretary Linh, Prime Minister Do Muoi and his predecessor and Party *éminence grise,* Pham Van Dong, had absented themselves from their own Independence Day celebrations and flown to Chengdu to meet Chinese leaders for the first time since the mid-1970s. The leadership 'officially forgot' the previous decade of antagonism, agreed to all China's demands for a solution in Cambodia, and made peace with Beijing in preference to Washington. The following year, at the Seventh Party Congress, Thach was dismissed from the Politburo.

However, in spite of Thach's exit, the modernisers still won concessions. The Congress endorsed both hostility to the imperialist West and also the policy of 'diversification' previously approved by the Politburo. The two-faced foreign policy continued at a crucial meeting of the Central Committee in June 1992. It ordained a hierarchy of countries – with communist friends like China, Cuba and North Korea at the top and the United States at the bottom – but also specified the country's top foreign policy priorities as regional co-operation and better relations with the world's economic powers. The gestures were in the direction of communist solidarity but the real movement was towards international integration. Within three years Vietnam had both joined the Association of Southeast Asian Nations (ASEAN) and established diplomatic relations with the United States. There were still big limits to relations with the old capitalist enemy, in particular over security co-operation. But then, on 7 March 1997, China pushed Vietnam into the arms of the US. It sent an oil-drilling platform, the Kantan III, into an area of the Gulf of Tonkin claimed by both it and Vietnam. In response the Vietnamese summoned all the ambassadors of ASEAN states to a briefing and then, in a ground-breaking step, it invited the Commander-in-Chief of US Pacific Command, Admiral Joseph Prueher, to visit Hanoi. A week after that visit, the Chinese withdrew the oil rig. A new phase in Vietnam's international relations had begun.

The Vietnamese elite are well aware of the realities of their relationship with China. The whole country is about the size of a single Chinese province, it depends upon Chinese imports for much of its industrial output and consumer needs and China has a larger and more sophisticated military. A full-scale confrontation would be disastrous. But Vietnam still has interests to defend; in particular its claims to territory and resources in the South China Sea. As a result it has chosen which battles to fight, and when, very carefully. In almost all of them it has lost ground in the short term, in the hope of picking up gains later. In 1990, for example, it conceded key points to China over the settlement in Cambodia. That allowed Hanoi to improve relations with the rest of Southeast Asia and remove the justification for the international economic embargo it was suffering under. The deal with China led, step by step, to a huge increase in foreign investment in Vietnam and a leap in economic development, and strengthened the Party's rule. But in subsequent years Vietnam has outmanoeuvred China's allies in Cambodia and ensured the government remains firmly pro-Hanoi. Short-term losses led to long-term gains.

The same kind of calculation seems to have taken place over the northern border. When the two countries agreed a deal on the penultimate day of 1999, the Vietnamese side conceded 114 square kilometres which China had gained by force in 1979.[12] The result caused a wave of anger in the country, and prompted a crackdown on dissidents who openly disagreed with the decision. But in return for the loss of a strip of mountainous forest, Vietnam was able to reduce tension, and its military presence, on the land frontier, open up cross-border trade and pay more attention to its other security issues. The benefits far outweighed the costs. Since then Vietnam and China have also agreed a border in the Gulf of Tonkin, a fisheries agreement and, in April 2006, the start of joint naval patrols in the area.

But tensions remain in the relationship; indeed, there remains a strong possibility of open hostility. Two issues stand out. One is quiet now but may prove to be more significant in the long run. Beijing is taking a greater interest in the Mekong River, which begins its course under Chinese control and ends it under Vietnamese. China is building up to 15 dams on the Mekong and its tributaries, which already appear to be reducing its flow. The other issue is the ownership of two island archipelagos in the South China Sea: the Paracels and, in particular, the Spratlys. Straddling China's main trading routes, thought to be rich in oil reserves and laden with contested history, the islands have become a focus for popular as well as official anger. On Sunday, 9 December 2007, Vietnam witnessed something it hadn't seen for more than 30 years – street demonstrations by angry nationalists. China had just announced it was incorporating the Paracels, Spratlys and another set of islands into a new local authority. This county-level department was, in China's eyes, responsible for about 2.5 million square kilometres of sea – its frontiers stretching as far as the coasts of the Philippines and Malaysia. Pulled together by emails, text messages and unofficial websites, around 250 people, mainly students, male and female, gathered in front of the Chinese Embassy, chanting 'Down with China' and waving Vietnamese flags. The protest was scrappy but passionate and seemed to be entirely spontaneous. There were no cadres marshalling people, and police treated foreign journalists with just as much suspicion as usual.

The Party appeared to have decided to allow the protest rather than provoke a confrontation in front of all the tourists visiting the military museum opposite. It also served a useful purpose, reminding the Chinese government that Vietnam was under pressure to defend its interests. The protests carried on for two more Sundays in both Hanoi and Ho Chi Minh City but became more orchestrated – with what were probably members of the Youth Union turning up in matching T-shirts bearing slogans condemning Chinese hegemony. The Party took control of the protests and allowed them to fizzle out. But before they were done, they'd been copied by overseas Vietnamese communities in the US, Australia, France and the UK. For once, all Vietnamese appeared united. If there's one thing the global Vietnamese community can agree on, it's a dislike of China.

* * *

China and the United States are not just countries that Vietnam has to balance; they are symbols of the two broad currents running within its leadership – one which favours more integration with the outside world, the other more suspicious of it. The integrationists' home is a bland block on a side street off one of the six-lane boulevards in the new university district of western Hanoi. There the Diplomatic Academy of Vietnam trains the Foreign Ministry's diplomats and thinks about the country's future. Ta Minh Tuan, from its Centre for European and American Studies, exemplifies its outlook: young, open-minded and comfortable discussing with foreigners issues that were once considered state secrets. His explanation of why Vietnam is pursuing closer ties with the US is, more or less, the modernisers' manifesto. 'Our policy is to maintain a peaceful international environment for our economic development and the US can play a very important role in that. People tend to think that the US is trying to lure Vietnam into its influence, to do some sort of counterbalance towards China, but I would say it's not true. Our consistent policy is to keep balanced relations between Vietnam and China, and Vietnam and the States. The US plays a very important role in this region and if we want to develop there must be closer, greater co-operation with the US. We need investment, we need security, we need friends and I think we're on the right track at the moment. The US can be a good partner.'

This is something which former Prime Minister Vo Van Kiet understood well. It was he who developed the idea that Vietnam must 'enmesh' as many international actors in Vietnam as possible. He argued that, rather than fearing foreign countries, Vietnam should engage with them. By uniting their interests with those of the Party, they would help protect both the country's independence and the Party's control of the country. And so it has come to pass. Compare Vietnam's position with that of Burma/Myanmar. Both are one-party states intent on remaining in power and both have regional strategic significance. But while Burma is subject to high-profile pressure from Europe and the US, Vietnam is receiving billions of dollars in foreign aid and investment. No US administration is likely to jeopardise the multibillion-dollar interests of Intel, Nike, Ford, GE and all the other US corporations who've invested in Vietnam, by pushing for change and instability. International capitalism is doing very nicely out of Communist Party rule in Vietnam and stability is a lot more important than the release of a very few troublesome dissidents. Vo Van Kiet died in 2008 but he must be chuckling loudly to himself in whichever part of the afterlife communist leaders end up.

The conservative wing of the Vietnamese leadership tends not to give interviews to journalists. Its supporters hide away in the security establishment, nurturing their suspicion of the outside world and their paranoia about imperialist plots. They see plots everywhere, in particular the threat of 'peaceful evolution' – nefarious plans by 'hostile forces' to undermine communism through 'soft' power and pressure to respect human rights. They can be forgiven: paranoia has served them well in the past. The revolutionary movement's success against the French, the Democratic Republic of Vietnam's survival in the face of superpower firepower and the Socialist Republic of Vietnam's continuing independence in spite of the plotting of its enemies are all evidence of that. American-based observers often express bewilderment at the degree of suspicion displayed by most Vietnamese policy-makers. But from Vietnam's position the suspicion is perfectly justified. The whole pre-1975 history of US involvement in Vietnam involved plotting, cajoling, lobbying, leveraging pressure and fomenting military coups – and that was just against Washington's nominal ally. The Vietnamese look at the contemporary experience of countries with close security ties to the US (Colombia, Egypt, Pakistan and the Philippines are good examples) and see loss of sovereignty, a distortion of national interests to favour Washington's and frequently the pursuit of short-term tactical gains which exacerbate systemic threats to the country's survival. Suspicion could be regarded as the proper and rational response to Washington's open-armed embrace.

The interplay, or even struggle, between these two groups – integrationists and conservatives – defines Vietnamese foreign policy, or more often the lack of it. Though these battles are about ideas, the fights aren't just ideological: both factions are seeking ways to remain in power in shifting circumstances. Some have decided the best way to preserve the regime (or just to preserve their own interests within it) is by maintaining a strong state and preserving an alliance with China in order to intimidate any potential adversary and resist change as much as possible. They find allies in the state-owned sector of the economy (who fear the consequences of freer trade) and the security forces. Their integrationist rivals believe the best way to remain in power is to open the economy, enmesh the country in the international political system and neutralise its adversaries. They find allies in the private sector and the

professional classes. The verbal battles between these groups employ the rhetoric of ideology – but these battles are as much about competing memories of
the past as they are about the present. There are still a few who talk the
language of anti-imperialism, and a very few who might still believe it, but this
language is now a cloak for other arguments. The real divisions are over tactics
rather than grand strategy, and cliques rather than ideology.

The paranoia of the hardliners/conservatives/security establishment
(call them what you will) has, at times, led them to bizarre conclusions. In
2003, following the US invasion of Iraq, some of them became convinced
that the all-powerful hegemon was about to do the same thing to Vietnam.
The American scholar Alexander Vuving interviewed several foreign policy
officials in Hanoi between April and September 2003 and found they were
much more concerned about a US invasion than about any other strategic
issue. At the same time, their rivals the modernisers were getting concerned
that US focus on Iraq was allowing China too much of a free hand in East
Asia.[13] The combined effect was possibly Vietnam's most crucial strategic
decision of recent years. At its Central Committee meeting in July 2003
the Party adopted a new 'Strategy of Fatherland Defence', formally
removing ideology from foreign policy. Countries were designated either
'partners' or 'objects of struggle' but these distinctions were based purely on
their attitude towards Vietnam rather than on their imperialist nature.[14]
Four months after the Central Committee vote, the Vietnamese Defence
Minister was visiting Washington and a US warship was making its first
port visit to Vietnam in 28 years. According to the then US Ambassador,
Raymond Burghardt, this was the moment when the two sides began to
discuss strategic issues.[15]

Things have moved on, slowly. Vietnam is being wooed by a succession
of American admirals in their best whites. Pacific commanders, fleet
commanders and a boatful of other senior officers have steered a course to
the grandiose new Ministry of Defence buildings in Hanoi. At each visit the
smiles get wider but the visits usually end with little substantive progress.
On his visit in January 2007, Admiral Gary Roughead, Commander of the
US Pacific Fleet, could only point to an offer to exchange information on
weather forecasting. Even combined search and rescue exercises, traditionally the thin end of the military co-operation wedge, appeared to be too
controversial. Admiral Roughead was adamant that he wasn't asking
Vietnam for access to the US Navy's former base at Cam Ranh Bay nor any

other basing rights. 'I have no desire for basing in Southeast Asia. We're bringing a nuclear-powered aircraft carrier into the Pacific, we're shifting submarines into the Pacific and we have our very responsive forward deployed force in Japan. We simply do not need that base structure in Southeast Asia.' But other analysts wonder why the US is making so much effort with Vietnam if it really isn't interested in basing. For its part, the top brass of the Vietnam People's Army has been happy to meet visiting admirals, even to attend conferences in Honolulu and San Diego. But its co-operation has been limited to hunting for missing servicemen from the war and the specific things it wants from the US: training and spare parts for all the American-made equipment it captured in 1975.

Military co-operation is now increasingly tied to movement on one of the most vexed issues between the two countries: the legacy of Agent Orange. Almost 80 million litres of Agent Orange and other defoliants were sprayed over Vietnam between 1961 and 1971. Based on a tactic used by the British in Malaya, the chemicals were used to kill vegetation around military bases, reveal Communist supply lines and deny cover to potential ambushers. Most of the defoliant used was contaminated with dioxin – one of the most toxic chemicals ever made. US records suggest that 2.6 million hectares were sprayed with defoliant, that more than half were sprayed at least four times and that between two and five million people were sprayed directly.[16] In at least 42 cases, emergencies meant that entire plane loads, 120,000 litres, were dumped in 30 seconds instead of the usual four to five minutes. Anyone underneath could have been soaked in dioxin.

The Peace Village outside Hanoi is one of 12 across Vietnam which look after thousands of children born with serious disabilities blamed on dioxin poisoning. Their parents either lived or fought in areas that were sprayed and later, sometimes years later, gave birth to children without eyes, limbs or organs, or with oversized heads, extra joints or serious mental disabilities. The Peace Villages are just the tip of the iceberg. Many tens of thousands of disabled children are kept out of sight by their ashamed parents in villages and towns where they get little or no therapeutic treatment and where the burden of care is so great that families usually remain mired in poverty. The link between dioxin poisoning and disease is well established in the West but the link between being sprayed with defoliant in Vietnam and becoming ill is strongly contested by those with the most to lose: the US government and the chemical companies that made the defoliants, in particular Dow and Monsanto. No US court has yet upheld a connection. In 1984 chemical companies agreed to pay $180 million (later increased) in an out of court settlement to American war veterans but without admitting liability. Fifty-eight thousand people received payouts from the chemical companies – averaging $3,800 each. In 1991 the US Congress directed the US Department of Veterans Affairs to pay benefits to vets suffering from a specified list of dioxin-related disorders – including spina bifida among their children. In 2000, benefits were being paid to 7,520 people. None of this has been extended to those Vietnamese who were in the same place at the same time.

In 2007 the US government conceded at last that it did indeed have some liability for dioxin contamination in Vietnam – but only for sites where defoliants were stored, not where they were sprayed. It's currently spending about $3 million a year to remove contaminated earth from the former airbase in Danang (now the city's international airport), to stop any more dioxin leaching into the local water supply. Further clean-ups are expected in two other former bases. It's not surprising that the US government has been reluctant to admit liability for the spraying of dioxin in Vietnam. If it were to take the same approach with the millions of Vietnamese who believe they have suffered health problems as a result of spraying as it did with its own veterans, the cost would easily reach several billion dollars. What's been more surprising has been the reluctance, until very recently, of the Vietnamese government to pursue the issue.

VAVA, the Vietnamese Association for Victims of Agent Orange, is not the main care-provider for people suffering dioxin poisoning; that's done, in so far as its resources will allow, by the Vietnamese Red Cross. VAVA is, in effect, the angry conscience of Vietnam finally coming to the surface. It was founded specifically to take a more combative role on the issue by those fractions of the Communist Party who felt the government was being too soft with the US. Hanoi was told early in the process of negotiating diplomatic relations with the United States that any attempt to link it to Agent Orange would get nowhere. While assistance with finding US soldiers Missing In Action was a priority for Washington, Hanoi wasn't allowed to discuss the mass poisoning of civilians. The contrast was obscene but Vietnam had little choice. The leadership wanted to end the country's diplomatic isolation so the whole dioxin issue was simply dropped. But unhappiness rose within parts of the military and the health establishment over the sidelining of the issue. Pressure began to build up from war veterans and others in the Party for something to be done. An initial attempt at a joint US–Vietnamese government investigation began in 2002, but fell apart amid rancour. The Vietnamese side was dominated by strong critics of the American conduct of the war and relations rapidly deteriorated. In 2003, with official progress blocked, they went away and founded VAVA to pursue the issue in a more aggressive way.

The group has good connections. Its Vice-President, Professor Nguyen Trong Nhan, is a former Minister of Health, a retired doctor who helps run the association in his spare time from his office in the Hanoi eye hospital. It gets little support from the government, though. To finance the legal action it's brought against Dow, Monsanto and the other chemical companies who produced defoliants, VAVA needs to organise concerts and other fund-raising efforts. Professor Nhan and the rest of VAVA take a combative approach to the issue. 'I'm continuing to help Agent Orange victims in Vietnam to sue chemical companies in the US,' he says. 'We're asking for compensation for the use of their products in Vietnam.' The actual case that VAVA brought in the Brooklyn District Court in New York City accused the chemical companies of war crimes. But it was a relatively simple defence for the companies to argue that the chemicals were not deployed intention-ally to harm civilians, nor were their side-effects widely known at the time. The case was rejected in 2005, at appeal in 2008 and finally by the US Supreme Court in 2009. More action is planned but the highly politicised approach that VAVA has taken, valid as it may be in the eyes of those it represents, is unlikely to convince an American court.

Neither has VAVA assembled enough expert evidence to prove a link between spraying and poor health. For Professor Nhan this just seems unnecessary. 'We estimate about three million people in Vietnam were victims of Agent Orange. We found they have very many serious diseases and there are many kinds of anomalies among their children and grand-children. Many years ago we examined the level of dioxin in blood and fat tissue with the help of laboratories in Germany, Russia and Japan and we know that the level of dioxin of these people was very high. But all scientists know that the level of dioxin in the body falls over time and that's why it's not necessary for the level of dioxin now to be very high to recognise the person as a victim of dioxin. We must recognise the people as victims if they were in the area where Agent Orange was sprayed.' This was not enough to convince the judges in New York and Washington. The court case has become little more than a diversion, to soak up the energies of those who would seek restitution from the United States. The Vietnamese government let VAVA and its supporters get on with the case while generally avoiding the issue itself.

But then, in late 2006, once Vietnam had completed negotiations to join the World Trade Organisation and the US Congress had approved Permanent Normal Trading Relations, the Vietnamese side realised that, at last, it had some leverage. A neat solution was found. Since it was the Vietnamese military pushing for tougher action, and since the US military was pushing for closer security relations, the Vietnamese government delegated the Agent Orange issue to the Ministry of Defence. If the US wants progress on military issues then it is going to have to make some concessions on Agent Orange. (Fortuitously, any lucrative research and remediation contracts will also have to go through the Ministry.) In November 2006 Agent Orange was discussed for the first time by the two countries' presidents and then in February 2007 the US announced it would fund the clean-up in Danang. The steps are small and the longer they take the fewer people will be eligible for any sort of compensation, but some progress is at last being made. The marginalisation of the more militant voices on the Vietnamese side, the ironing out of yet another wrinkle in the appearance of smooth relations, facilitated progress. Once again, difficult memories have been suppressed in the interests of a strategic *rapprochement* with the US.

* * *

If Vietnam's relations with the United States are characterised by repressed memories and those with China by invented ones, then a third group of relationships are characterised by recovered memories. Vietnamese leaders usually avoid the rhetoric of anti-imperialism now, but they still make use of links established in the Cold War. Vietnam continues to buy most of its military hardware from the old eastern bloc. Russia supplies ships, jet fighters and missiles, Ukraine has sold aircraft and upgraded naval vessels and Belarus provides sinister internal security equipment. Even NATO members Poland and the Czech Republic have sold Vietnam second-hand Soviet-built tanks.[17] The queues outside the Eastern European embassies tell the story of guest workers who went abroad, married and settled, of business links between import-exporters, of smuggling operations among extended families and of continuing ties between socialist parties of various hues.

Old ideological links are a significant part of Vietnam's two most significant military alliances: with Russia and with India. All three have declared themselves 'strategic partners' of the others.[18] Russia is Vietnam's biggest weapons provider and India is helping Vietnam to build up an indigenous arms manufacturing base.[19] They both have investments in Vietnam's offshore oil industry and they share several attributes which Vietnam finds attractive: they're large, they're players in the new multi-polar world, they're far away and they've both had conflicts with China. In other words, they'll assist Vietnam but they won't dominate it. Vietnam could be to India what Pakistan is to China: a partner on the border of its regional competitor. The Vietnamese military know the most likely location for any future conflict it might have to fight will be far offshore in the South China Sea, where it currently lacks the ability to project significant power. Both Russia and India have plenty of experience in projecting power at sea and they're both supplying Vietnam with ships and missiles. India's navy now makes port visits to Vietnam at least as often as the US.

Vietnam isn't seeking to turn these relationships into alliances of the kind it had with the USSR. Instead it wants to use them, and relations with other parts of the world, to prevent itself being sucked too closely into the orbit of either the US or China. An unpublished paper produced by the Institute of International Relations in Hanoi (the previous name for the Diplomatic Academy of Vietnam) put it this way:

> Given Vietnam's low profile on the agenda of great powers and the country's constraints in terms of strength and position, Vietnam by itself cannot establish a firm balance with China or the USA. Therefore, partnerships with Russia, India, Japan, EU and ASEAN . . . are all required as a counterweight to China and the US, thus striking a balance in the relations with these two powers.[20]

Of the five counterweights, ASEAN has proved the most significant. By joining the organisation and quickly resolving all its border disputes with ASEAN members (except its vexed sea border with Cambodia and those parts of the Spratlys dispute which involve Brunei and the Philippines)

Vietnam created a new set of allies to bolster its dealings with China. Once ASEAN and China agreed their 'Declaration of Conduct' in the South China Sea in 2002, the Spratlys dispute became an issue for ASEAN as a whole to discuss with China rather than Vietnam alone. In trade too, Vietnam has lobbied for ASEAN-wide agreements with China to mitigate the impact of the industrial superpower on its northern border. Of course, Hanoi continues to nurture its 'special relationship' with Beijing but, by involving ASEAN, Vietnam has increased the potential costs which China might incur if it sought to turn up the heat in the South China Sea.

Another 'counterweight', the European Union, has played a less significant role than Vietnam would have liked. The EU is as important to Vietnam's economy as the US: it receives almost as much of Vietnam's exports as the States (17 per cent and 18 per cent of the total respectively), provides almost as much investment as Japan (15 per cent and 17 per cent respectively) and a huge amount of development aid. European companies are big investors in oilfields, financial services and supermarkets. But Vietnam doesn't feature as high on the EU's list of priorities as the EU does on Vietnam's. For some time Vietnam has been pushing for a Partnership and Co-operation Agreement (PCA) with the EU. The two agreed a strategy paper in 2005 but the Vietnamese side wants something stronger. The EU is happy to go along with the idea but does not see it as a priority. 'It's not necessary,' says one European Commission diplomat. Part of the reason is that all PCAs must include six paragraphs defined by the European Parliament – including one on protecting human rights. This seems to be the sticking point for Hanoi. Nonetheless, Vietnam continues to seek a formal piece of paper to underscore its relationship with Europe, another counterweight to the gravitational pulls of the US and China.

* * *

Vietnam's attempts to find some kind of position between these various gravitational pulls epitomises the new multi-polar global order. It wants to give the big powers a stake in Vietnam's future but not too great an influence over it. Perhaps it would be helpful to see Vietnam, and in particular its elite, as motivated by competing xenophobias based upon rival memories of the past: between China the eternal oppressor and China the twentieth-century liberator, between America the twentieth-century destroyer and America the twenty-first century investor. One part of the country is familiar with the old world, with the Soviet Union and China and the old ways of doing things. They suffered during the 'American War' and found meaning in the calls for international socialism. Abandoning those dreams now is, for them, a betrayal of everything they and their dead comrades fought for during those glorious, miserable years. The other group is familiar with the West and enjoys the benefits of capitalism. They see China not as a guardian, but as a threat, and they believe international integration will bring both riches and greater security.

As more and more Vietnamese encounter the outside world, the integrationists are getting stronger. Official delegations, study tours, tourism and the influence of overseas Vietnamese are all changing the mindsets of the national leadership. They're sending their children to study in the West and doing deals with western businesses. It seems to be a one-way street. The last bastion of opposition appears to be the security apparatus. But who knows what will happen? It might seem, in its efforts to please everyone, in its breathtaking rush forward, that Vietnam is forgetting its past, suppressing the traumas of previous centuries. But in a country with an ancestors' altar in almost every home, the past is never totally suppressed. For decades the public presentation of the past has been efficiently managed by the Communist Party but the spread of new technologies is causing it to lose control. The dogged pursuit of the Agent Orange case and the spontaneous protests over the South China Sea suggest that memories are reappearing. Perhaps a younger generation might revive them and disrupt the smooth development of international relations. In the meantime no Vietnamese government could be stridently anti-US, nor overtly anti-China. Without the support of both, Vietnam's economy couldn't provide the jobs and rising living standards its people demand. Then the regime's survival would be in jeopardy and that's far more important than the preservation of anyone's memories: real or imagined.

10

Schisms and divisions

Nguyen Thi Nhu Hoa's finger hovered over the return key. When her finger came down she would break a national taboo, set off a furious online 'blog war' and reveal long-suppressed tensions in Vietnamese society. This wasn't her plan. All she wanted to do was share a few home truths about the differences between her home town of Saigon and the capital, Hanoi. All her life she'd heard about Hanoi, beautiful Hanoi, home of the nation, its source of culture. And then, in November 2006, she went there. She couldn't believe her eyes. She saw 'dirty and ugly streets . . . old fashioned motorbikes . . . slow internet connections . . . bad food . . . slow service' and a deep lack of sophistication. She told her online readers it was no place for a trendy young Saigonese. Her blog entry was called 'Fucking Ha Loi', a scathing reference to the accents of provincial northerners who pronounce 'n' as 'l'. Adding further insult, the change of letter changed the meaning of Hanoi's name from 'inside the river' to 'wading in the dirty river'.

Nhu Hoa, one of the millions of young Vietnamese posting their thoughts on the Yahoo 360 site, offered her comments under the nickname 'Be Crys' – Little Crys. But it wasn't long before news of her blog spread and her real identity was revealed. Crys/Nhu Hoa was a 17-year-old pupil at Saigon's highly respected 'Secondary School for the Talented', a state-run college which only accepts the cream of the academic crop. It's intended to mould the future elite – the high achievers of tomorrow. She was a very middle-class rebel. Within days, around 9,000 comments had been posted on her site: a real blog war was under way. She was bewildered by the attention. All she'd done was say what everyone already knew. The difference, of course, was that she'd done it in public.

Her shocked reaction to the 'backwardness' of the capital (a 'backwardness' – it's worth saying – which most foreigners find charming) was provoked by the sudden collapse, in her eyes, of the image created by years of official propaganda. That image was sustainable so long as travel restrictions and poverty kept people confined to their locality, but more and more Vietnamese are travelling around the country and discovering the contrasts between north and south. However, the taboos against openly discussing them remain strong. The trauma of the war, the fear of reopening a split in the nation is too strong among the older generations. It took a 17-year old to prick the national bubble.

Hanoi's assumed supremacy is the basis of the collection of stories which make up what is, in effect, the officially approved national Vietnamese history. The 'Official History' teaches Vietnamese that the spiritual home of their country is the north and that the south only became a part of the national story once northerners arrived there just a few centuries ago. Even the official name of the majority ethnic group, 'Kinh', implies northernness – it's derived from *kinh do*, meaning 'capital'. This national myth predates Communist Party rule, but is one of its main buttresses. Its maintenance helps legitimise Hanoi's dominance over the reunified country, but it's also a major reason why significant minorities maintain grievances against the majority.

In the 'Official History', Vietnam was born in the third century BCE when ethnic groups with a unique 'Vietnamese' identity settled in the northern Red River Delta. In this version, the 'Vietnamese' Kinh maintained their uniqueness through centuries of Chinese colonial rule before emerging as an independent people with their own state in 938 CE. In subsequent centuries they gradually extended their rule – and the lands of Vietnam – southwards, a period officially referred to as the 'March to the South'. The account is a classic 'founding myth', a national story with an ideological purpose. Historical evidence shows that Vietnam's development was considerably more complex. Different rulers controlled different parts of the country, empires ebbed and flowed, and relations with China varied over time. No state called 'Viet Nam' existed in Indochina until Emperor Gia Long declared one in 1802 (and even he had wanted to call it something different) nor was there a coherent sense among the population that they were part of a country called 'Viet Nam' until well into the twentieth century.

Most problematically, this history of Vietnam suggests that the centre and the south were empty lands until the Kinh arrived. In fact, they were controlled by two different civilisations for centuries. The Cham, an Indian-influenced people following Hinduism and later Islam, ruled central and parts of southern 'Vietnam' from approximately 200 CE until 1471. Some parts of the Cham held out much longer. One corner of south-eastern Vietnam, around Ninh Thuan province, only became part of 'Vietnam' in 1832. The rest of the south was home to the Khmer. They controlled the Mekong Delta and areas adjacent to it, including what became Saigon, until they were forced out by advancing 'Vietnamese' forces. Saigon itself became an outpost of the 'Vietnamese' court in 1698 while still formally a part of the Khmer Empire, and was captured by France in 1859. At most, the settlement was part of an independent 'Vietnam' for just 161 years. All this suggests that the history of the Cham and the Khmer should be seen as just as important a part of the history of Vietnam as that of the various groups which controlled the north, but that isn't the view of the 'Official History'.

Significant Cham and Khmer minorities remain in southern Vietnam with quite different interpretations of their history. The Khmer in particular continue to nurse grievances against their marginalisation by the Kinh. They still call themselves Khmer Krom – 'lower Khmer' – separated from the 'upper Khmer' in Cambodia. Almost all that remains of the Cham empires which ruled southern Vietnam for more than a millennium are huge brick towers around the city of Nha Trang (some of which have recently been officially vandalised in the guise of 'restoration') and a museum of fabulous sculpture in the city of Danang. There are just over 130,000 Cham people left, mainly Muslim, scattered across the south. Other minorities feel similarly excluded from the 'Official History'. In the Central Highlands and the mountains of the north-west, dozens of ethnic groups have completely different interpretations of the past, speak different languages and feel minimal connection to Hanoi.

To be fair, Hanoi has made great efforts to accommodate the country's minorities. From its beginnings in the 1930s the Communist Party recognised their existence and their rights – something which other countries in Southeast Asia – Thailand and Laos, for example – long failed to do. But since the establishment of the state the dominant attitude has been patronising. The authorities regularly describe minority peoples as 'backward' and introduce policies to 'civilise' them by 'developing' their agriculture and banning their customs – with effects which that become familiar from other examples of similar civilising missions around the world: community break-down, resentment and occasional outbreaks of anti-state violence.

* * *

The presence of a sizeable population of minorities (around 15 per cent of the national total) is one reason for the strong sense of solidarity among the majority Kinh. The founding myth – the belief that Vietnam was forged in struggle against outsiders and needs to be defended – remains strong. But there are plenty of differences among the Kinh, most often expressed in jokes. The punchlines vary but the themes are constant. Southerners are open-minded and generous, northerners are conservative and cold, and people from the centre are hard-headed and tight-fisted. In one, a boy drops a bottle of fish sauce in the market: a northerner tells him off for being care-less, a southerner gives him the money to buy a new bottle and someone from the centre crawls around with a spoon trying to collect the drops.

Such stereotypes are always exaggerated but they do tell us something about life in different parts of the country. Life is easier in the south. The fertile soils of the deltas have created abundance and its different civilisations have created vigorous trading networks and prosperity. Harsh living conditions in the centre of the country are a major reason why people are so poor and one reason often given for the political success of so many who come from the region. Environmental differences like these aren't the sole reason for different political cultures in different parts of the country, but it is striking that society is organised in quite different ways in different places. In the north, where the flow of the Red River is fatally unpredictable, villages evolved in ways which would help them survive both drought and flood. Even now, they tend to be walled, centralised communities managed by hierarchical institutions with strong and conservative rules of behaviour. The flow of the Mekong, however, is quite different. The natural reservoir of the Ton Le Sap, the vast expanding and contracting lake in the centre of Cambodia, restrains the Mekong's flow – absorbing the excess in the wet season and releasing it during the dry, making flooding and drought less problematic. It's too simplistic to say that this is the only reason why villages in the Mekong Delta tend to be more open and less hierarchical and society less conservative, but it is clearly a part of the explanation.

Both Hanoi and Saigon are built on rivers but Hanoi has turned away from the mighty stream at its back door. The Red River's unpredictable flow has created a ribbon of blighted territory along its banks occupied by the poor and marginal. The city faces inwards, clustering around the lakes in its centre, a giant version of the walled villages in its hinterland. Symbolically it seems to be keeping outside influences to a minimum. In Saigon, the river is the city's focus: the trade and new ideas it brings are welcomed into the heart of the city. The Saigon River has brought merchants here for centuries, making it both entrepôt and melting pot, home to mosques and Hindu temples as well as pagodas and churches. It also brought French colonialism to Saigon earlier and established it more thoroughly than in the rest of the country.

Cochinchina, comprising Saigon and the Mekong Delta, was annexed as a French colony while the rest of the country remained nominally under the rule of the Nguyen monarchy – albeit 'protected' by France. While the distinction might not have been obvious to the average peasant, Cochinchina was under French law; which meant there was, for example, greater freedom of the press. The colonial economy – plantations, commodity markets and globalisation – penetrated society more quickly and more deeply than in the north or centre. Combine all these factors with the later arrival of the Kinh people, and their mixing with the pre-existing Cham, Khmer and other populations, and it's easy to see how a society with a structure and outlook quite different to other parts of the country could have evolved. Sometimes though, this is overstated, particularly by those who still seek to justify an old war.

The biggest untruth of the 'American War' was that it was a fight between one country called North Vietnam and another called South Vietnam. It was not. It was a fight between two political elites, both of which claimed sovereignty over the whole country, but had different visions of its future. One was based in Hanoi, the other in Saigon, but that was intended (by the 1954 Geneva peace accords) to be a temporary arrangement, pending national elections; not a formal partition of the country. It's strange that this very basic fact needs to be stated so baldly, but the weight of Cold War propaganda has left such a deep impression upon so many people that it colours their views of the country to this day. Vietnam is not a homogeneous country, and this chapter is about the schisms and divisions which lurk behind the official façade of unity – but neither is it one which has been eternally divided at the middle, nor one whose existence is threatened by a contemporary clash of civilisations. The Vietnamese combatants in the Vietnam-American War were not fighting because they hated 'northerners' or 'southerners'. Both sides were heirs to nationalist movements which stressed their attachment to national unity. Their divisions were over ideology, the role of the state in society, religion and many other political issues.[1]

In this long view of Vietnamese history, the 21 years between the division of the country into capitalist and communist in 1954 and its reunification under communism in 1975 seem less important than what went before and after. But those 21 years meant there was continuity in the south between the freewheeling capitalism of French Cochinchina and that of the 'American' Republic of Viet Nam (RVN), which was never truly suppressed after reunification before economic reforms began in socialist Vietnam in 1979. Capitalism is a relatively recent introduction in the north but it has been southern Vietnam's default position for almost all of the past 150 years.

When the communist People's Army crashed through the gates of the Presidential Palace in Saigon in April 1975, it seemed, in the minds of the northern leadership, to confirm Hanoi's superiority: militarily, ideologically and historically. The north had beaten the Americans. Triumphalism reigned. Hanoi sent another army to the south, an army of northern bureaucrats which tried to remould it into an image of the north without regard to its very different economic situation. But bureaucratic ideology met its match: capitalism was never truly eradicated. More humiliatingly for the ideologues, in those parts of the country where socialism prevailed, hardship endured. Gradually they had to face up to the reality that Hanoi communism couldn't solve all the country's problems. Hubris would soon be humbled.

Even now, the extent to which Hanoi's rule was saved by the south is unacknowledged in public discourse: the 'Official History' of Hanoi's supremacy endures. But if it hadn't been for that legacy of southern entrepreneurialism, Vietnam might have collapsed. Despite Hanoi's draconian campaigns in favour of collectivisation and against 'comprador capitalists' (mainly ethnic Chinese), old trading arrangements survived. In 1979, when the failure of Hanoi's policies had become obvious, southern leaders, such as the then Party boss of Ho Chi Minh City, Vo Van Kiet, authorised 'pragmatic' steps to make ends meet. The city authorities bought rice from farmers at market prices and allowed those Chinese entrepreneurs who hadn't fled the country to make contact with traders in Hong Kong, Singapore and Taiwan to keep imports and exports flowing. Such fence-breaking broke the rules imposed by Hanoi, but kept the economy alive.

When, eventually, the failure to make state socialism pay the bills forced Hanoi to open up the economy, the south was ready to take full advantage. The first foreign investors to arrive were the trading contacts of the Chinese community. They found the south more conducive to business: less rule-bound, less ideological. In addition the south had the benefit of roads and ports paid for during the war years by American taxpayers. Between 1990 and 1994, 60 per cent of all foreign direct investment went to Ho Chi Minh City and three of its neighbouring provinces: Binh Duong, Dong Nai and the 'oil province' of Ba Ria-Vung Tau.[2] These advantages for the southern provinces were multiplied by a curious arrangement, initially begun as an incentive to encourage economic growth.

The Vietnamese government allowed (and still allows now) provinces to retain any revenue they earn above a set target. In the north, most provinces tried to boost their income by developing the state sector. But leaders from those four southern provinces – more open-minded, less suspicious of foreigners – looked abroad for investment. It worked. Labour-intensive industries such as textiles, garments and food processing flocked in and the taxes and tariffs they paid made their host provinces rich. The surplus (after deductions for kickbacks and patronage) was reinvested in better infrastructure and services, which encouraged other investors to locate there, creating a virtuous circle of growth. Southern leaders, who had been largely excluded from the pinnacles of power since reunification, knew they were unlikely to make it to the top of national politics. Instead, they concentrated on keeping their own constituents happy, untroubled by the need to break national rules to keep the income flowing.

While some in Hanoi disapproved, they couldn't stop the fence-breaking because the country needed the cash. In the 1980s provinces had depended upon the central government for the allocation of subsidies from the Soviet Union. By the early 1990s the central government was dependent upon the surplus being generated in the south. The quid pro quo was a strong policy of redistribution. Southern surplus still funds government spending across the country, lifting the standard of living in northern and central areas closer to the national average and helping to preserve national unity and the Party's hold on power.

There are currently 11 provinces which generate a surplus. Four are in the north, including Hanoi itself, two are in the centre but five are in the south and, together, these five generate half the provincial income of the entire country. Increasingly they set the agenda for the country as a whole. As northern workers flock to the assembly lines and building sites of the south, there has been a 'march to the north' by southern political leaders. The current President, Nguyen Minh Triet, began his rise to the top by turning Binh Duong into an industrial powerhouse. The current Prime Minister, Nguyen Tan Dung, is also a southerner. Since 2006 southerners have, for the first time, filled two of the three most powerful political positions. There are now more southerners than northerners in the Politburo. As the Vietnamese say, 'The north beat the Americans, but the south beat the Russians.'

So what is left for southerners to complain about now? Not everyone is happy. The Party may have recognised the failings of northern hubris internally, but it still hasn't done so externally. For the time being there's only one acceptable version of recent history, the 'Official History' in which the north saved the south. The role of the southern communist Viet Long is downplayed and those who fought for the RVN are treated as traitors. Former soldiers and civil servants from the RVN, and even their children, are still discriminated against. They find it difficult to get jobs in the state sector and rarely achieve promotion. While wounded soldiers from the communist side receive a modest pension and other benefits, those from the RVN side are left without either, forced to depend upon charity for survival. RVN military cemeteries are abandoned and derelict. All these things rankle deeply with a small but significant section of the population.

However, the areas with most to grumble about now are the areas outside the country's two growth poles: Ho Chi Minh City and Hanoi. Although the government is trying to redress the balance, other places are being left behind. The city of Danang may be doing well, but most of the central region still finds life tough. Hue was once the capital of the whole country; now it's a backwater, its position usurped by upstarts in the north and south. In the past, one of the big three political leaders was always from the centre; currently none of them is. But there's also a more dangerous pattern emerging. Increasingly the differences are not between provinces but *within* them. As the majority Kinh population advances, it is the ethnic minority populations – the ones who've always been on the receiving end of the thrust of the 'Official History' – who are being left behind.

* * *

The bride-to-be teetered up the hewn-log steps, trying to reach the wooden platform above her head. Soaring over the platform like a great sail was the roof of the communal house, sides so steep they appeared almost vertical. Inside, there was enough space to seat a whole village. Great bamboo rafters towered into the air, meeting at a sharp apex high above. Outside, along the roof ridge, ritual objects waved in the wind, warding off evil spirits. But none of this bothered the bride-to-be too much. She'd given up trying to reach the platform. Her high heels were too spindly and her big white dress too flouncy. The photographer was just going to have to take her picture half-way up the steps. Her husband-to-be gallantly posed below her, trying to support his bride while simultaneously looking besotted for posterity.

The gardens of the Vietnam Museum of Ethnology in Hanoi have become one of the most popular places for the city's wealthy soon-to-be-weds to have their photographs taken. Every weekend, dozens of couples show up in silk and suits accompanied by a small army of stylists, shoe fitters, make-up artists, dress designers, photographers and assistants. They make a circuit of the garden, posing on the steps of the communal house (built by the Bahnar people), standing next to the long house (built by the Ede people) or, if they're feeling a bit naughty, joking by the sexually explicit tomb statues (carved by the Gia-Rai people). Round and round they go, each ethnic group providing a bucolic backdrop to their conspicuous consumption. The results, posted in an album, will be circulated among their guests on wedding day. And why not? The Ethnology Museum is one of the few well-managed pieces of peaceful green space in the capital, its trees and ponds an easily accessible reminder of a rural past increasingly inaccessible to dwellers in the expanding city. The institution gets a nice income from the photography fees – helping to make it the best modern museum in the whole country – and the couples get some nice pictures.

But there's something unsettling about all these Kinh couples choosing to display their sophistication by posing in front of the homes of people whom they would usually go to great lengths to avoid. The Museum's former director, Nguyen Van Huy, shakes his head at the irony. A quiet but bold man, Professor Huy has dedicated his life to understanding and celebrating the country's ethnic minorities. The simple fact that somehow, in the teeming quarters of Hanoi, space was found to construct the Museum suggests that there are others in the political system who support his work. That's partly a tribute to Professor Huy's father – the founder of Vietnamese ethnology who helped the Communist Party understand the minorities, a crucial contribution to its wartime victory. The road outside the Museum is named after him. 'Many people have these patronising ideas,' says Professor Huy. 'TV documentaries call the minorities "backward" and "aboriginal" and the places where they live "neglected".' He's critical of the way such ideas are perpetuated to benefit the tourist industry. 'For example, tourist promotion enterprises talk about "love markets" among the people of the north-west highlands. But among the minority peoples there's no such phrase as "love market". It's just invented to attract tourists. It's very offensive', he says.

The town of Sa Pa, high up in the north-western hills, is the centre of the 'love market industry'. It has acquired a reputation among many Vietnamese as a town of loose morals because the Kinh-dominated local authorities have deliberately marketed it that way. The myth of the 'love market' – a place where boys and girls from minority groups are supposed to come and find partners – has been propagated as an alternative to the superficially more conservative morals of the lowland Kinh. There is some basis to the myth; gatherings of young people did take place in market towns. But they are not ancient rituals – the oldest one seems to date only from 1919.

Although Sa Pa is surrounded by minority villages, the town has built a theme park at 'Dragon's Jaw Hill' so that visitors can experience minority culture without the indignity of travelling down into the valley. After buying a ticket, visitors walk up the hill past a run of souvenir stalls to a sturdily built stilt house in which ethnic Kinh dancers dress up in different minority costumes and perform versions of tribal dances. There's plenty of talent on display, the entertainment and the view make it worth the small entrance fee, but the effect has been to remove the minority peoples even from their own culture. As with the bridal photographs, they have become a backdrop on to which the Kinh can project their own imaginings. The only place left for the Hmong people in Sa Pa is the street. Unable to borrow from the

Kinh-dominated banks or get the necessary permits from Kinh-dominated local authorities to open permanent businesses, they stalk the sidewalks expertly hunting down foreign visitors to hawk bracelets and trinkets. These girls come up from their villages, rent a room in town sleeping five to a bed and eke out a living to supplement the family income. The families are grateful for the money but, not surprisingly, resent the Kinh community's greater success.

The Hmong find themselves at the wrong end of the Vietnamese ethnic spectrum. Relatively recent arrivals – they migrated from China just two or three hundred years ago – they are regarded by Kinh much as Europeans often regard Gypsies: as dishonest, subversive and primitive. Their slash-and-burn cultivation is blamed for destroying the forest, for encroaching on the land of other minorities and upsetting the status quo. At the other end of the spectrum, some minorities are much more highly regarded. They adapted well to the arrival of the Kinh and have become, as the French colonialists would have said, evolué – evolved to the point of civilisation. The most powerful man in the country, Communist Party General Secretary Nong Duc Manh, is a member of the Tay minority. Originally from the north-eastern highlands, the Tay controlled that part of the border with China. School-books portray them as powerful and heroic. In most aspects of their lives they, and another group, the Muong, are barely distinguishable from the Kinh.

The Vietnamese state has officially defined 53 ethnic minorities, ranging in size from the Tay and the Thai with around 1.5 million members each, to the Brau, Odu and Romam with just 300 or so. Almost from its inception, the Communist Party adopted a benign attitude to them. Even before it fled to the hills to fight its guerrilla war against the French, it had adopted Lenin's views on so-called 'national minorities'. According to Professor Huy, the Party's 1935 Resolution 'to consolidate communities in favour of liberation' still guides its policy to this day. In their fight against the communists, both the French and US militaries played the classic colonial game of divide and rule. They bolstered the minorities' social position and encouraged their sense of grievance against the Kinh. In the north-west, the French created autonomous zones for the Muong and Thai. Further south, in the Central Highlands, they created the 'Pays Montagnard du Sud Indochinois' (the Montagnard Lands of South Indochina) to try to foster a collective 'Montagnard' (the French word for 'highlander') identity among the disparate minorities of the Central Highlands. The whole point of this

Montagnard identity was to unite the minorities and emphasise their differences from the Kinh-dominated nationalist forces. The effect has been long-lasting: in the Highlands the dream of autonomy has lingered on.

When the French left, the RVN ('South Vietnam') drastically reduced the highlanders' autonomy and began to encourage Kinh migration into the region. In response, some highlanders joined up with the Communists, who promised to reinstate their autonomy. Others eventually formed FULRO, the United Front for the Liberation of Oppressed Races, which took a jaundiced view of all Kinh – but then split into communist and American-backed factions. The war in the Central Highlands became bitter and bloody. Communists used the region for bases and supply routes. The US declared large areas 'free–fire zones', defoliated them with Agent Orange and blew them to pieces with B-52s. Some 200,000 highlanders are thought to have been killed and 85 per cent of the population fled their villages.[3] During this terrible time a section of the Highlands' population took to calling themselves 'Degar' to distinguish themselves from the Kinh but also from other groups who'd previously been grouped under the Montagnard umbrella. The word was derived from *Ede Ga* – the name Ede people use to describe themselves. An extra 'r' was added to stretch its meaning to include other groups such as the Bahnar and Mnong Gar. 'Degar' represented a new ethno-nationalism, which attempted to unite minorities of very different origins mixing mythical history, evangelical Protestantism and new demands for autonomy.

Once the war was won, the Communists stopped acting like a revolutionary movement carefully cultivating the support of a complex mix of minorities and started behaving like a typical modern state trying to secure its borders. Kinh migration was increased. Land was cleared and New Economic Zones (NEZs) were created, with state farms to create jobs and grow commercial crops. Party members, volunteers, political prisoners and Chinese traders in need of 're-education' were transported from the Lowlands and told to make the Highlands safe for socialism. Upland minority groups had traditionally practised 'swidden' (slash-and-burn) agriculture – using the land for short periods and then moving on to allow the poor soil to recover before returning many years later. But given the Montagnards' previous links to US Special Forces and their ongoing resistance to Communist control, Hanoi wanted them to be pinned down, stuck in one place where the Party could keep an eye on them.

The results were a success for the state: 25 NEZs were established in the Highlands, the Degar uprising was contained, Vietnam rose to become the world's second-largest coffee producer and hundreds of thousands of jobs were created. Somewhere between four and five million people are thought to have migrated to the Highlands in the years after 1975. Even after the NEZ policy was abandoned, migrants kept on moving, attracted by the lure of easy money from coffee; 'brown gold', they called it. But for the highlanders all this was disastrous. Minorities made up almost half the population of Dak Lak province in 1975. By 2002 they were just a fifth.[4] At the same time, the Party, in the tradition of 'mutual assistance', had been bringing the benefits of socialist (i.e. Kinh) culture to the highlanders. Some things – singing, dancing and handicrafts – were preserved, but 'backward ways' such as swidden agriculture, communal living and animist religion were suppressed. Unhygienic burials were banned and marriage rituals modified to be 'less wasteful'. Even the words of traditional songs were changed by Party functionaries and taught anew to children.[5]

The highlanders' situation had been just about tolerable when land was under collective ownership. Traditional lands were managed communally. But once economic reform began, the land was bought, squatted or stolen by Kinh people. The government frequently argues that the dramatic fall in poverty in the Central Highlands is evidence that they've improved life there for everyone. But the numbers tell a different story when broken down by ethnicity. In 1993 (according to World Bank figures) 45 per cent of Kinh there were in poverty versus 95 per cent of minority people. By 2004 the Kinh poverty rate had fallen to 15 per cent, but for minorities it remained at 75 per cent. When the global coffee price crash came in 2001 (largely the result of Vietnamese over-production), things turned very sour indeed.

Unable to practise their way of agriculture, forced off their ancestral lands by lowland migrants, losing their traditional culture, stoked up with Evangelical fervour and egged on by radical supporters in the United States, many Degar have become more militant. In 2001, and again in 2004, feelings boiled over into rioting. Prompted by conflicts over land, a security clamp-down and the repression of unregistered (and therefore illegal) house churches, thousands of people marched long distances from their villages to the major cities of the Highlands. So many turned out, they overwhelmed the security forces. There they demanded an independent state and religious freedom before they were dispersed by the police and army.

During the Easter weekend in 2004 the protests were bigger – some estimates put the total number involved at 30,000 – and met with a more vicious response. Up to ten people were killed by security forces and Kinh settlers. In their wake, security forces put the Highlands under what amounted to martial law, with soldiers on the roads and police checkpoints in every village.

It's clear that the protests were not entirely spontaneous. The ground had been laid by supporters of the US-based Montagnard Foundation Inc., an organisation run by militants who'd once fought with American forces. The MFI is an overtly Christian organisation, which sees itself as the heir to FULRO and demands autonomy for the Highlands. Around half the minority population of the Highlands are now Christians. Bereft of the spaces, animals and ritual objects used in their traditional animist ceremonies, and simultaneously under constant cultural assault from local officials, most Degar have abandoned the rituals which were once the foundations of the old life and turned to Evangelical Protestantism to fill the gap. The Word is being spread by local pastors and broadcast in local languages from transmitters in the Philippines – all subsidised by American Christians. The choice of religion increases the paranoia of the authorities, linked as it is to right-wing interests in the United States, but that seems to be a conscious part of the attraction. Unlike Catholicism or other forms of Christianity which have working relationships with the Communist authorities, Evangelicalism clearly demarcates the Degar from the Kinh.

A few Western experts with extensive knowledge of the Central Highlands say they believe there really is a genuine desire within the Party for a new approach, but the cadres just don't know what to do. Many of the policies adopted – with the support of international aid donors – to improve the highlanders' lives are simply extensions of those which created the problems in the first place: forced settlement of traditionally mobile peoples, market-based trading in place of subsistence agriculture and the channelling of funds through corrupt and racist local officials. The situation in the Highlands already seems to have moved beyond the point where these will resolve the crisis: too much land has been taken from the minorities. The mass adoption of Protestantism, an individualistic religion, has undermined the social basis for the collective ownership of land.

The future for most minorities in Vietnam appears bleak. Remote villages remain desperately poor but the easiest route to a better living – migration to the cities – is hard for people without much education or the networks to find work and accommodation. Many minority people from the north-west are migrating instead to the Central Highlands, exacerbating the problems there. The situation is likely to get worse. According to the World Bank, in 2004 ethnic minorities made up 39 per cent of Vietnam's poor. They're being left behind, some lost in despair, alcohol and drug addiction, others becoming more militant. Something needs to be done, but given Vietnam's record of racism towards minorities it's only an even chance that it will be the right thing.

* * *

Groups like MFI often argue that the problems of the Central Highlands are caused by the Communist Party's hatred of religion. But the Party doesn't have a problem with religious belief *per se*; what it objects to are autonomous religious organisations. This isn't particularly surprising given that fractions of all the significant religious groups in the country – Buddhist, Catholic, Evangelical Protestant and Vietnam's two unique religions, Cao Dai and Hoa Hao – have agitated, resisted and in some cases taken up arms against the Party or the state at one time or other. In spite of this, the Party didn't try to eradicate religion. It propagandised against 'superstition' and 'back-ward practices', obstructed the work of religious groups and discriminated against believers but it generally took a very pragmatic view, regarding religion as something to control rather than suppress.

Change came with the crisis of the early 1980s as the northern ideologues' confidence cracked. Just as they were forced to recognise (at least privately) the strength of the southern economic model, so they had to come to terms with the failure of their confident atheism to satisfy the country's spiritual and social needs. It was the end of the triumphalist socialist narrative, of the Party's claim to be able to meet all of society's desires. Ever since then it has sought ways to co-opt religion as another buttress to its rule. The declining effectiveness of socialist ideology as a means of mass mobilisation has prompted a search for new ways to govern people's behaviour in an era of mass consumption and for a convincing new national identity in the face of globalisation.

Old symbols are being reinterpreted, old traditions reinvented and ideas which were once thought backward and superstitious are being given new respect. So the Temple of Literature in Hanoi, once portrayed as an example of reactionary Confucian elitism, has been refurbished and given a new role to mark the eternal importance of education in Vietnamese civilisation. Confucianism has obvious attractions to a ruling elite that wants to teach its citizens the importance of respect and proper behaviour. However, it's a conservative social philosophy and doesn't touch the souls of the masses in contemporary Vietnam in the way that newly revived folk religious practices do.

These folk beliefs have the power to move extraordinary numbers of people, and their joyful anarchy can be bewildering. The shrine of Ba Chua Xu – the Lady of the Realm – just outside the city of Chau Doc on the border with Cambodia receives over a million visitors a year.[6] They travel there for a host of reasons but usually to pray for some kind of intercession in the material world: for fertility, wealth, happiness or just a good exam result. According to an official guide, 75 'mother goddesses' are worshipped in Vietnam and each locality has its own special deities – guardian spirits who performed some meritorious duty in a bygone age and are now venerated in the local temple or communal house. These are the same buildings that were once used as village stores by Party cadres keen to stamp out superstition. Fortune tellers, spirit mediums, geomancers – all have sprung up anew to service a growing demand for spirituality. Urban professionals shyly admit to consulting fortune tellers about why they can't find a boyfriend and to burning effigies to satisfy an angry ancestor.

The same customs that half a century ago were blamed for the loss of the country to colonialism are now being revived to protect the national identity against the forces of globalisation. The official cultural organisations – the Institute of Folklore and cultural and tourist bodies up and down the country – have been reinterpreting and re-describing once-taboo activities and finding within them the essence of national culture.[7] Annual village festivals, condemned in the past for reinforcing the domination of the landlord class, have been revived – partly as community activities, partly as tourist attractions. But the enthusiasm with which these new-old festivals and 'superstitious practices' such as ancestor worship have been taken up proves that they are seen by a very large number of people not just as pieces of a new state propaganda but as something authentic and special.

The revolution appears to have come full circle. As Marxists, Party cadres used to regard these old rituals as symbols of fear: performed by people who could not control nature and so venerated it instead. But now the Party has recognised that it too is unable to control the forces of nature. Globalisation is bashing down the door and the Party is seeking support – albeit in a different way – from the rituals. In the intervening years the Party has liquidated the old landlord class and put itself in their place; the rituals no longer represent something opposed to the Party but something compatible with it. Shorn of their 'objective' class basis they can now be celebrated with Party functionaries at the head of the processions and everyone is welcome to join in.

Folk belief is usually a focus of individual and family spirituality and riotously disorganised. The Party has had to take a quite different approach to the management of organised religion. Hanoi's most prestigious Buddhist institution is the fifteenth-century Quan Su Pagoda. On religious festivals such as Vesak – 'Buddha's Birthday' – its small yellow-painted compound is packed with people lighting incense sticks and placing them in the great urns in front of the prayer halls. It's impossible for late-comers to get into the halls; even the steps up to them are packed with worshippers. Inside, brown-clad monks and nuns chant, the rising murmur loud enough to drown out the motorbike noise outside the walls. At the back of the hall and on its veranda dozens of women, wearing the same brown robes as the nuns but clearly younger and better-coiffed, sit in front of open prayer books, joining in the chanting. These women are some of the most important patrons of Vietnam's Buddhist revival.

They give time and money to the pagodas, often to the chagrin of their families. They have become the butt of television jokes and occasional critical remarks by state officials, but these middle-class women have found meaning and, above all, status through their ostentatious displays of piety. With extravagant gestures, audible prayers and loud breathing they attract attention within the pagoda in ways that would be quite unseemly outside its walls. Large groups organise coach trips around the country to pray in different pagodas. Within their homes devotion can take on extraordinary proportions: some have filled one entire room of their two-room houses with elaborate altars. All of these things would once have been regarded as wasteful, backward practices. Party cadres would have called at the houses to remind these women of their obligations to their family and society and to ask them to devote their time and money to more constructive purposes. No longer. Now they are free to do as they want – and their generosity is helping to rebuild pagodas across the country.

On Buddha's Birthday in 2006, a few metres away from the clamorous worship, a quiet meeting took place in a long, thin meeting room. Down one side sat a row of men in grey. Facing them sat a row of men in saffron and brown. The Party and state had come to bring their greetings to the official Buddhist church. Ornate bunches of red flowers stood ready on the grey side of the room and at the appointed hour the Most Venerable Thich Thanh Tu, Standing Vice-President of the Vietnam Buddhist Sangha, entered, to be greeted by Mr Ngo Yen Thi, Chairman of the Government Committee on Religious Affairs. The two men sat down on a bench, held hands and exchanged seasonal pleasantries. Then the government representative handed over the flowers to the monk and all the men in grey and saffron applauded. This was the picture which made it into the newspapers, not the conspicuous devotion next door.

The Quan Su Pagoda is the headquarters of the only authorised Buddhist organisation in the country. In November 1981, representatives of nine denominations from across the country were 'persuaded' to come to the Pagoda and merge into the Vietnam Buddhist Sangha under the motto, 'Dharma, Nation, Socialism'. Since then, the Sangha has been a member of the Vietnam Fatherland Front, the body which extends and amplifies Communist Party rule through the trade union, women's union, youth union and the other 'mass organisations'. The Sangha's membership of the VFF gives it a couple of seats in the National Assembly, the monks' saffron robes and woolly hats brightening up the sea of grey suits and military uniforms. This is the kind of religion with which the Party is happy to coexist: quiet, obedient and loyal.

There is another group of Buddhists of whom the Party takes a very different view. The Unified Buddhist Church of Vietnam exists in limbo: formally banned, severely restricted, but also tolerated. The UBCV represents a peculiarly militant strain of Buddhism with its roots in the central region of Vietnam. Monks from Hue and Danang have opposed every modern Vietnamese regime. Dozens set themselves on fire in 1963 in protest against (southern) President Diem's anti-Buddhist policies and the UBCV continues to uphold the tradition of resistance. Its headquarters is in Paris, but its most important Vietnamese outpost is the Thanh Minh Zen Monastery in Ho Chi Minh City. The building, which looks like an office block from the outside, is located just off the main road between the city centre and the airport. Right opposite is a police station, a handy base for the officers keeping an eye on the monastery's most famous resident: Thich Quang Do, who is kept there under 'pagoda arrest'.

Do and the UBCV persistently demand the right to follow the dictates of conscience rather than state. 'It's impossible to be both a Buddhist and a communist,' Do told me by telephone. The Party fears the Church's potential strength. When its former leader, Thich Huyen Quang, died in July 2008, the UBCV claimed that 6,000 monks, nuns and lay followers attended his funeral. The Church may be illegal but the Party doesn't want to risk a confrontation. There was a heavy security presence at the funeral and foreigners were kept away but the ceremony took place without interference. However, when the UBCV tries to support farmers' protests, as it did in the summer of 2007, or even when it tries to organise relief efforts for typhoon victims, the state takes a firm line. Praying in a monastery is acceptable; taking the message on to the streets is not.

Every religious body in Vietnam needs official approval from the Government Committee on Religious Affairs. Each congregation of that religion then has to register and report each of its members. In this way the government 'knows' – on paper at least – exactly how many authorised religious believers there are in the country. Unregistered churches aren't allowed. Negotiating this system has been particularly tricky for the Catholic Church, but Church and state now seem to have come to a working arrangement. In January 2007, as the bell of St Joseph's Cathedral clanged out its call to prayer across central Hanoi, the thoughts of the priests and the 70 worshippers inside were firmly on developments on the other side of the world. Their Prime Minister, Nguyen Tan Dung, was sitting down with their spiritual leader, Benedict XVI, in the Vatican for the first ever meeting between a Pope and a communist Vietnamese official.

For decades the Communist Party had regarded the Catholic Church as a tool of colonialism and its believers as potential fifth columnists. In 1951 Vietnamese bishops had issued a public letter restating the Vatican line that it was impossible to be both a Catholic and a communist. At independence almost a million Catholics fled south to escape Communist rule. In 1958 the Vatican 'embassy' in Hanoi, the Papal Nunciature, was closed down. In the years that followed, seminaries were shut, restrictions were placed on priests, the Church's education and social services were taken over by the state, and church buildings fell into disrepair. Nonetheless, Catholicism was never banned and the Church just about kept functioning. Then, under pressure from abroad to allow greater religious freedom, the Party had an epiphany – realising that the Catholic Church was no longer a hostile agent of imperialism, but a centralised, hierarchical organisation just like theirs. They could do business.

The only Catholic organisation to which believers can legally belong is the 'Solidarity Committee of Patriotic Vietnamese Catholics'. As with the Buddhist Sangha, the Committee is a part of the Vietnam Fatherland Front and therefore under the direct supervision of the Communist Party. However, the Church's leadership, the Vietnamese Council of Bishops, is not part of the VFF; it's directly in communion with the Vatican. Through this uneasy compromise, which gives both the Vatican and the Party a veto over the appointment of priests and other church activities, both sides have been satisfied. It's a quite different situation to the one in China and that's one reason why the Vatican has been pushing things forward with Hanoi, hoping to persuade Beijing that it too can find a 'Vietnamese Way' to balance Church and state. Vietnam has a small crop of troublesome priests such as Father Nguyen Van Ly, who have agitated against local officials and the Party at large (see Chapter 6 for more on Fr Ly) but the Church as a whole has kept itself wholly separate from their political activities and avoided any repercussions.

Increasingly, however, the formal structure supervising the Church, the Patriotic Committee, is becoming irrelevant as priests deal directly with whichever branch of government they need to get something done. So long as the state knows what the priests are up to it's been happy to leave them alone. A spate of church renovation in the north has been funded with resources quite out of proportion to any that could be raised locally. The state must have turned a blind eye to large sums coming from abroad. On other questions of property though, there remains more heat than light.

The Church wants to recover some of the land it held before the Communists took power. Its holdings used to be a very large, particularly in the south. Even in Hanoi, the Church could potentially lay claim to two of the city's biggest hospitals – one still called St Paul's, the other now known as the Viet-Cuba – both of which were originally Catholic foundations. In September 2008 two disputes over church land made international news. One was at the site of the former Papal Nunciature, a block south of the Cathedral, and another in the south-western Dong Da district. In late 2007, rumours began to circulate that the state planned to sell both pieces of land to developers. The timing appeared strange; relations with the Church had improved in so many areas that it seemed bizarre to provoke a row. Tensions rose, leading to clashes between police and parishioners at both sites in late 2008. But after having ramped up tensions, the Party clearly decided to ramp them down again. Neither piece of land was sold. Both were declared to be public parks – implicitly making their future a subject for negotiations. The parishioners who'd been arrested were given suspended jail sentences, keeping them out of prison but giving everyone a warning not to overstep the mark. A marker was put down for the Church too: not to assume that it will easily recover its former holdings.

Relations are far more co-operative on the subject of the Church's role in providing social care, although issues still remain. The state doesn't have the resources to cope with the burgeoning social problems of the new, rapidly urbanising society. To fill the gap the Party has encouraged the 'socialisation' – actually the privatisation – of social care. The Church has been allowed to extend its outreach work to the chronically ill, disabled, elderly and homeless people, street children and, in particular, those with HIV or AIDS. According to the government's own figures, the Church runs over a thousand charitable or humanitarian centres. Much of this work is not formally registered but it is certainly encouraged by overwhelmed local authorities. During 2008 the Party took a big step towards formalising these arrangements by re-licensing the Church's care organisation, Caritas Vietnam, for the first time since reunification. However, there is one area into which the Church desperately wants to move, but can't: education. Legally, anyone in Vietnam can set up a school. Religious groups have applied but no permits have yet been granted. For the time being the state seems determined to preserve its monopoly of the means of mass indoctrination, but perhaps, in time, this too will change.

* * *

The murmuring in the pagodas and the speaking in voices at spirit medium ceremonies are audible evidence of the growing sophistication of Communist Party rule in Vietnam. Its cultural cadres have engineered a renaissance of organised and folk religion which buttresses its position. The Party has allowed believers to revive rituals which tie them to something much larger – a community of believers, a lineage of ancestors, a nation of Vietnamese, the state and ultimately, although obscured from view behind these screens, the Party. That's not to imply that these beliefs are false, just that they are now followed in ways that are different from those of the past and that those differences are, to some extent, the deliberate result of Party strategy. By distinguishing 'good' Buddhists and Catholics from 'bad' ones and substituting itself for the landlord class in village spirit ceremonies, the Party is trying to create a 'post-political' position for itself. If all goes to its plan religion will become a way of demonstrating loyalty to the state and to the elite now in charge of the state.

But if it has successfully found a new *modus vivendi* with religion, the Party is still a long way from doing the same with certain ethnic minorities. Those who found themselves on the wrong end of the 'March to the South' and the drive to control the country's remote mountains have a quite different view, not just of the Party, but of the state too. It would make little difference whether Party rule continued indefinitely or dissolved tomorrow; the same grievances would remain. Indeed, it's not too hard to imagine that if ever central authority broke down in Vietnam, one result would be acts of genocide in the Central Highlands as settlers and highlanders fought over the land. It would take some currently unthinkable acts of restitution and reconciliation by representatives of the Kinh majority to set things right. They're unthinkable because to get to that point would require the unstitching of what I have called here the 'Official History'. This collection of stories underpins the Kinh people's self-confidence, their right to rule and, with that, the Party's right to rule too.

To write a new, inclusive 'History' would demand a critical reappraisal of the last two millennia of Indochinese history and throw into doubt many of the accepted truths about the country's development: in particular the twin ideas of the steadfast struggle by an immutable people against a succession of invaders and the Kinh people's 'redeeming mission' to extend their rule to the frontiers of the land. It hardly needs to be said that such a revision would throw into question the nationalist legitimacy of the current state. There's no place in the 'Official History' for any resistance to northern forces – whether in the first century, the tenth or the twentieth. If the story that the Vietnamese have been a single nation for 2,300 years is questioned, then Hanoi's right to rule the whole country, or any part of it, could be questioned too. This helps explain why no new history of the country has been published in Vietnam for many years. The War remains the great unspoken, the great unhealed. It lingers still.

Could anything change? Possibly, but it would require a greater sense of confidence about the future than the Party currently displays. If it believed the strings tying together the 'Official History' could be relaxed without undoing the country at the same time, then it might be possible. But that would require a reconciliation between the Party and its enemies – at home and abroad. Until now the Party has insisted that its enemies reconcile themselves to it rather than the other way around. But perhaps this will change. Vietnam still has the capacity to surprise.

Epilogue

There's nothing inevitable about what happens next in Vietnam. Whether the country thrives or stagnates will depend upon the choices made, in the main, by the Communist Party. The ingredients of national success are already in place. Some are easy to measure: a young population, widespread basic education and plenty of foreign investment. Others are less tangible, in particular the optimism, energy and acquisitiveness of the people. But these ingredients could easily be wasted or allowed to spoil. The country is storing up troubles – the entrenchment of the new elite, the hollowing out of the state, the over-exploitation of the environment, ethnic inequality and the others I've described in the preceding pages. All of these problems are solvable, but the longer they remain unaddressed, the worse they will become. The question is whether the Party leadership has the will to tackle them in time.

I don't believe the Party is on the road to liberal democracy, probably not even towards 'managed democracy'. Both those terms imply some kind of sovereignty for the people and that isn't the way the Party thinks. The Party is prepared to allow greater participation in the management of the state, especially at village level, but it isn't prepared to let the people rule. All the evidence suggests the Party intends to remain in charge of policy-making. Citizens have the right to raise the alarm about abuses and inefficiency, but not to blame Party leaders or their protégés for their creation or perpetuation. The real causes of problems like corruption, pollution and financial instability are being swept under the carpet, ignored until they turn into crises.

Since independence the Party has maintained control over the country through extensive networks of surveillance and mobilisation. But as the country becomes richer these systems will become more difficult to maintain. Rising wages will make the cost of maintaining an omniscient security system unaffordable and give citizens with independent incomes greater ability to ignore it. Younger people, absorbed by the myriad distractions of urban living, are less easily mobilised by Party directives. Without its traditional duties of surveillance and mobilisation the local Party-state will hollow out and its authority will ebb away. The Party will need new institutions to help it manage the new society. It has a crucial ally in Vietnam's strong traditions of family and community obligations but the quid pro quo will have to be greater respect for their autonomy.

For the past couple of decades the Party has won loyalty by providing economic growth and creating jobs. Output of agricultural and industrial commodities and manufacturing industry has soared but the costs have been borne by the environment. Fisheries have been destroyed, rivers killed by toxic waste and cities choked by pollution. Now the price is being paid by the people. The current pattern of growth is literally unsustainable. If the regions around Hanoi and Ho Chi Minh City are to become vast industrial conurbations they will need much tougher environmental protection or they will become, quite simply, unliveable.

Growth is delivering greater benefits to cities than to rural areas and more to Kinh people than minorities. As remote areas get left behind and as ethnic inequality widens within them, minority groups will feel more excluded. Economic grievances may become ethnic ones. The situation in the Central Highlands is already bleak and most likely to get worse. The situation for other minorities, such as the Khmer in the Mekong Delta, or groups living in the North-west Highlands and the south-central coast, while not as bad, could easily evolve into political problems.

So far, the Party has managed the country's transition reasonably well. Vietnam has travelled from Stalinism to a market economy without the fratricide of Yugoslavia or the 'shock therapy' of Eastern Europe. But every day society becomes more complex and its problems more intricate. The Party cannot solve them alone. Increasingly the challenges it faces, like widening inequality and endemic corruption, are not technical but political, and solving them will require facing up to parts of the new elite. The Party has, over the past few years, been able to rein in vested interests when they've threatened national stability but its ability to do so may be weakening. The Party's membership is becoming more urban, more bourgeois. Top families and provincial bosses have created patronage networks which are making them untouchable. The vested interests are taking over.

Through more than 70 years of evolution the Communist Party has developed a strong ethos of national leadership and of collective responsibility. It has maintained discipline among the elite and kept differences within manageable proportions. Its internal democracy has allowed different interests within society to debate and find some consensus. The biggest question facing the country is whether the Party can continue to play that role as society becomes richer and more diverse. If the Party becomes a tool of the business elite then other groups, particularly workers, may choose to act outside Party structures. Moreover, new forces are emerging in society, outside the Party. If the Party doesn't find ways to incorporate them into decision-making, they may become restive.

None of these problems will be addressed unless there is pressure to do so, but cosy networks of influence are preventing serious analysis of them. Is Vietnam's fate to become just another Southeast Asian oligarchy? It's a distinct possibility but it doesn't have to be so. The Party has long constrained freedom of speech in order to prevent challenges to its rule. Increasingly, though, expression is being constrained for the personal benefit of those at the top. Their personal interests are taking priority over the country's. Those who still prioritise the national interest need support. They need the media to be able to seek out unpalatable truths, they need public figures to air grievances and they need to be able to mobilise pressure on the leadership. If Vietnam is to join the ranks of the tiger economies it needs to unshackle freedom of expression. It may cause problems in the short term but in the end it will prevent a great many more.

Notes

Introduction: Another Vietnam

1. Gore Vidal, *Reflections, Upon a Sinking Ship*, Boston, MA: Little, Brown, 1969.

1: The communist capitalist playground

1. This account of the early years of economic reform relies on the work of Adam Fforde. See Chapter 1 of his *Vietnamese State Industry and the Political Economy of Commercial Renaissance: Dragon's Tooth or Curate's Egg?*, Oxford: Chandos, 2007.
2. Preamble to Government Decree 188–HDBT, quoted in ibid., p. 36.
3. Adam Fforde ascribes the first published use of the term to two Vietnamese economists: Dam Van Nhue and Le Si Thiep in a 1981 article in *Nghien Cuu Kinh Te*, Vol. 5, no. 10.
4. Nguyen Tri Hung, *The Inflation of Vietnam in Transition*. Discussion paper 22, Centre for ASEAN Studies, University of Antwerp, January 1999, http://webh01.ua.ac.be/cas/PDF/CAS22.pdf.
5. David Dollar, Paul Glewwe and Jennie Ilene Litvack, *Household Welfare and Vietnam's Transition*. World Bank Technical Paper 389, 1998.
6. Fforde, *Vietnamese State Industry*, p. 43.
7. Vietnamese government statistics quoted in ibid., p. xxiii.
8. Martin Gainsborough, 'Key issues in the political economy of Doi Moi', in Duncan McCargo (ed.), *Rethinking Vietnam*, London and New York: Routledge Curzon, 2004, p. 43.
9. Agence France Presse, 15 December 1999. Quoted in Carlyle Thayer, 'Reform immobilism: the prospects for *doi moi*'. Paper presented at Nitze School of Advanced International Studies, November 2001. http://www.vpa-inc.org/conference/pdf/thayer1.pdf.
10. Carl Thayer, 'Vietnam's integration into the region and the Asian financial crisis'. Address to EuroViet 4 Conference, Passau, Germany, 16 September 1999. http://www.unsw.adfa.edu.au/hass/images/politics_pdf/pol_ct/vietnam.pdf.
11. Gainsborough, 'Key issues', p. 50.
12. Scott Cheshier and Jago Penrose, *Top 200: Industrial Strategies of Vietnam's Largest Firms*, Hanoi: UNDP Vietnam, 2007.
13. Ibid.
14. Jago Penrose, Jonathan Pincus and Scott Cheshier, 'Vietnam: beyond fish and ships', *Far Eastern Economic Review*, September 2007.
15. Jonathan Pincus and Vu Thanh Tu Anh, 'Vietnam: a tiger in turmoil', *Far Eastern Economic Review*, May 2008.

16. 'Embarrassment for Vinashin as Graig Handymax springs leak', Lloyd's List, 10 April 2006.
17. David Dapice, 'Fear of flying: why is sustaining reform so hard in Vietnam?' Paper presented at the 4th High Level Roundtable Meeting – Assistance to the 20-year review of *Doi Moi* in Vietnam Project, Hanoi, 15–16 June 2006.
18. Scott Cheshier, *State Corporations, Financial Instability and Industrialisation in Viet Nam.* UNDP Viet Nam Policy Dialogue Paper, Hanoi, 2009.
19. Ibid.
20. Quoted in Scott Cheshier, Scott Robertson and Bill Stoops, 'SOE Sector: the number one challenge, *Vietnam Focus*', August/September 2008. Dragon Capital, Ho Chi Minh City, Vietnam.
21. 'Vietnam to issue legal framework on operations of state-owned corps', *Nhan Dan* (The People) newspaper, 15 September 2008.
22. Katariina Hakkala and Ari Kokko, *The State and the Private Sector in Vietnam.* Working Paper 236, European Institute of Japanese Studies, Stockholm School of Economics, June 2007.
23. D.C. Nguyen, A.T. Pham, V. Bui and D. Dapice, *Why Don't Northern Provinces Grow Faster?*, Hanoi: Central Institute for Economic Management (CIEM) and United Nations Development Program, 2004.
24. Jonathan Pincus and John Sender, 'Quantifying poverty in Viet Nam: who counts?', *Journal of Vietnamese Studies*, Vol. 3, no. 1, pp. 108–50.

2: Selling the fields

1. VietNamNet Bridge, 'Exporting Rice at low prices, a bitter lesson', 5 August 2008.
2. VietNamNet Bridge, 'Worries about rice prices', 30 September 2008 (*Saigon Business Times*).
3. Inter Press Service, 'Vietnam: Good harvests don't bring good sales', 6 November 2008.
4. VietNamNet Bridge, 'Rice price plunges into chaos', 18 September 2008 (*Saigon Times*).
5. Ibid.
6. Asian Development Bank, 'Linking the poor with rice value chains', www.markets4poor.org Briefing 1.
7. Asian Development Bank, 'Markets for the Poor' (the participation of the poor in the value chain for tea), www.markets4poor.org Briefing 4.
8. Dang Nguyen Anh, Cecilia Tacoli and Hoang Xuan Thanh, *Migration in Vietnam: A Review of Information on Current Trends and Patterns and their Policy Implications.* UK Department for International Development: London, 2003. www.eldis.org.
9. Sandra S. Huang, 'Situational analysis on urban migrants in Vietnam – a report for Oxfam International'.
10. Hy Van Luong, 'Wealth, power and inequality: global market, the state and local sociocultural dynamics', in Hy V. Luong (ed.), *Postwar Vietnam: Dynamics of a Transforming Society*, Lanham, MD: Rowman & Littlefield, 2003, pp. 81–106.
11. Pamela McElwee, 'From the moral economy to the world economy: revisiting Vietnamese peasants in a globalizing era', *Journal of Vietnamese Studies*, Vol. 2, no. 2, pp. 57–107.
12. Hy V. Luong, 'Introduction', in Hy V. Luong (ed.), *Postwar Vietnam: Dynamics of a Transforming Society*, Singapore: Institute of Southeast Asian Studies, 2003.
13. See McElwee, 'From the moral economy', p. 92.
14. Dimitrios Konstadakopulos, 'Environmental and resource degradation associated with small-scale enterprise clusters in the Red River Delta of northern Vietnam', *Geographical Research* 46(1), November 2008. See also Mike Douglass et al., *The Urban Transition in Vietnam* Honolulu, Fukuoka and Hanoi: UNCHS/UNDP: University of Hawai'i, Department of Urban and Regional planning January 2002, Chapter 1.

3: Living on the streets

1. William Turley, 'Urbanization in war: Hanoi 1946–1973', *Pacific Affairs*, 48, Autumn 1975, pp. 373, 379. Quoted in William Logan, *Hanoi: Biography of a City*, Sydney: University of New South Wales Press, 2000, p. 136.

2. There are more than 36 streets in the old part of town: '36' is just a number that Vietnamese used colloquially to mean 'a lot'.

3. Lisa Drummond, 'Street scenes: practices of public and private space in urban Vietnam', *Urban Studies*, Vol. 37, no. 12, 2000.

4. I am grateful to Erik Harms for these insights. See Erik Harms, 'Vietnam's civilizing process and the retreat from the street: a turtle's eye view from Ho Chi Minh City'. Paper submitted to *City and Society*.

5. David Koh, 'Negotiating the socialist state in Vietnam through local administrators: the case of karaoke shops', *Sojourn*, Vol. 16, no. 2, 2001, pp. 279–305.

4: Grandfather is watching you

1. For a full account of the development of the *ho khau* system, see Andrew Hardy, 'Rules and resources: negotiating the household registration system in Vietnam under Reform', *Sojourn*, Vol. 16, no. 2, 2001, pp. 187–212.

2. *Birth Registration in Vietnam*. Country Report prepared for the Fourth Asia and Pacific Regional Conference on Universal Birth Registration, 'Record, Recognise, Respect', Bangkok, 13–17 March 2006. http://www.plan-international.org/pdfs/vietnamcp.pdf.

3. WHO, 'Vietnam's helmet law saves lives', Associated Press, 14 December 2008.

4. Interview with Do Trung Ta on Vietnam Express website, trans. in VietnamNet Bridge *Witnesses of Historical Internet Moments*, 22 October 2007.

5. VietnamNet Bridge, 'Internet in Vietnam tops in growth', 12 November 2007.

6. VietnamNet Bridge, 'Ten persons who brought internet to Vietnam', 29 November 2007.

7. Ministry of Foreign Affairs press briefing, 10 August 2006.

8. The Citizen Lab at the Munk Centre for International Studies, University of Toronto; Berkman Center for Internet & Society at Harvard Law School; the Advanced Network Research Group at the Cambridge Security Programme, University of Cambridge; and the Oxford Internet Institute, Oxford University.

9. OpenNet Initiative, *Internet Filtering in Vietnam in 2005–2006: A Country Study*, August 2006. www.opennet.net/vietnam.

10. Amnesty International, *Viet Nam: A Tightening Net: Web-based Repression and Censorship*, 21 October 2006, Index Number: ASA 41/008/2006, p. 7. (www.amesty.org).

11. Joerg Wischermann, 'Vietnam in the era of Doi Moi: Issue-oriented Organisations and their relationship to the government', *Asian Survey*, Vol. 43, no. 6, November–December 2003, pp. 867–99.

12. Ibid.

13. Thaveeporn Vasavakul, *Rebuilding Authority Relations: Public Administration Reform in the Era of Doi Moi*. Adam Fforde and Associates Pty Ltd for the Asian Development Bank, submitted May 2002.

14. I'm grateful to Mark Sidel at the University of Iowa for insights into the history of the Law on Associations.

15. Andrew Wells-Dang, 'Political space in Vietnam: a view from the rice-roots'. Paper presented at University of Birmingham, UK, September 2008. Most of the information about the Park campaign comes from this paper.

16. 'Farmers' organizations in Vietnam – rural members in an emerging civil society?' in *Towards Good Society*, documentation of a workshop of the Heinrich Böll Foundation, held in Berlin 26–27 October 2004. http://www.boell.de/downloads/asien/Towards-6.pdf.

17. Dpa Minsk Belarus planning training for Vietnam's police, 30 January 2007.

5: 'Greet the Party, Greet Spring'!

1. For more on this see Mandy Thomas, 'Out of control: emergent cultural landscapes and political change in urban Vietnam', *Urban Studies*, Vol. 39, no. 9, 2002, pp. 1611–1624.

2. For more on this process see Mark Sidel, *Law and Society in Vietnam: The Transition from Socialism in Comparative Perspective,* Cambridge University Press: Cambridge, UK, 2008, p. 45.
3. Matt Steinglass, 'Vietnam elections attract candidates from outside Communist Party, but few win', Voice of America website, 17 April 2007.
4. Edmund Malesky and Paul Schuler, 'Why do single-party regimes hold elections? An analysis of candidate data in Vietnam's 2007 National Assembly Contest'. Paper presented at the 2008 Annual meeting of the Political Science Associate, Boston, USA.
5. Ibid.
6. Quoted in Bristol-Vietnam Project, *Vietnam after the Tenth Party Congress: Emerging and Future Trends,* University of Bristol, May 2006.
7. Martin Gainsborough, 'Corruption and the politics of economic decentralisation in Vietnam', *Journal of Contemporary Asia,* January 2003.
8. For more on this see David Koh, *Wards of Hanoi,* Institute of Southeast Asian Studies, Singapore, 2006.
9. C. Thayer, 'Current dynamics of Vietnamese society and external challenges'. Paper presented at the Conference on Sustainable Development in Vietnam, Maryland, 13 November 2003.
10. Quoted in Bristol-Vietnam Project, *Vietnam after the Tenth Party Congress.*
11. Nhan Dan, 15 January 2007. See http://www.nhandan.com.vn/english/life/150107/life_v.htm.
12. Karen Valentin, 'Mass mobilization and the struggle over the youth: the role of Ho Chi Minh Communist Youth Union in urban Vietnam', *Young,* 15, 2007, p. 299.
13. I am grateful to Eddy Malesky for pointing out this piece of hidden history. See his 'Gerrymandering – Vietnamese style: escaping the partial reform equilibrium in a non-democratic regime', *Journal of Politics,* 71: 1, 2009, pp. 132–159.
14. Martin Gainsborough, 'From Patronage to 'Outcomes': Vietnam's Communist Party Congresses Reconsidered', *Journal of Vietnamese Studies,* Vol. 21, pp. 3–26, 2007.

6: The rise and fall of Bloc 8406

1. The purge is probably more accurately viewed as a campaign against those who prioritised consolidating socialism in the Democratic Republic of Vietnam (North Vietnam) over extending the armed struggle in the south.
2. For more on Hoang Minh Chinh's life see Zachary Abuza, *Renovating Politics in Contemporary Vietnam,* Boulder, CO: Lynne Rienner, 2001, and Robert Templer, *Shadows and Wind,* London: Little, Brown/Penguin, 1999, Chapter 7.
3. Letter from Hoang Minh Chinh to CPVN Secretary-General Nong Duc Manh and others, 2 December 2005, available online at www.avhrc.org/pdf/hmc_urgent_report2.pdf.
4. This and other comments from Dai and Le Thi Cong Nhan come from interviews with the author conducted in Hanoi in autumn 2006.
5. Committee for Human Rights in Vietnam, News Bulletin, December 2006 http://human-rightsvn.blogspot.com
6. Interim Platform, Vietnam Progression Party, 8 September 2006. available at www.vietnam progression.org
7. Press release from Committee for Human Rights in Vietnam, 9 February 2007 (probably written by Nguyen Van Dai himself).
8. The others involved were Hoang Tien, Nguyen Khac Toan, Duong Thi Xuan and Bach Ngoc Duong.
9. Reform call by ex-Vietnamese PM, BBC News Online, 10 May 2007, http://news.bbc.co.uk/1/hi/world/asia-pacific/6638347.stm.
10. Press conference by Ambassador Michael Marine, Hanoi, 13 December 2006.

7: A sharp knife, but not too sharp

1. 'Senior officials investigated for allegedly taking bribes in Vietnam corruption scandal', Associated Press, 13 April 2006. See also 'Forgotten moneybag suggests deputy minister received bribes', *Thanh Nien,* 13 April 2006.
2. VietNamNet Bridge, 'NA corridor buzzing over journalist arrest case', 14 May 2008.
3. 'Report on the trial of four defendants who are former reporters and ex-police investigators', *Thanh Nien,* 15 October 2008.
4. Russell Heng has written about this in his chapter in David Marr's book, *Mass Media in Vietnam,* Monograph 25 Canberra, Dept of Political and Social Change, Australian National University, 1998. See, in particular, CPVN Directive 79 of 11 March 1986 allowing the press to write about Party self-criticism sessions and Directive 15 of 21 September 1987 entitled 'Better utilisation of the press in the struggle against negativism'.
5. 'Vietnam vows not to privatize state-owned media', Associated Press, 1 December 2006.
6. See, for example, Iain Finlay and Trish Clark, *Good Morning Hanoi,* Simon & Schuster Pymble: NSW, Australia, 2006, p. 117.
7. Roger Mitton, 'Chronicle of a death untold', *Straits Times,* Singapore, 22 June 2006.
8. 'Vietnam must regulate blogs, say officials', AFP Hanoi, 25 December 2007.
9. Ibid.
10. 'Vietnam tightens controls on bloggers', Agence France Presse, 23 December 2008.
11. Data from alexa.com. Accessed 1 June 2009.
12. Popular Vietnamese blogger fired by newspaper. Associated Press 27 August, 2009.
13. 'Vietnam press advances alongside the people', commentary by Quang Son, Voice of Vietnam radio website, 10 January 2007.
14. Quoted in Catherine McKinley, 'The Press in Vietnam: to what extent does the state-owned press combat corruption?' Unpublished MSc dissertation, Centre for Economic and Management Studies, University of London, 4 November 2007.

8: See it before it's gone

1. 'Vietnam's top coal port resumes operation', Reuters, 11 August 2008.
2. E.J. Sterling, M.M. Hurley and Le Duc Minh, *Vietnam: A Natural History,* New Haven and London: Yale University Press, 2006.
3. Nguyen Van Song, 'Wildlife trading in Vietnam: situation, causes & solutions', *Journal of Environment & Development,* Vol. 17 (2008), p. 145.
4. World Bank, *Going, Going, Gone . . . The Illegal Trade in Wildlife in East and Southeast Asia,* July 2005.
5. Nguyen Van Song, 'Wildlife trading in Vietnam'.
6. Ibid., p. 145.
7. Keith Barney, *Central Plan and Global Exports: Tracking Vietnam's Forestry Commodity Chains and Export Links to China,* Washington, DC: Forest Trends, 2005. www.foresttrends.org.
8. Dara O'Rourke, 'Community-driven regulation: towards an improved model of environmental regulation in Vietnam', in Peter Evans, *Liveable Cities: The Politics of Urban Livelihood and Sustainability,* Berkeley: University of California Press, 2002.
9. Agence France Presse, ' "Cancer village": the dark side of Vietnam's industrial boom', 1 December 2008.
10. Dasgupta Susmita, Benoit Laplante, Craig Meisner, David Wheeler and Jianping Yan, *The Impact of Sea Level Rise on Developing Countries: A Comparative Analysis.* World Bank Policy Research Working Paper 4136, February 2007.
11. ICEM report, 2008. Jeremy Carew-Reid, 'Rapid assessment of the extent and impact of Sea Level Rise in Viet Nam International Centre for Environmental Management Indooroopilly', Queensland Australia, February 2008.

9: Enemies into friends

1. 'Two US Navy ships dock in former Saigon: sailors to celebrate July 4 in Vietnam', Associated Press, 2 July 2006.

2. Le Dung, official government spokesman, Ministry of Foreign Affairs press briefing, Hanoi, 10 August 2006.

3. Matt Steinglass, 'Two nations held captive by a distant war', *The National*, 17 October 2008. http://www.thenational.ae/article/20081017/REVIEW/214822325/1008.

4. For more on the strategic usefulness of remembering and forgetting see Gerrit W. Gong, 'The beginning of history: remembering and forgetting as strategic issues', *Washington Quarterly*, Vol. 24, no. 2, Spring 2001, pp. 45–57.

5. Alexander B. Woodside, *Vietnam and the Chinese Model*, Cambridge, Mass.: Harvard University Press, 1971. Quoted in Benedict Anderson, *Imagined Communities*, London: Verso, 1991.

6. Odd Westadds and S. Quinn-Judge (eds), *The Third Indochina War: Conflict between China, Vietnam and Cambodia*, London: Routledge, 2006, p. 5.

7. Robert S. Ross, *The Indochina Tangle: China's Vietnam Policy 1975–79*. New York: Columbia University Press, 1988, pp. 24–6.

8. Ibid. pp. 240–3.

9. James Mann, *About Face*, New York: Knopf, 1999, pp. 98–100. Mann says that Deng Xiaoping cleared the 1979 attack on Vietnam with Carter during his visit to the White House in late 1979.

10. United States Pacific Command, *Asia-Pacific Economic Update*, Vol. 2, Honolulu: USPACOM. Quoted in Jorn Dosch, and Ta Minh Tuan, 'Recent changes in Vietnam's foreign policy', in Duncan McCargo (ed.), *Rethinking Vietnam*, London: Routledge, 2004.

11. Alexander Vuving, 'Strategy and evolution of Vietnam's China policy', *Asian Survey*, Vol. 46, no. 6, November/December 2006.

12. Alexander Vuving, 'Grand strategic fit and power shift: explaining turning points in China–Vietnam relations'. Paper presented at the conference 'Living with China', organised by Rajaratnam School of International Studies, Nangyang Technological University, Singapore, 8–9 March 2007.

13. Raymond F. Burghardt, *Old Enemies Become Friends: US and Vietnam*, Washington, DC: Brookings Institution, November 2006. http://www.brookings.edu/fp/cnaps/commentary/burghardt20061101.htm

14. Vuving, 'Strategy and evolution'.

15. Burghardt, *Old Enemies Become Friends*.

16. Jeanne Mager Stellman et al., 'The extent and patterns of usage of Agent Orange and other herbicides in Vietnam', *Nature*, Vol. 422 17 April 2003.

17. Carlyle A. Thayer, 'Vietnam People's Army: development and modernization'. Presentation to Brunei Institute of Defence Studies, 24 July 2008.

18. Russia agreed a strategic partnership with Vietnam in 2001, India agreed one with Vietnam in 2007. India and Russia have had their own strategic partnership since 2000.

19. Thayer, 'Vietnam People's Army'.

20. Institute for International Relations, Ministry of Foreign Affairs of Vietnam. Unpublished official study on Vietnam's policy towards great powers. Quoted in Pham Quoc Dat, 'Vietnam coping with China and the limitations of balance of power politics'. Unpublished MA thesis, London Metropolitan University, December 2004.

10: Schisms and divisions

1. For more on this line of argument see Christoph Giebel, 'National liberation and the Cold War in Viet Nam: spatial representation of war after 1945.' Paper presented at the Sixth EuroViet Conference, Hamburg, June 2008.

2. Edmund Malesky, 'Straight ahead on red: how foreign direct investment empowers sub-national leaders', *Journal of Politics*, Vol. 70, no. 1, January 2008.

3. Gerald Cannon Hickey, *Free in the Forest: Ethnohistory of the Vietnamese Central Highlands, 1954–1976*, New Haven: Yale University Press, 1982.

4. Sylvie Doutriaux, Charles Geisler and Gerald Shively, 'Competing for coffee space: develop-ment-induced displacement in the Central Highlands of Vietnam,' *Rural Sociology*, Vol. 73, no. 4, 2008.

5. Oscar Salemink, 'The King of Fire and Vietnamese ethnic policy in the Central Highlands', in Ken Kampe and Don McCaskill (eds), *Development or Domestication? Indigenous Peoples of Southeast Asia*, Chiang Mai: Silkworm Books, 1997, pp. 488–535.

6. For more on the shrine see Philip Taylor, *Goddess on the Rise: Pilgrimage and Popular Religion in Vietnam*, Honolulu: University of Hawaii Press, 2004.

7. Philip Taylor, 'The goddess, the ethnologist, the folklorist and the cadre: situating exegesis of Vietnam's folk religion in time and place', *Australian Journal of Anthropology*, Vol. 14, no. 3, 2003.

Suggestions for further reading

In contrast to the many thousands of books about aspects of US involvement in the Vietnam conflict, there are surprisingly few non-specialist books about the history and culture of the country. I was inspired to write this book by a previous correspondent's account of the country. Robert Templer's *Shadows and Wind: A View of Modern Vietnam* (Little Brown/Penguin, 1999) describes a sclerotic country struggling in the wake of the 1997 Asian financial crisis – a very different Vietnam. Another reporter to have written about this period but with a more optimistic perspective was Murray Hiebert, in *Chasing the Tigers: A Portrait of the New Vietnam* (Kodansha, 1996). The former Hanoi correspondent for the *Los Angeles Times* David Lamb revealed some of the country's charms in *Vietnam, Now: A Reporter Returns* (PublicAffairs, 2003).

Vietnam is inspiring a growing number of travelogues and memoirs. Two in particular stand out: *Catfish and Mandala: A Two-Wheeled Voyage through the Landscape and Memory of Vietnam* by Andrew X. Pham (Picador, 2000) and *The House on Dream Street: Memoir of an American Woman in Vietnam* by Dana Sachs (Algonquin Books, 2000).

Remarkably for a country which engaged so much international attention for so long, there is no easily accessible general history. A forthcoming book by Yale History professor Ben Kiernan *A History of Vietnam From Earliest Times to the Present* (Oxford University Press, 2011) should go a long way to filling the gap. In the meantime, Stanley Karnow's *Vietnam: A History* (Penguin, 1997) is probably the best known (it accompanied a US PBS TV series) but in spite of the title it's not so much a history of Vietnam as of the war, although with overview chapters about earlier epochs. The twentieth-century story of Vietnam is told through the lives of one family in *The Sacred Willow: Four Generations in the Life of a Vietnamese Family* by Duong Van Mai Elliott (Oxford University Press, 2000). International scholars have published plenty of detailed works intended for specialist readers. Among them are *The Birth of Vietnam* by Keith Taylor (University of California Press, 1991), the most authoritative account yet published of the early history of Vietnam up to the tenth century. Other important historical works include David Marr's series of books about twentieth-century Vietnam, including *1945: The Quest for Power* (University of California Press, 1995).

Books on the American perspective on the 'American War' fill shelves and warehouses. For balanced perspectives, readers might consult the many works of William Duiker, including his textbook *Sacred War* (McGraw-Hill, 1995). For a (Hanoi) Vietnamese perspective, Bao Ninh's *The Sorrow of War* (Secker and Warburg, 1993) stands out as one of the greatest war stories ever written. *A Time Far Past* is by Le Luu (University of Massachusetts Press, 1997), who has been described as James Jones to Bao Ninh's Kurt Vonnegut. The diaries of Dang Thuy Tram, a military doctor who was killed in 1970 at the age of 27, were translated by Andrew X. Pham and published as *Last Night I Dreamed of Peace: The Diary of Dang Thuy Tram* (Harmony Books, 2007). Both books tell the story of the war from the perspective of those who hid in bunkers and fought for national liberation. Two recent books by Heonik Kwon, including *Ghosts of War* (Cambridge, 2008) explore the cultural legacy of war through remembrance and spiritual encounters with lingering ghosts.

Local Vietnamese literature has long suffered the corroding effects of official censorship. One writer stands out as the boldest: Duong Thu Huong fought in the war before publishing her first books in the 1980s. Her best-known work *Paradise of the Blind* (Penguin Books, 1994) focuses on the excesses of the 1950s land-reform campaign and the demise of the Communist Party's hopes for a better society, but it's just one of a series of excellent books. Another writer who fell out of favour with the authorities is Nguyen Huy Thiep whose story *The General Retires* caused a scandal on publication (Oxford University Press, 1992). A more recent collection is *Crossing the River: Short Fiction by Nguyen Huy Thiep*, edited by Nguyên Nguyêt Câm and Dana Sachs (Curbstone, 2003). A good collection by other Vietnamese writers is *Love after War: Contemporary Fiction from Viet Nam*, edited by Ho Anh Thai and Wayne Karlin (Curbstone Press, 2003).

Huynh Sanh Thong's *An Anthology of Vietnamese Poetry* (Yale University Press, 2001) is a great introduction to the subject. The Viet Nam Literature Project (www.vietnamlit.org) has many more recommendations.

Anyone seeking a more in-depth overview of developments in Vietnamese society than is found in this book would do well to look at one of two books intended as undergraduate readers: *Rethinking Vietnam*, edited by Duncan McCargo (RoutledgeCurzon, 2004) and *Postwar Vietnam: Dynamics of a Transforming Society*, edited by Hy V. Luong (Rowman and Littlefield, 2003). Finally, deeper insights into Vietnamese culture can be found in the works of anthropologist Philip Taylor, including 'Fragments of the Present' (Hawai'i, 2001) in *Vietnam: Journeys of Body, Mind, and Spirit*, edited by Van Huy Nguyen and Laurel Kendall to accompany an exhibition at the American Museum of Natural History (University of California Press, 2003) and *Understanding Vietnam* by Neil L. Jamieson (University of California Press, 1995). *Vietnam Today: A Guide to a Nation at a Crossroads* by Mark A. Ashwill and Thai Ngoc Diep (Intercultural Press, 2004) is a quick guide to the country.

And anyone looking for more depth on any of the subjects in this book would do well to track down the books and journal articles listed in the notes at the end of each chapter which have greatly illuminated my understanding of Vietnam.

Index